Sixty Years an Athlete

The life and times of an extraordinary amateur athlete

By

Mike Harris

An autobiography of a most energetic life

Typeset in Mercury

Design, editing, typesetting and publishing by UK Book Publishing

UK Book Publishing is a trading name of Consilience Media

www.ukbookpublishing.com

ISBN: 978-1-910223-66-6

I would like to dedicate this book in remembrance of my childhood friends, particularly from Stobswood's little School whose lives were so tragically cut short by either illness or accidents. You were a truly meaningful part of my life when we were all so young, and you remain ever present in my memory as I age.

Acknowledgements

On a cold and glum January day in 2016, I sat deep in thought whilst looking at our house telephone. Alongside me was a self-penned manuscript consisting of around 93,000 words. Over the preceding three or four months, I had sat quietly and diligently recording details of my life to date. Feeling a little uncomfortable due to my raw inexperience, as I sat next to the phone it was 'crunch time', and I had a decision to make. The decision was whether to call the number I had found while browsing on-line, and which I'd hurriedly scribbled onto a piece of scrap paper with a view to looking at the feasibility of turning the manuscript into a book, or conversely, simply place the whole thing into a box file and put it on hold indefinitely! Although at the time the latter of the two appealed, nevertheless probably due to the close proximity of the phone and with little to lose, I picked up the receiver, swallowed, and rang the number.

There was an immediate response with the customary 'Hello' followed by, 'UK Book Publishing'. 'Oh hello,' I responded before getting straight to the point. 'I have written an autobiography, and am looking at the feasibility of perhaps turning it into a book – or something.' Naively and somewhat uncertain I then added, 'Are you able to help?' And so began my association with Jay, Ruth, Judith and Dan at UK Book Publishing in Whitley Bay. Although I fully accept our relationship is first and foremost business, I earnestly feel it only but proper to acknowledge the assistance in its various forms that I received from that tentative phone call and onwards. From the moment we met, this amateur and budding author was treated with the utmost respect, and I felt immediately at ease with these experts as we went on to discuss the possibilities of having my work published. It was indeed fortuitous that the UK Book Publishing number was the first I tried and I am very grateful for initially your genuine interest, and thereafter your continued assistance throughout, ending with turning my 93,000 word manuscript into a readable and professional publication. Thank you.

I would also like to thank Gary and Kerrie Hall for taking the time to read an early draft version of my manuscript, and the resulting encouragement given at a time when I had so many reservations about it all, such as the recurring thought of who the hell am I to write a book? – about myself?

My gratitude also to two local authors, Neil Taylor and Mike Kirkup, for your time, your valuable comments and encouragement.

Thanks also to Morpeth Harriers for my initial brief, but invaluable, early 'apprenticeship' and for my welcome back after service life.

Finally I would like to sincerely thank Barnesbury Cycling Club for the countless cycling events you have staged over so many years in my native north east. If I have been in any way successful in pursuit of sporting achievements within both triathlon and cycling your presence has been monumental.

Additionally, although nothing to do with this publication, nevertheless, may I also take the opportunity to thank Mark, Mike, and Arron at Breeze Cycles, and Eileen Baron at Eclipse Training for your very obvious areas of expertise, and also for 'just being there'.

Contents

Prologue

The exact date is not important; it's just another Saturday in 2014. I'm 63 years of age now and I'm about to set off again for a fairly lengthy journey down the motorway, this time it's for yet another 25 mile cycling time trial. For me it's just another event, one of thousands of competitions I've completed over many decades. The difference today, and it's not unusual at the moment, is that I really don't want to go; in fact I wish something would occur to prevent me from going, something out of my control (sounds ridiculous I know!). My enthusiasm for today's lonely, lengthy journey is nonexistent, the heat and all the traffic together with the customary queues act as another deterrent. After 45 years of driving I still find it a laborious but unavoidable chore; I really don't like sitting very still behind a steering wheel. More to the point, for some reason, at the moment my current form is not good. Today I feel total lethargy, partly because the weather is so warm and windy, and instead of my normal excitement my mood verges almost on dread! I know the pain and discomfort I will put myself through during the race will once again be brutal.

As my thoughts dwell on the negatives rather than the usual positives I look to the skies; the weather is always so crucial in cycle time trialling as you strive to go faster than you've ever gone before in search of that oh so often elusive Personal Best. It's a southerly wind today by the looks of it which means on this course the first 12 plus miles will be out into a very stiff uncompromising head wind. It's likely that both the wind and the ever present draught from the traffic will make it a difficult day to steer and manage my bike as it sways to and fro, left to right, and forwards and backwards as the lorries and general traffic pass so close to my fragile machine. The deep section front wheel and antiquated disc wheel on the back (too old now to run true) will ensure that riding in a straight line today will be impossible. At the off, the discomfort of the first couple of minutes, as my superbly fit body begins to adjust to the intense physical anaerobic effort, will at best be uncomfortable, and at worst almost unbearable! Regardless, 60 plus years of racing will ensure I'll operate on automatic. I'll adjust my gears accordingly in search of something suitable, not for ease of effort, but rather for increased speed to propel myself forward as fast and as efficiently as possible.

Somewhat stubbornly, as befits my character I suppose, I don't use the current trends of 'must have' power meters and pulse monitors, nor do I use a computer like all the rest; never had one, don't need one, I see them all as distractions. I will just do what I have always done and try as hard as I possibly can, from countdown to finishing flag, and the best power meter and computer in the world isn't going to change any of that – for me only effort matters!

I'm good at this type of event though; after all, now in my 60s I have 80 plus wins behind me in similar cycle races, as well as literally hundreds of top three placings. As a former Royal Marine I revelled in punishing physical pursuits, I'd never come close to quitting. In another era as a runner I've 'raced' and won marathons, as a boxer I've won boxing bouts – and more importantly, I was never stopped. As a triathlete I excelled, winning British titles and had almost 50 triathlon wins, and been a former British Ironman record holder. I don't think anybody has ever trained as consistently hard, as I have, or for so long. I've won all my events by myself with no outside assistance, and with very little support from any quarter, never even had a coach to mop my brow or discuss my highs and lows of athletic participation. I've won, not because I'm a talent, but rather because I'm tough, hard as nails, ultra-determined, disciplined and possibly above all full of personal pride – as such I can only ever give my best. Every race and sporting competition I've done endorses my individual identity, it proves who and what I am.

So, back to this Saturday in 2014, and regardless of my negative feelings and reservations about today's event, *of course* I'll go anyhow, and will do my absolute best, and when it's all over, despite the fatigue I'll somehow feel better for it. The drive home will be easier, strangely it won't seem as long as the outward journey did, nor will it be as tense. I'll listen to some blues, Albert King, Otis Rush, Junior Wells or Buddy Guy, the weather will be cooler, the traffic will be lighter, and tonight in bed, despite tossing and turning whilst subconsciously reliving the event, I'll rest more content! At home as usual there will be little, if any, interest in my performance. No one gives a toss really; on reflection few ever did, and why should they?

Such is the life of this amateur athlete!

Introduction

Writing an autobiography, as I've discovered, is not easy. Maybe that's because none of it is fiction – you can't make things up as you go to spice up the story: it was what it was, and it is what it is! The content has got to be truthful otherwise there is absolutely no point to it all. My concerns while writing this are that I somehow unintentionally upset someone and that most certainly isn't my aim and where I have been a little critical I have purposefully left out names, mainly because there isn't an immediate right of reply, as there would be in, say, a meeting. But what follows is a true reflection on my life to date, the way I saw it as a 4 year old and the way I see it today as a 64 year old.

In my home village I am probably viewed simply as a guy who rides a bike! Or maybe as a guy who used to run, or perhaps – "didn't he used to do triathlons or something?". Some may even say whatever he was he plays a canny 'blues harmonica'! But how many small villages similar to mine have within the community a multi-national medal winning champion, or a guy who, whilst always working full time, has represented Great Britain for a decade, yet whose local identity remains so obscure? Lengthy books have been written about Widdrington, its people and its sporting history, and I don't warrant a mention, not a solitary word! The former is just one of the reasons for writing this. As the title of this personal journal states, I've been an athlete for 60 years almost to the day, and up till now, a very quiet one, and an *amateur* in every sense of the word. Like many people I guess, my personal life is somewhat unique; certainly there can be very few, if any, who have competed in sport for so long and at such a level, and even fewer who have done it my way.

One of the reasons for writing this book now is that I believe I've had a life so very different from anybody else I know, or anybody else I have even read about. No one, as far as I'm aware, has had a life so varied in the general sense, whilst so athletically intense in the sporting sense. If I don't write my story now whilst I'm able, it'll disappear and die with me when I eventually go, and for me and perhaps future generations of my family and relations, I think that would be a pity, for there is much to tell. If I have a 'slight' sadness about my life in sport, it's simply that very few have ever really been interested in me from the sporting context, although some have indeed shown a fleeting interest from time to time as identified in my congested personal scrap books, and the occasional but brief comments. But if you read my book you'll discover that my life has indeed been different and you will also see elements about me that even family and friends don't know, some relating to thoughts, feelings and emotions, and others just too plain fact – fantasy has no place in an autobiography! People have rarely, if ever, asked about me, and maybe it's part of being a 'Geordie' but it's so very difficult to talk about yourself unless there's an outside prompt. Likewise, I've also discovered how difficult it is to say good or positive things about yourself without feeling somewhat pompous or even arrogant; we'd much rather someone else said any such niceties. My 60 years of sporting anonymity is not likely to end now, and so I've decided to take the bull by horns and record the detail myself. If you have any initial doubts about the uniqueness of my life though, then momentarily take a look at the title for a starter – **'60 years an athlete'!**

Although I have decided on this, the title itself could be a bit misleading. It may suggest that the content is solely about sport, as such; for many who aren't sporting types the content may appear at first glance unattractive or potentially rather boring, particularly as I'm not 'a name' who is instantly recognisable. So, it is pertinent to mention at this stage that the sporting content of this book is only part of the story. The bigger part is the life I have led whilst quietly trying to fulfil my sporting ambitions. **This is a story about an 'amateur' athlete, an athlete a million miles different from the full time 'professionals' who have materialised over the past 20 or 30 plus years.** I am, indeed, very ordinary, except perhaps for my sporting CV.

For as long as I can remember I have always been a real sporting enthusiast; however, I have to sadly admit currently (and maybe it's an age thing) to a personal 'falling out' with sport as it has developed over the preceding years and to where it has arrived at today especially in relation to so called 'top level' sporting competition. Currently, most of our medal winning sporting 'stars' have never had a job as many of us ordinary mortals recognise the meaning of the term. Today's sports performers are as much at home as 'show biz celebrities' as they are as sporting types. They happily saturate all elements of a willing media with their perceived brilliance, whilst continually elaborating on all the 'sacrifices' they've made! It does appear that 'any' air play and media exposure from any willing source (not always sports related) is essential to bolster their already well developed self-esteem! Alas, medals it seems are no longer enough for some. Guys will pose naked and girls will spend hours preparing for a photo shoot for a Sunday newspaper supplement, in an attempt to identify that they aren't just blessed with wonderful sporting talents, but are additionally blessed as beautiful Adonis types as well! Additionally many of our sporting stars have written an autobiography before they are 30 years old (with some by all accounts having written several), which of course begs the question, if they have only gone to school, trained for a relatively short time and won a few competitions, before collecting their obligatory MBEs etc. – how much can there be to tell? Well there is always the current norm, where they elaborate on the aforementioned many sacrifices they have made on their arduous road to winning their medal/s, whilst at the same time graciously hoping that their amazing success will 'inspire' others to do as well, and of course they will further extol how proud they are to have won medals 'for Great Britain' whilst in the process managing to secure quite substantial personal financial rewards. Yet despite their success, many of our top sports people appear so utterly miserable, some complaining that the notable recognition and acclaim they've received is apparently just not enough when compared to the elevated status of some other stars. Sadly, I fear sport, like pop music, is now a business, and the athletes are nothing other than the employees within the business. Fame and monetary gain is apparently just as important, if not more so, than the sporting achievements. Not dissimilar perhaps to 'pop music' where some 'singers', just like some 'athletes', very quickly make quite large amounts of money before they go out of fashion – or, in the case of the sports star, fade very early in their lives from athletic competition.

The latter type stars of today are all so very different from my early childhood exposure to past sporting greats, most, if not all of whom, appeared so discreet, humble, well-mannered as well as proud. The past masters of sport even appeared genuinely embarrassed by their newly found and often fleeting fame. In fact the sporting stars of my childhood and youth were often perceived as 'normal' members of society who had made good, despite the necessity to work full time in order to feed and clothe their families, just like their neighbours. Today of course many of our stars of sport often receive generous handouts from the National Lottery, Sporting Bodies or their Personal Sponsors, as well as considerable 'back-up' support. When looking back it seems that there was little difference between the sporting icons of yesteryear and the spectating public, apart from their wonderful sporting achievements.

My story could not be further apart from today's sporting celebrities, and is much more in line with the amateur sportsmen and women of my youth, because like them I have remained an amateur athlete throughout my working and sporting life. If there is a difference though, as you will see, it is my *longevity* as a sportsman, because I have been an athlete of sorts since I was four years old and I'm now 64, which fortuitously (for the title of this book) is 60 years almost to the day. What perhaps makes me so different is I've never stopped being an athlete. Athletic competition has never been my job, therefore I have never sought or gained any monetary rewards from it; I simply love athletic competition in all its varying forms and always have! But I have little to show in terms of possessions for my 60 years of effort, except numerous memories and as many mementos. But I've few regrets, although I would like to have been able to 'rest' more!

I have been married for 37 years and been with the same woman for 40 years and we have two wonderful sons, a super daughter-in-law and extended family, and a heaven sent little grandson. I have always worked full time since the day I left school just before my 15th birthday, and have never as far as I can recall had a single day off sick from work or from school in my entire life. **I've never been unemployed and never had benefits of any description. I have never taken a 'performance enhancing drug' or collected a 'life enhancing benefit'. With drugs and benefits I just wouldn't know where to start and that's a fact; I am proud that acquiring either has never been even a lukewarm consideration.** For over 35 years I haven't even taken a pill of any description, not even an aspirin. I have bin bags brimming over with so many cups, plaques, and medals that we really don't know what to do with them all, so we store them safely out of sight in the loft and that's their place no doubt till I die. Once I go, I fully expect that they'll all go unceremoniously to the nearest refuge tip, and rightly so because they'll mean nothing at all to anyone who perhaps stumbles across them. But for me, in a life which I will be brazen enough for the second time to call unique, every one of those awards is drenched with effort and has a story, and each will carry an invisible covering of honest sweat.

I have always been a dreamer, and as I attempted to turn my very personal dreams and resulting ambitions into realities I regularly trained three times a day, pre-work in the very early morning, midday during lunch breaks and then in the evenings when the day's work was over – this amounted to some 25 hours of training every week, and was always in tandem with full time employment and a fairly hectic but normal family life. *As you will see, since my first race as a four year old, I have literally never stopped.* Unlike some other successful athletes I have never had excessive luxuries. I had 'old bangers' for cars which lay on the drive because they wouldn't start, and always lived in modest houses, and for the most part (even when representing Great Britain) I lived life on a real monetary budget, always too proud like many others of my generation, to ever have had debt. I quietly and anonymously trained seven days a week, year after year after year.

I have, I think, achieved much to be proud of, more so because I was born and remain very ordinary in terms of talent. Despite my all out physical efforts I found it difficult to win a race at school, yet went on as you will see to win big events later, including British Championships (I have 18 'national medals') – additionally after a sporting apprenticeship at my little school in the woods I had top 10 placings in European competitions in foreign climes, and attained top 15 placings in World Championships, all whilst representing Great Britain for 10 years or so. But I have never been invited onto radio or television shows and never secured lucrative sponsorship. **I am an 'amateur' athlete in the true sense of the word, and proud of it! As for the so called 'sacrifices' (our stars so often mention), never, I wouldn't dream of mentioning the word, for no one forced me into my mad and often chaotic life; 'I chose it'!** It is also likely that if I had been a 'professional' sports person, my career would have ended 30 plus years ago, before or shortly after I had reached 30. For me, when I reached 30, I still had another 35 years to go before I got to where I am today! *And I'm still 'trying'!*

'Show me the boy and I'll show you the man'

In this book, I have spent quite a lengthy time describing my childhood and formative years as I remember them, because I assume this period and those times may be of 'general' interest, being as they were, so very different from today's IT-obsessed, physically inactive, static world. It seems we physically move now, not because we want to, but because we have to. Whereas at one time many years ago we moved because it was joyous; in simplistic terms movement felt good and was perceived as normal. Taking the stairs these days as opposed to the escalator results in strange or suspicious looks, so abnormal has it become to walk when you can ride!

Who knows why we are all so different, and in our own way so unique. Likewise, I wonder why one man's meat is another's poison; certainly from both the physiological and psychological perspective I believe we are all born pretty much the same. Maybe our 'early years' (as I've hinted) at least hold some of the clues as to our life's future journey and why we choose to take a particular path. We are all so open to influence, especially when so young, and certainly the *Nature Nurture* debate has a lot of substance for consideration. Were we born this way? Or were we schooled that way? Well, my view is that at birth we are all athletes, it's just that at that particular time we aren't in training. But surely one baby is born physically similar to the next, that is a unit of flesh and blood which instinctively thrives on movement, and some of us continue to thrive on movement, whist others see the same physical activities as cumbersome chores. What about me? When you spend, as I have, so many thousands and thousands of hours alone in isolation you tend to think a lot, you get lost in your thoughts. I sometimes wonder: How did I become an athlete? I can think of no good reason as to why I would choose to pursue such a continuous and arduous sporting life and for so incredibly long. I wasn't pushed into it and apart from my school days and time spent in the Royal Marines, nor was I ever encouraged to do it. However, it will become clear to any interested reader, how much I loved physical activity as a child, and maybe, just as night follows day, such a passion and love of all things physical then, would naturally continue through the years and leading up to where I am now.

As children, with no former life to reflect back on, we must surely be open to all sorts of influences, both conscious, and beneath the surface, subconscious. The latter is one of the reasons why I have written such extended chapters on my early years, such as the chapter I've labelled **The start line.** Then there's the 'growing up' period including school life. I believe it very likely that somewhere in my childhood the seeds were sown which would entice or even compel me into a lifetime of competitive sport. My 'efforts', rather than my results, have, I believe, resulted in affording me with a pretty unique identity, the latter resulting in who I became and indeed who I am now. I have discovered that from the outset of this project, and with the help of my many *indispensable training diaries*, the more I write, the more I remember, and one occurrence quite naturally leads right into another, hence we have a story that has a start, a middle, and an end (but the latter not quite yet I hope); such is life I suppose and there is a varied pattern for us all.

One of my regrets in my life is not having sought, when I had the chance, enough information about my grandparents and even their fathers and mothers. It's almost too late now, but in writing this account of *my life*, maybe someday in the distant future someone whilst rummaging through some long redundant dusty drawers, will come across these memoirs of an unknown and pretty ordinary guy from another time, and whilst browsing through the pages may be heard to murmur – bah*!*

Having said all the latter, this seems like a pretty good time to move on.

The start line 1955

The beginning of a sporting journey that goes on even today in 2016!

Sometime in the autumn of 1955, shortly after my 4th birthday I had my first taste of competitive sport, in the form of a foot race along a piece of pavement in Widdrington, Northumberland. Unbeknown to me at that time, **this race, which was over in the blink of an eye, would in its own unique way probably affect and shape the remainder of my life!** For the 60 years following this innocuous and very brief event, I would automatically and without any conscious thought, relive on literally thousands of occasions the same feelings and emotions I first experienced on that autumnal night on Widdrington's dark, chilly streets!

Linda, John (rear) and me around the time of the first race

In the brief timespan it took to cover those 20 or 30 yards I instinctively learned the harsh reality and lessons of competitive sport that I would experience and repeat time and time again throughout my life, from the age of four years to my current age of 64, with so many highs and as many lows and with emotions which ebb and flow like the tide. Emotions of excitement and anticipation, absolute joy and jubilation, the warmest feeling of satisfaction and relief (when the pain subsides), but also emotions of trepidation and fear, disappointment, and even a feeling of shame and loneliness that can accompany that desolate feeling of defeat!

The build-up, as I remember it!

It is hard to believe in today's life entombed as it is in so much 'information technology' and all that that stands for, that in the post-war British households of the early 1950s very few houses had what would today be considered essential items. But in the world I entered into during the 1950s, telephones, fridges, toasters, central heating systems, music centres, laptops, credit cards and cheque books, household cameras (hence a lack of any childhood sporting photographs) and even cars, were commodities not yet common. Additionally a fairly high proportion of homes were not furbished (as yet) with televisions either. Although the Harris household was no poorer than others, we were one of those who for a time didn't possess a television. As such, a cousin, John (three years my senior), would call on myself and my sister Linda (18 months my senior), at which point the three of us would briskly make the short 400 yard trip up to 39 Elizabeth Street, occupied at this time by a family called 'the Brodies' where we'd watch their 'telly'. Mr and Mrs Brodie were lovely homely people (several years later I would knock on their door and pester them repeatedly for a loan of their record player and records, and they would always oblige). The family lived at the time next door to Cousin John's house. Once in the house, several of us kids from neighbouring families, would sit crossed legged on the floor as the room lights were extinguished, curtains were ceremoniously drawn, and at precisely 5pm 'children's hour' would commence on the tiny black and white television screen! Episodes of Champion the Wonder Horse, Poncho and Cisco, Robin Hood, the Lone Ranger, and Billy Bunter to name but a few, were viewed with innocent excitement, as the flickering embers from the coal fire and the light from the tiny television set lit up both the children's faces and the darkened sitting room.

'A sweet anyone?'

I fully remember on one of these occasions as we sat in anticipation on the floor, Mr Brodie (we called all adults Mr or Mrs in those days) came in from the kitchen with a tray of what looked like countless bony coloured wrapped sweets, and invited us all to take one each. A real treat, as sweets those days were really quite a rarity. As I hurriedly unwrapped mine, much to my dismay I found it to be nothing other than a pebble from the garden! Of course we all looked at each other in confusion and considerable disappointment only to hear the fits of laughter coming from the kitchen! Needless to say we didn't see the joke! In fact, if it had happened today, I may well have chinned him!

Back to the race!

Anyhow, it was on one of these journeys from 79 East Acres up to 39 Elizabeth Street that a 'race' was hastily organised by Cousin John. The pavement measured (and still does) approximately 25 yards, top to bottom. Directed by John (the Alpha male of this small group due to his seniority), Linda and I took our designated places on the start line alongside him, before the command of **'ready, steady, GO'** was given, at which point the three rookie 'athletes' ran as fast as our unprepared spindly little legs would carry us. Of course John reached 'the finish line' first, followed by Linda, with myself a distant third from three! John, pointing to each of us in turn, proceeded to point at himself accompanied by a gleeful proclamation of '1st, the winner', before jabbing a pointed finger at Linda '2nd' and then almost as an afterthought outstretched an arm in my direction proclaiming me '3rd'! On this occasion, and my first race, **I was last**! For the first time in my short life I experienced the empty feeling of failure. I would quietly, and without fuss, experience the same feelings again throughout my early schooling years. It wasn't that I was a poor athlete – far from it, I was always at least better than average (as witnessed on all my many school reports where I 'always' got either a B+ or an A for PE and Games) – but I instinctively realised that for me at least, only winning would ever matter, and sadly perhaps only winning would make me smile. The latter is not in any way looked upon as an attribute, oh no, rather a cumbersome weight I would drag around with me my entire life. Even today as I write this piece, 19th September 2015, I am deflated having ridden my bike flat out over 26 miles around one of my personal training courses, given it my all, only to discover at the end that I am two minutes slower than last week! *Oh to be normal!*

Anyhow, on completion of the evening's entertainment we would all depart and go our separate ways; John went home, next door, and Linda and I headed back down to number 79! Regardless of the merriment of the evening's entertainment, as we journeyed home the shame of the defeat began to take effect on me, **beaten by my sister, a girl!** What could possibly be worse? As we hurried along in the dark, I began to challenge Linda to another race, and another, and another until through exhaustion on her part rather than any newly acquired speed on my part I finally beat her, before pointing a victorious finger at *my* chest 1st, followed by a similar gesture to Linda 2nd! Oh what Joy!! By hook or by crook, and so quickly after my devastating recent defeat, I had won my first race. **The win didn't come easy and over the next 60 years, they never would!** More importantly perhaps, and unbeknown to me then, the race had taught me a valuable lesson, even at that tender age: **never give in, there is always hope!**

In a strange way, if you never give in you are never beaten either, regardless of the result, because the saga is ongoing. A competition lost is only a very temporary hitch, as long as you have self-belief, and tomorrow as the saying goes is another day, and another day allows you to start all over again and renew your quest as more opportunities present themselves.

Mike Harris Personal Sporting Achievement Record

- Three times British Triathlon Champion
- Three times runner-up in British Triathlon Championships
- Two times 3rd in British Triathlon Championships
- Additionally five other top eight placings in British Triathlon Championships
- 10 times British Masters Triathlon Champion
- 10 times Northern Triathlon Champion
- Former British Ironman record holder
- Top 10 placings in European Championships
- Top 15 in World Championships
- Member of Great Britain Team for 10 years
- Winner of 47 open triathlons
- North Eastern Counties Marathon Champion
- Winner of 80 open Cycling Time Trials races (most whilst in my 50s)
- National age group Ultra Fit Champion
- Former Royal Marine with representative honours in Boxing, Hockey, Athletics, and Cross Country
- Represented School in football, rugby, athletics, cross country, cricket and was part of school gymnastics display team
- *Remained a working amateur athlete throughout athletic career. Whilst always being 'self-coached'!*

Early life and growing up in 1950s England (and racing the bus!)

Early photo from Margaret Street
Linda (on left), friend (centre) and me

For reasons unknown to me and so difficult to explain I have been blessed (so far at least) with an incredible, but rather baffling long term memory, a memory for intricate and apparently 'meaningless' detail. I say baffling because many of my early childhood memories appear to have no specific reason for recall. Close friends whom I went to primary school with, starting in 1956 having just turned five, often 'take the mick' whilst looking bemused as I regularly recall the most ludicrous of memories. The precise colour of pudding plates in the canteen in 1956, being a recent one? I can recall so many different occurrences at various local venues and even the words spoken in those distant times, some more than 60 years ago. I can even guess with a degree of certainty the times and even the dates of many of my early memories. The latter is possible by reflecting on where I lived at that specific time, or what class I was in at school. *For example:* I can recall as a six year old, as if it was yesterday, sitting in Standard 2 at Stobswood School next to a childhood friend, Alan Morton (many years later I would have the honour of being Alan and his lovely wife's Lynn's best man at their wedding). Following 'assembly' (daily prayers and hymns) and prior to a probable lesson on tens and

*Early photo from 25 Margaret Street
Mother, Nana, me and Linda*

units, or pounds, shillings, and pence, or something similar, we took our seats and were directed by Mrs Gagie, the form teacher, to write in the margin of our little blue books, the date, at which point Alan turned to me and whispered "22 days to Christmas"! Why I would remember that I've no idea! Numbers have never been a strong point for me; however, I am able to state with a degree of certainty the date and time of Alan's comment and arrive at the 3rd December 1957, at approximately 9.20ish! I mention this as an example of my memories of so long ago (and I have so many others) by way of proving the accuracy of my recollections, such as my first race. In other words, I relate this simply as an example of the memory I am blessed with which has been so important while writing this. Having said that, the sporting elements of this book are taken almost direct from my many training diaries. I could never have stored so much precise detail.

Winding the clock back to August 11th 1951 (**not a great month to be born if you wanted to win early school races!*)

Arrived back from Malta

I was born in Malta on the 11th August 1951. My father (Robert) at
the time was a Petty Officer in the Royal Navy, having gone through
the Second World War, enlisting as a boy Junior Signalman. My
mother (Margaret) was a former Wren, and together with my elder
sister Linda we were all housed in married quarters in Sliema a
couple of miles from Valetta. I have no memories at all of that period,
perhaps not surprisingly, although my mother over the years had told
me much about life in Malta that I was so oblivious of. My mother
would shake her head from side to side as she remembered me as a
baby. A somewhat robust laddie by all accounts with a will of my own
and a temper to match! Seemingly keeping sheets on my cot was an
impossibility as my legs kicked continually for all they were worth.
Even now my bed's a wreck when I wake. When I was old enough to
crawl a few months later, I was regularly out of sight if left alone for a
minute or two on the floor. When I could walk or stumble, and climb,
I was by all accounts into absolutely everything. Around this time
I was regularly controlled when 'out and about' with a set of 'reins'
which were strapped across my chest as I toddled along. On one of
these occasions I leapt forwards without warning (no doubt trying to
escape!), at which point the straps snapped, sending me crashing face

down on to the pavement. Most of my newly developed teeth were shattered and with my face covered in blood I apparently caused much panic and consternation! None the worse for wear, a short while later having learned the joy of running I went absent for lengthy periods causing major alarm and worry. Always in a hurry! Strange as it must sound I have always read books and magazines back to front, and still do – same principle, I suppose: it cuts unnecessary corners and it's quicker!

After several months in the heat of Malta, the family returned to the freezing cold of England, where we took up residence at 25 Margaret Street, Widdrington, sharing a council house with my Grandad and Nana Barnfather, along with my Uncle Robert, when he was not away serving with the Black Watch, and occasionally my Great Grandad. Probably because my Dad was still in the navy at the time I have few memories of him from that period.

Grandad Barnfather ('Nicky the Ghost') and his dad!

My grandparents on both sides were wonderful caring people, great role models for me now that I too am in that category; I have nothing but great memories of them all. My grandad Barnfather (affectionately known locally as 'Nicky the ghost' because his house in Choppington Colliery was apparently haunted), was built like a brick outhouse, very sturdy, and apart from his time in the armed forces during the wars, was a miner for the rest of his life. He was certainly a comical figure; he taught me how to ride my first two wheeler bike. To this day I remember him riding (and showing off) this tiny two wheeled bike, while wearing his customary trilby hat and raincoat. He very much resembled a clown in a circus, so small was the bike that he sat so precariously on. Although I can't remember this, he once brought a monkey home from abroad, although the likelihood is that he got it from a pet shop, and once in the house it was released to go anywhere it pleased. For a short while the monkey ruled the house, everyone frightened to go near it. It would hang upside down from my nana's best curtains apparently, before scampering across the floor, while the family fled – must have been a sight though. Not at all sure what happened to it. My grandad once came home from the working men's club drunk, got the wrong house, went upstairs, stripped, and got into bed with the woman next door. The woman, by all accounts, thought it was her husband until it dawned on her that he was in first shift at the pit. Turning around she was looking directly into the eyes of *'Nicky the ghost'* and screamed the house down. My grandad stumbling out of the bed before fleeing half naked while leaving a trail of his clothes. People didn't lock their doors in those days, so I suppose it would be a relatively simple mistake to make whilst 'under the influence'. But I wonder? His dad, my Great Grandad, lived with us for a while by all accounts, but I have no memories of him at all. My mother used to say as old as he was, and much to the embarrassment of the family, he was 'courting' a woman half his age, down the 'Mile Road' and he would stay out regularly all night, coming home with a self-satisfied smile on his face! A dapper dresser by all accounts, always well turned out, he carried a distinctive white cane which went well with his bowler hat!

Unfortunately there are bits of the above that I can't remember. My first memories of this period are once again baffling bearing in mind that at that point I must have been between one and three and a half years old, and why would I clog up my memory storage system with such triviality? Regardless, I can clearly recall one morning after some overnight rain, dancing around some petrol spillage outside number 25 with other kids. I even remember being told the bonny colours from the spillage were the residue of 'fairies' wash', the fairies having been there through the night before fleeing at daybreak. I can remember going looking for them under bushes, and inside dust bins, with no luck I hasten to add. I can also remember looking for four leaf clovers at the bottom of our garden in the sun with Linda (my ever present bodyguard) and neighbours Freddie and Andy Coulthard. After the rain, we used to purse our young lips and run them along the iron railings outside our house whilst sipping the rain water. I also remember having a small multi coloured three wheel bike, which got run over and squashed by a grocer's van – good job I wasn't on it at the time, otherwise this journal wouldn't have even started! It must appear to some like a very long time ago when I relate to the Co-op horse and cart delivering groceries around the streets, and the French onion man selling onions draped over his bicycle cross bar. Shoe repair men shouting inaudible words as they trailed the then quiet, traffic free streets looking for business. Despite the risk of being sued, I can also vaguely remember being scolded having taken a hammer to Margaret Fogo's head! Maybe the frustrating result of another race I'd lost?

It did seem to me in those carefree early childhood days that all our houses were 'open doors', people coming and going, for much of the time, busy little havens. There must have been an air of optimism as well in those days with World War II having finished only a handful of years before, although I believe some 'rationing' was still on. Most married women in those days were housewives, tending the house, cooking, washing and looking after us kids, while the men went to work. Also the kitchen with its roaring coal fire was the main focal point in the house, that's where we all gathered (often with a 'wireless' on), probably because there was little of interest in the sitting room. In Widdrington there were very few cars (great for playing football, on traffic free streets). Perhaps one of the reasons for the lack of cars (apart from cost) was that most men worked at the local colliery (the pit), or the adjoining brickyard, or opencast or on several of the farms in the area; as such there would be little need for transportation other than perhaps a 'black' BSA push bike – all bikes seemed to be black then as I remember. Indeed a while later there was a daily procession of men and school children all walking in the same direction to work and school respectively, and for the most part we were all known to each other one way or another. Another memory of those days was being fascinated with the amount of 'bonny' coloured 'spit' we dodged on the paths – the spit had come from, in the main, miners who were regularly coughing up the stuff which would be all colours, green, red, and with copious amounts of coal dust! But honestly, whenever I think of those days I smile, a small healthy child, loved and cared for, always outside, with a zest for life and blessed with a phenomenal amount of raw healthy energy, with as yet few if any fears, anxieties or worries.

On the 'very rare' occasions in the past when my sporting prowess was discussed 'briefly' in the house (i.e. where did it come from, because it wasn't obvious?) my mother, who had very little time for sport, used to say as only she could – **"you were born healthy, Michael, you never ailed anything, son"** and she was so right – even at school I never had a day off as I recall, and still have books awarded and given to me at the end of term for 100% attendance. Good habits die hard, and in my last job with Northumbria Police I worked for almost 24 years and never had a single day's sick leave. Likewise year after year as an athlete, I never missed an intended training session! As witnessed by my many detailed training diaries, collected over several decades.

Little Dan

As I write, I have a beautiful blond haired little grandson now, Dan, and at two and a half years of age he is identical to the description outlined above. I also find that I can readily enter his current narrow little world. He has an occasional ferocious temper, just like his grandad, but for the most part he's much the same as I seemingly was. Even showing early signs of being left handed like his grandad. He's a healthy, wonderful little lad, loved and cherished by us all, with the gift of good health and a hive of natural god-given energy, put to good use in his haste to explore this brand new world he has recently entered into with all its current innocent attractions.

Our own house!

When I was about three or four years of age we moved out of the jovial, busy little house in Margaret Street and moved into our first very own, newly built council house about 400 yards from my Grandparents. A two up two down at 79 East Acres, with a large uncultivated garden, which would remain a large uncultivated garden, certainly for as long as we lived there anyhow! The house was (and still is) adjacent to a long area of grass which was known locally as the 'bottom green'. The green runs parallel to the main Kings Cross to Edinburgh railway line. This area was our very own Olympic Park; we raced on there, played football and cricket, raced our bikes, and even raced the steam trains while trying to make conversation with the train drivers as they chugged along. I say 'tried' to make conversation as the drivers probably had no idea what we were saying in our Geordie slang! I remember the grass on the verges often catching fire either from the sparks or from the coal ashes thrown out by the engineers. Good fun though helping to put the small fires out. The Flying Scotsman and the Mallard were regulars on 'our patch' and the Queen must have occasionally viewed our games of football as she travelled to and fro from London's Kings Cross to Edinburgh's Waverley Station. Part of our staple diet as we played in those days was running into the house from time to time, having a cup of water, before hurriedly consuming a couple of 'sugar and bread' sandwiches, ugh! Quickly reenergised, we were back out before recommencing our activities.

My remaining pre-school days were spent playing almost always outside, (there was truly nothing to keep us indoors) with friends in the locality of my home and the 'bottom green'. On the odd occasion when we weren't allowed out I would play indoors with Linda. I would hide, normally in the cubby hole under the stairs and wait for Linda to come for me whilst uttering 'Fe, fie, foe, fum, I smell the blood of an Englishmun'! God, the fear, as I trembled while draping the coats over my head in an attempt to become invisible!

Directly outside our front door was the remnants of a sand heap which had been left by the builders of our houses; many hours were spent there, pushing and pulling a variety of little dingy cars around on our makeshift sandy roads. I also recall with friends, pushing a pedal car up the hill outside my house and once at the top as many of us as it would take jumped on board and hung on for dear life as we hurtled downwards towards the bottom, stopped dead in our tracks by the curb adjoining the green, before repeating the same manoeuvre over and over again. Strange when you are young, happy times always seemed to be accompanied by sunshine, I can't remember at any time playing in the rain! Although I do remember walking to school in the rain and windy days and snow falls, and carol singers singing their carols underneath the lamp post outside our house in the dark, while watching them in pyjamas from a bedroom window. Another memory is of being obsessed with a steel drain outside the house – I was convinced there was a frog 'trapped' inside and unable to free itself; as such I mercifully and repeatedly tried to make contact with it through the vents of the steel grate using two pieces of wood like chopsticks, all to no avail. Whether or not there was a frog in there at all I've no idea. I recently went around there again and the same drain that was there in 1954/1955 is still there, as is the aforementioned lamp post. Whether it was due to the frog incident or not, even today I have a fondness for frogs, the most passive and unemotional of animals, a living, sensitive creature seemingly trapped into the most undemonstrative of bodies. I have always been profoundly interested in nature, seeing it in all its forms as I ride, run and walk every day. Although I consider myself a hard man, I abhor cruelty and turn the television off, hiding from it, if I know elements of animal cruelty or suffering are about to come on.

A sign of things to come!

As a child at Christmas I always received two or three 'sports books' which invariably were the catalyst for many of my future sporting aspirations. David Coleman's Grandstand, Norris McWhirter's Christmas Sports Almanac, or the World of Sport. Not guided by anything in particular I would quickly leaf through the pages till I found a photograph which caught my attention and lured me into reading the accompanying story. It was during these times that I'd marvel at the exploits of sporting greats such as Emil Zatopek, Vladimir Kuts, Paavo Nurmi, Jim Thorpe, Jesse Owens, Sydney Wooderson, Gordon Pirie, Derek Ibbotson, Herb Elliott and Peter Snell, Fanny Blankers-Koen. Together with youthful pictures of Bobby Charlton, Tom Finney, Wor Jackie Milburn, Hughie Gallacher, Stirling Moss, Mike Hawthorn, Jacques Anquetil, Freddie Trueman, Brian Close, Floyd Patterson, Jack Brabham, and so on! In days when the media influence was so restricted the stories were almost like fairy tales, strangely, even with a sense of romance about them. Sport then wasn't the 'business' it has become. Above all, these people were not apparently well paid, and many remained amateurs throughout their sporting years, unlike today's celebrity and image obsessed 'professionals'.

Having written the last sentence I now feel as if I should apologise. I love my country and the ongoing success we reap makes me smile, I'm just a bit sad about the one-upmanship manner by which we attain it! We are not some gifted Aryan race with superior innate athletic ability; we've won nothing at football since 1966 which would suggest that when other nations are our equal in terms of wealth, and support, we are quite ordinary. We don't train harder than other nations, what our athletes have is an unfair advantage in terms of a lifestyle unhindered as it is by a need to work and support one's self. What we have is often superior and advanced equipment, with quite in depth back-up teams, and a freedom to travel the world in search of superior training venues. All is not equal in sport, as was once the sporting ethos; maybe it never was? Grassroots sport still makes me smile though, so much more honest. If you want to reaffirm your liking of sport, go and watch a Cross Country Harrier League event! All age groups and genders digging out blind, each giving their best!

At some point around this time I have vague memories of running around our block on a summer's evening, with loads of other kids. As we finished each lap another one or two would drop out, until finally I was running around alone; it made me feel good as they all clapped each time I came round. I also remember it coming to a quick end as my Nana met me at her gate shouting 'You'll wear your socks out, laddie!' and threatening to murder me if I came round again!

Racing the bus! (first time around)

Similar to the above I can also well remember going to Sunday School for a while with Linda and a few other childhood friends. The church we attended on this occasion (we went to others at various times) was a Presbyterian in Widdrington Village, about two miles from our home, and I would be six or seven years old then. We were given our bus fare for the journey there and back and although I used the money legitimately to get there, when we came out I'd keep my return bus fare firmly in my pocket, and as the others queued for the bus I'd 'leg it' and often be waiting at the bus stop at the other end for the others as they got off. The mile jog up the road and additional mile walk home seemed just another triviality, although the money issue was a bit deceitful I suppose! On the Monday on the way to school I'd get four halfpenny 'chews' at the co-op for the previous day's efforts! *All part of 60 years an athlete!*

Another passion I have always had for as long as I can remember is *music*. I remember us all sitting on a Saturday evening watching *'the Six-Five Special'*, one of the very first pop shows to appear on British television. As soon as it came on with its very own theme tune (*the six-five special coming down the line, the six-five special right on time ...!)* our Budgie would sing so loudly (presumably as excited by the music as I was), that we had to put him out into the hall, till the programme had finished. Music excited me even then, and had me singing loudly (Tommy Steele's Nairobi being one I can remember) in the bath while banging my elbows off the bath sides. To this day I still have my mother's antiquated 'green hair brush' which I used to pretend was a makeshift guitar all those years ago. Today I play proper guitars, I hasten to add, having gathered a fine collection – they are my pride and joy, and hours are spent just looking at them like an artist would view a masterpiece of a painting. Guitars have always intrigued me for some reason. When I was a small child we had a very small, pink banjo on our Christmas tree, always placed out of reach though, a little higher than the rest, out of reach of my clumsy little hands, but it was always my favourite.

As mentioned previously, children are often oblivious to certain things happening around them in the earliest stages of their lives with the world as yet not having revealed its darker side. Certainly I have very few negative childhood memories from those early years. However, I do have a very clear memory, not so happy, of going into the house one day around this time and seeing my mother sitting on the settee crying, with the few contents of her purse scattered around next to her. Asking what the matter was, she dried her eyes, smiling up at me as she put the pennies back, and mumbled her reply which unusually I can't recall. Many years later I tentatively mentioned that scene to her, and she was genuinely shocked that I could recall that moment so long ago. She went on to explain that at that time we had very little money and with bills to pay and groceries to buy she was struggling to make ends meet. She wouldn't have been alone in that regard though at that time for sure.

My formative years were very busy, I ran as and when I felt like it and slept like a log at the end of the day, exhausted by my physical antics.

Early school years

(And a great imagination!)

I still have a 'Stories' school exercise book from September 1958 (I would just have turned seven at the time) in which I wrote a story about a school trip to Edinburgh. At the end Mrs Tait gave me 9 out of 10 and a 'red' star, followed by 'How do you know all this? You weren't there'! Rightly so, I didn't go, I don't know why, maybe we were hard up or it was Linda's turn? Anyhow when my classmates came back the next day, we all had to write about the trip. I wrote enthusiastically about the train journey, the castle, the zoo, what we had for lunch etc. – and I wasn't even there! Always have had a great imagination, saves a lot of money I suppose!

In September 1956 I began my school education, at Stobswood School, a small cluster of red-bricked buildings which nestled on the fringe of mature woodland. *As ridiculous as it may sound now, but looking back it's probable that I actually started my athletic training right back then, as a five year old in September 1956.* Although there is no doubt that even before this date I had led an energetic life, and certainly up to this point I didn't have to be encouraged to run, and loved being outside, it all came very naturally, as I am sure it did with all my mates. However, from the moment I started school I had a fairly lengthy walk there and back and in all weathers, initially in hand-me-down hob nailed boots, clanking along like the Gestapo. On arriving at school – the journey probably took about 45 minutes – we all joined a line in the yard, and had our hands inspected before being allowed inside. In anticipation of the inspection, as we walked through the gates we used to spit vigorously on our hands, accompanied by frantic rubbing in an attempt to remove all the engrained dirt accumulated on our journey through the woods.

The school was within about 20 metres from the main London to

Edinburgh railway line. It was also within touching distance of Stobswood 'pit' and the local brickyard, both of which provided a very high proportion of the work for Widdrington and Stobswood folk.

Starting school ensured that discipline took over from the jovial carefree days of pre-school infancy, and as mentioned that discipline began and ended each day's schooling with a fairly lengthy walk there and back. I recently retraced that journey and it took 30 minutes at a brisk pace and that's as a fit adult; as a five year old I would guess it would take an estimated further 15 minutes or so, resulting in a 90 minute hike every school day. Add to that three highly energetic 'play times' between lessons and the odd PE lesson (which we did in the clothes, shoes or wellies we wore for school that day) and you can begin to appreciate why I refer to this period as 'athletic'. I would also add, these early daily excursions were by the most direct route; however, once we were familiar with the journey, we would zig zag along while calling on friends as we went, climb trees, and do some birds nesting etc. The indirect route through the fields and the woods was always my favoured route. We were one of the few families in Widdrington at the time who had a car. A big black Hillman (not dissimilar to the Al Capone Chicago era) with sills along the sides and the ever present internal smell of the all leather seats! Despite the latter I can only ever once remember being offered a lift from my dad and that was one morning when the snow had fallen in buckets. As Linda and I prepared to leave the house my dad said, 'Stay where you are and I'll run you along.' Sitting back down again in our wellies, hats, gloves, and coats, watching the falling snow while Dad finished his breakfast, I can remember becoming increasingly agitated as the time went by, as in those days if you were late for school there was a price to pay (more on that later!). Eventually we followed our dad out, sat freezing on the back seat while he took out the starting handle and after several energetic attempts to unsuccessfully turn the engine over he gave up, which was followed by a blunt directive encouraging us to *get your skates on and be quick otherwise you'll be late'!* To this day I remember running along in the snow with Linda, by ourselves due to the rest of the kids having long gone. I remember also waiting on Linda whilst encouraging her to go quicker, as unlike our first race, it was she who couldn't now keep up with me! As we proceeded along Grangewood Terrace on the 'final lap' the school bell rang; picking the pace up one last time we made it by a handful of seconds! I have many memories of winter school days, our wellies leaving red painful circles as they rubbed continuously on our bared upper calves, woollen bobble hats, gloves and balaclavas recently knitted by our Nana. Dark early morning skies, loads of snow, icy roads, huge icicles hanging precariously from the upper drains, and attempting to knock them down to suck as cheaper versions of tasteless ice lollies, and the school milk bottles with the frozen milk protruding a couple of inches from the top, frozen solid. Despite the quite hostile winters we seemed to have in those days, our little brick school with very few mod cons was never closed due to winter weather. Unlike today whereby if there is a dark cloud on the horizon all schools pull down the shutters – for health and safety reasons of course.

Back to that first day!

I can, like many others I would imagine, remember quite a bit about my first day at school, almost 60 years ago. On that first morning, new starters were initially escorted to school by our mothers or elder brothers and sisters, and picked up later at the end of the day. As mentioned previously, my journey was a lengthy one for a five year old – we lived at the farthest point away from school in Widdrington. Following the first day's trek we would make our own way there and back for the remaining school years.

That first day I have memories of what could be described as a kind of mayhem, lots of noise, kids crying, people running around, coming and going etc. At some point that morning as I stood as an interested bystander minding my own business, I was approached by Mrs Dixon, the class teacher, and as a reward for good behaviour, was given the honour of sharpening all the red pencils. Anyhow sharpen them I did, using the never before seen pencil sharpener with the bulky handle, attached to the desk by a couple of screws. In fact I sharpened the pencils so well I quickly reduced them all to half inch spelks! I hadn't been there a half hour and already had my first 'dressing down' in front of all the other kids. On hindsight it would probably be the case back then that there were few funds for classroom equipment, and sitting here now, I wonder how Mrs Dixon explained to Mr Clark, the Headmaster, the demise of all her pencils within half an hour of us beginning a new term! Many years later, I had a Sgt Major in the Marines, Sammy Fink (*see below) who once menacingly told us all 'you might not like me, but you'll never F...ing well forget me' (true!). It is likely Mrs Dixon, who was quite elderly, never forgot me either. I can also somewhat embarrassingly (even now) recall in the coming days 'filling my pants' so to speak in class (I mentioned this years later to my mother who replied without any sign of humour and quite proudly 'well, you were always regular, Michael'!) and her taking me up to the staff room to 'clean me up', just as the bell rang for playtime and all the teachers entered before retreating in somewhat of a 'hurry'. Around this time I also had my first minor playground 'tussle' with Alec Neal, which was broken up by a teacher taking hold of the two of us by our arms and shaking us vigorously whilst telling us this behaviour would not be tolerated! I genuinely look forward to seeing Alec; clearly we go back a long way – he's never changed, a good friend, probably better looking now than he was then and he's still ugly, despite all the Botox and cosmetic surgery!

An early acquaintance at school was Ronnie Gibbard. Ronnie was an ever constant companion of mine at school; as far as I can remember going way back we sat next to each other every day, in every school and class we attended. Primary, Secondary and Boarding school, much in common, the two of us loved sport, had little time for lessons, laughed or smirked regularly and when it was all over we left together at 15. A talented footballer, Ronnie went on to have trials for Burnley when they were a top team; he still plays, a lot to be said for the Stobswood school dinners – liver, tetties and cabbage!

Before I forget, the aforementioned Sammy Fink used to bet money on me in the Sergeants' Mess, that I would win boxing and running competitions, frightening me to death in the process, as his Sgt Major's 'encouraging' voice was heard bellowing a million decibels in excess of all other 'spectators'! I have a photograph to remind me of those times, which shows our cross country team crouching down having a team photo taken having just won the unit championships, and there I am with my 1st place 'winnings', rolling some dollars between my fingers, having just been 'paid' – happy days!

In those early school days I also quickly discovered that I was different from most of my other classmates. I was, and am left handed, well almost. I write left handed but to complicate things I do most other activities right handed, I also kick footballs right footed and throw balls right handed! I have clear memories of attempting to write using my favoured left hand, but confusingly being told by teachers to look at how everyone else was using their right hand, as such being advised to do likewise (bet Prince Charles never had that type of hassle though). As soon as she was gone of course I reverted back to my favoured left side. This strange phenomenon would cause me all sorts of problems during instructional life as all things were demonstrated from the right side and I had to somehow transfer the demos on to the other side!

A good hiding!

It is hard to imagine today, but all the way through my schooling days we were liable to be hit, a hand on the back side or quick clip on the side of the head, the belt, the ruler, the cane, the sandshoe and even the cricket bat. Even now I have no issue with any of that, as long as it was justified. After all 'pain is a big de-motivator'. However we occasionally got smacked not for doing something wrong but more because we didn't learn either well enough or quick enough. I can remember one such chastisement, in Mrs Gagie's class. One morning we were handed back our 'sums' books which she'd marked overnight. However on this occasion she had an issue with my untidy work; she called me out front before writing zeros on the blackboard, while telling the class this is how Michael Harris writes his noughts. My zeros hadn't 'joined up', in other words they looked more like tear drops or small lemons than being totally round! Not content to humiliate me in front of the class, she then proceeded to drag me around the classroom by my hand, up and down the aisles, whilst vigorously smacking my backside. Once back to my seat she shoved me down on the chair. At this stage as I remember she glared at me as I met her gaze; there were no tears from me and I'm convinced this made her even angrier. For me the humiliation (while I sat looking at all the others as they looked at me) came from the class and not from the vigorous hiding. But rightly or wrongly, my noughts were always joined up after this 'telling off'!

I was to spend large periods of my future life as a teacher. Part of the role of a teacher, tutor or coach is finding out what works best for each individual. Clearly we are all very different. For me 'praise' was the key, I worked better feeling as if I were valuable; harsh treatment rarely worked. I can be very stubborn; I needed to feel important, the more praise I received the greater would be the effort. Looking back on the above scenario (which is clearly still with me almost 60 years later) it seems clear that the beating I received achieved very little, and if it achieved anything at all, there was most certainly a better way, e.g. 'do it this way, Michael, good lad, you are better than this'! Yet much against the grain these days, I have no issue at all with a reasonably gentle tap on the backside, should it be deemed appropriate or necessary.

School traditions and making pocket money in rural Northumberland!

In the days of my childhood there were clearly marked out 'seasons' such as 'blackberry' week, and a 'conker' season. As far as the latter was concerned, we'd put all our gathered conkers onto a piece of string before hammering the hell out of an opponent's stringed pride and joy! We played simple boyhood games like 'marbles', and collected rosehips from the numerous hedgerows which adjoined the lanes, roads and fields around Widdrington. The latter was a valuable pastime following on from the war years, when vitamin C was in short supply. For us kids though it was a highly attractive way of making some pocket money, receiving as we did three pence a pound from our school. We also did 'tetty pickin' (potato picking) where even as kids we could make in excess of 10 shillings a day in the fields of local farmers, a small fortune then for children who were used to three pence twice a week if you were lucky! Another money making venture was putting people's coals in. I think it fair to say that most of the men folk where I lived worked for the National Coal Board; as such they were entitled to regular loads of free coal, the coal being delivered in lorries and deposited on the road and path adjoining the house. Us

Me, Stobswood School,
about 10/11 years old

lads would stand on the Store corner, wait till the coal lorry went past, at which point we would run behind it to the delivery point. Once the load was tipped, we would walk up to the door of the occupant and ask if we could put the coal in (that is from the road to the coal house); if we got the nod we'd be provided with a barrow or pails and proceed to lead the coals into the coal house. On conclusion we'd be paid generally about 2 shillings or a half crown – hard work but good money! I can well remember on one occasion Trevor Barnes and I, having finished the job, knocking on the lady's door and waiting patiently for our anticipated monetary reward before being handed a 'hard-boiled egg' each, no money! Totally unimpressed, we seriously considered returning after dark and 'unloading' all the coal and putting it all back on the road, but due to the work involved we changed our minds and ate the bloody eggs instead! I can also remember going up with John Douglas to Ulgham Church which was covered in daffodils in the spring; we would then gather as many daffs as we could, before bundling them under our jumpers and returning to the streets of

Widdrington to sell them round the doors for tuppence a bunch. To the disdain of people now I am sure, we all had birds' egg collections, but growing up rurally that's what we did, it was the 'norm' then. Climbing trees or searching hedgerows for birds' nests, a boyhood hobby passed down through the years from previous generations, it all seemed so very innocent then, we didn't know any different! Even then though, we had moral or ethical values and never took the eggs from a bird if you already had one of that species in your collection!

The vast majority of us kids often wore 'hand me down' clothing and shoes; there was never any shame in that, we just got decent clothing attire from our relations as they grew out of them. Knitting was also a common pastime, particularly with Grannies, supplying as they did quality jumpers, hats and the likes. Some even got knitted swimming trunks, which immediately dropped to the knees when subjected to the chilly waters of Ulgham Burn or the freezing Druridge Bay seawater! At Ulgham Burn we used to play 'duffs' where you would challenge each other to do the most spectacular stunts which always resulted in us falling in the Burn, returning home late in the day – stinking!

A sign of the times perhaps, but in those days you could take a fishing net and scoop handfuls of fish out of the Burn at Ulgham without trying; occasionally we'd take them home in jam jars. My mother couldn't bear to see them swimming around in circles in such limited space so we would walk the mile or so back up before releasing them back into their natural environment.

Night times were spent traipsing the mile long journey back to Stobswood 'boys club' for gymnastics, road running or occasional games of billiards or table tennis. Another very energetic pastime was playing 'tally oh' outside in the dark and frosty streets. I can remember fleeing other kids on opposing teams (notably Longca Reed, Banty Moore, Trevor Barnes), with my lungs absolutely bursting and chest heaving in the process whilst blowing out copious amounts of vapoured white air into the frosty star-lit night. So many times whilst being chased I remember being so close to my physical limit that another few yards and I would have had to give in, collapse, or be caught, but even then I seemed to find a little extra strength and willpower from somewhere, until the heavy panting and following footsteps of my pursuers gradually faded, leaving me to stumble on in a real state of exhaustion, until the next similar encounter! In athletics terms the latter is called 'interval, or fartlek training'!

'Michael has other qualities other than academic!' (*Mr Clark, the headmaster's comment, on an end of term school report*).

My education at Stobswood School was, I think, made more difficult in so much as my sister Linda preceded me through the classes. Linda was a 'cute, good looking lass' (and still is I hasten to add) and a very bright pupil, who would go on to pass her 11 plus exam and go to grammar school (as expected). Always top of the form and even (much to my embarrassment) standing on a bench in assemblies to read a chapter or two from the bible in front of the whole school. Just as Linda was awarded with end of term books for scholarly work, I was awarded with similar books for what amounted to 'turning up regularly' Ha! (Otherwise known as 100% attendance.) When I mentioned previously that my education was made more difficult I simply mean that, Linda Harris's name always preceded Michael Harris's name through the class year groups. I am sure because of that I was labelled with scholarly 'potential' even before I got there. I can recall even now, listening to a conversation between my mother and nana and my nana stating quite categorically (after viewing a very 'ordinary' term's school report), '*Well, you can't get blood out of a stone, Margaret*'! I listened but at the time had little understanding of what she meant.

Covered in Spit!

A little escapade took place around this time which highlights in simplistic terms how Linda's academic prowess and reputation affected my early school life. On this occasion, together with two friends, Ossie Moore and Trevor Barnes, we used our lunchtime break to chase each other around the playground while repeatedly 'spitting' on each other while laughing like maniacs. As we rushed into the toilets to escape each other, Trevor ran into a cubicle whereby Ossie and I climbed up the cubicle walls and dangling over the top we rained even more spit down on the hapless Trevor! At which point a teacher caught us and with apparent unbelievable disgust and disdain at our antics marched the three of us upstairs to Mr Clark's office. There we were, the three of us covered in spit, head to toe, standing heads bowed in disgrace while getting a good telling off before getting our punishment, the dreaded cane. Ossie first, Trevor second, and then myself. As he arrived at me he made a comment that would follow me through my school years and way beyond even to this day (and emphasises how Linda's' name was associated with mine) 'and Michael Harris, Linda's brother'! No sooner had the three of us left the Head's office than both Ossie and Trevor looked at me and repeated Mr Clark's comments 'and Michael Harris, Linda's brother' accompanied by their evil little grins!

Linda!

Like many younger brothers I guess, whilst growing up I was a regular embarrassment to my older sister. Finding an example of what I mean isn't difficult, as many spring to mind. Here's one though! About three or four days prior to going on end of term leave from my boarding school at Bellingham, we all went on a school trip to Edinburgh. Entering a pet shop in the city, I couldn't resist the temptation of buying a couple of cute little

domesticated 'white mice'! I didn't have the money to buy a cage so for the next few days, whilst keeping my secret purchase out of sight of the teaching staff, I kept the mice in a coat pocket – till I got home, at which point they were transferred to the luxury of a shoe box. While going through my washing, my mother quickly identified my coat was in need of special attention due to its outwardly 'scruffy' state, hence Linda was tasked with taking it to the nearest dry cleaners. Queuing up in the shop Linda eventually got to the front where she was directed to 'check the pockets, pet', for any left-over items! Placing her well-manicured 16 year old hands into a pocket, she immediately, and in full view of the entire shop, withdrew copious amounts of claggy mouse's 'shit'! Obviously embarrassed and lost for words, she was handed a tissue, before repeating the same manoeuvre on the other side with an identical result, at which point the employee, in full view of all, turned the pockets inside out emptying four days of mouse diarrhoea all over the shop floor! You can only but imagine a fashionable, very attractive 16 year old young lady, standing there in full view of all, covered in mouse's dung, apparently from 'her' very own coat pockets! Wished I'd been there though! Oh yes, hilarious!

Despite her brother's unpredictable behaviour, Linda went on to make a real success of her life, bearing in mind the humble beginnings from where it all began at Stobswood's little school. As mentioned previously, she passed her Eleven Plus exam and went on to Morpeth's Grammar School for girls, then on to College, following which she moved to London, before gaining employment all over the world. She finished her working life as the *Personal Assistant to the Director General of the World Health Organisation (the latter was a former Prime Minister!)*. Married twice, she has two smashing sons and four wonderful grandchildren. Michael, her eldest, has a very demanding job, and like his mother did before him travels the world, additionally like his Unc' does triathlons including Ironman events. Christian, her younger, recently received an 'Oscar' (yes, an Oscar!) for writing the script for a Danish film called 'Helium'! Amazing! My only regret with Linda is that we have for most of our lives lived many miles apart; currently we meet perhaps once a year although we write weekly via emails. I have much respect for her first husband Henrik who I class as a friend, and have a great relationship with Tom, her current (or should I say 2nd) husband, an American Lawyer. She now lives in Florida amongst alligators, snakes and geet big hairy spiders!

Ugh! Can you imagine? While I live in the serenity of Widdrington alongside sparrows, starlings, and robins! I am indeed very fortunate!!

School sports days and a sign of things to come!

Apart from that very early family race at the age of four, it is very likely that my obsession for sporting competition was cemented at Stobswood School. Like at many schools, from about the age of eight or nine we were all put into 'sporting houses' (teams). At Stobswood there were four such houses, Portland (green), Cresswell (blue), Percy (yellow) and my own designated house Widdrington (red). If you had elder brothers and sisters in the school you inherited their house colours. The houses were all named after prominent Northumbrian families. In the hall where we had our daily morning assemblies prior to lessons, I remember being intrigued and drawn as if by an invisible magnet to the various sporting plaques on the wall behind the teachers showing all the sports day House winners over the preceding years. The successful houses being represented by little coloured bands stuck on to the plaques. Mr Clark, the school headmaster, was obviously very proud of the school's sporting prowess – as such there were always football and netball matches taking place as well as class, house, and occasional inter-school competitions. And before area tournaments he even supervised Rounders training himself, Rounders being one of his passions due to the school's very successful winning history.

Annual school sports days were for me a highlight of the year, and always seemed to take place on sunny days. You knew it was coming because all of a sudden the beautiful smell of freshly cut grass would breeze in through the classroom windows. This would then be followed by 'Benny' Nicholson (school handyman, and a friend to us all, who often joined in playtime kick-arounds in the yard) marking out the track lanes on the grass multi-purpose field. Even now the same smell gives me a shot of adrenalin as I cast my mind back to those simple days, days before spikes and 'proper' running apparel were the norm. The beauty of competition in those days was that all of us kids were identical in terms of clothing, footwear, and even wealth; the only thing that separated us was the coloured band we wore to identify our respective school house. There were no spikes, starting blocks or fancy shorts or singlets, no stop watches or fancy drinks, and as far as I can remember *we just rolled up our sleeves and got stuck in!* I can well remember one year being told by my mother that she would be going to Ashington to get us sandshoes in anticipation of the forthcoming sports day. The norm then (although not 'carved in tablets of stone') was that boys wore Woolworth's black canvas sandshoes and girls wore white. Anyhow all day I couldn't wait to get home from school and try my new 'running' shoes out, on the 'bottom green'! As soon as I got in I looked for the box, but the only ones I could find were white! *'Where's mine?'* I excitedly *enquired.* 'They didn't have your size, son, you'll have to share the white ones with Linda,' came the reply. *'They're girls','* I shouted. *'I can't wear them, they're white, they'll all laugh!'* 'Don't be so silly, that's all there is so get on with it.' Once again, years later, out of devilment and playing the hard done by waif, I raised this issue with my mother, but this time with a smile, my mother told me at the time she just didn't have the money to buy two pairs, but couldn't tell me – bless her!

Some years later my Uncle Robert, a PTI in the Black Watch, and my childhood hero, told me of a similar incident which happened to him. As he grew, he asked his dad, my grandad (who hadn't long left the RAF, after the war), if like the other lads he could start wearing 'long trousers'. After continuous badgering, he was thrown a pair, 'Here you are, son', at which point he hurriedly tried them on to make sure they fitted before going off to bed. Getting up the next day he proudly put on his first pair of 'long' trousers! And off he went to school. Later in the day, as the school bell rang for break time off he went to the toilet for a pee only to discover there was no front zip or button to release his 'tiddler' (got a way with words eh?). Baffled by this and now the focus of attention as he pulled his pants down to his knees, he was crassly informed by others 'Hey Barny, you've got WRAF's pants on'!! Think that's funny? He informed me his 'next 'pair of long trousers was a pair of 'cricket whites' which as you can imagine didn't exactly go well with his hobnailed black boots!

In anticipation of the approaching school sports day, PE lessons would switch from football, rounders and cricket to running, jumping and throwing (cricket balls) events. Competitions were designed to identify kids with ability who would then represent their respective houses in the forthcoming sports day. Sitting in class, and listening to the distinctive sound of the high jump bar hitting the sand pit at this time was torture for me, itching as I was to get out and away from the laborious 'sums' lessons.

There were people there whom I had the highest regard for, and even now I am still in awe of their sporting school triumphs. I will even go as far as to say I would willingly swap one of my 18 British Championship medals for one of those tiny innocuous cups they won. Margaret Kelly, Johnny Smith, Lynn Bolton, Keith Tweddle, Heather Farrell, the Clark brothers, Kathleen Moore were all winners of a school cup awarded for those accumulating the most points in running (only sprints in those early days), jumping, throwing and relay competitions. The cups (male and female) were presented at the conclusion of the day's competition while we all gathered around and applauded. What I would have given then to have taken a cup home!

*(see page 20 – born in August!) I was always very active in the sports, taking part in just about everything, but despite my best efforts for some reason which frustrated me more than I can say, I lacked the speed to contest the sprints at the front end. *It was years later I realised that in my year group I was the youngest pupil, having been born in August. There were people in my year who were (but for a week or two) a full year older than me – clearly that's a full year's growing and with it maturity, strength and additional speed! Likewise in the year below me there were many who were very close to me in terms of age – if I'd been born a week or two later and therefore in another year group I would have been right up there!*

I can remember that following the school sports day's initial excitement, and feelings of euphoria, together with triumphant expectations, coming back down to earth with a bump and utter disappointment at not having won anything. This, despite as always having tried my absolute best. Returning home in such a foul mood and being unable to explain that I was simply not good enough, and a bad loser! I'd be threatened with 'a good hiding' if I didn't cheer up. I never got used to being beaten in sports, and even at 64 I am exactly the same now as I was then, only now I hide it better. **But those years at 'Stobby' School I am sure helped make me what I became later, one of the best amateur athletes in the country! And in my chosen pursuit of triathlon THE best in Britain for a handful of years. Built around incredible singular and prolonged effort, rather than outstanding talent!**

I wonder though, how much of my future athletic prowess was nurtured or harnessed during those long energetic days and nights of my youth, and even by those early 'failings' in school sport?

I can't be too specific about the exact date; however, it would be around about this time when I was nine or 10 years old that my mother and father separated. This came as a shock, I hadn't noticed a breakdown in their relationship, but then I probably wouldn't (too busy, I suppose, running around). Certainly I didn't fully understand any of it. Sounds strange now to even say it, but in the days of my youth and for many years thereafter separations were nonexistent, as were divorces – they just didn't happen in our part of the world. At the moment, politically, there is much talk of cuts in tax credits and how the proposed cuts will affect families. There does seem to be a very repetitive narrative currently where single mothers with one, two, three or more children will suffer extensively if the Chancellor reduces their benefits. Where I lived as a child and I'm sure throughout the North East generally, this scenario (so many single mums) would very rarely have happened, or if it did it would have been viewed as extraordinary or at least very unusual. In today's ever changing world it seems as if lone parents with so many children are almost more common than families with a mother and a father in the same household. I'm not knocking single parenthood, just attempting to draw anyone reading this into the period in which I grew up. Having set the scene though it must appear contradictory as the Harris household was soon to become one of the latter families, single parent! Although we lived with my mother I am quick to point out that my dad always sent some money to help with our upkeep. But certainly my mother received nothing in relation to benefits (or tax credits) apart from a meagre 'family allowance' that every family received. Anyhow the separation resulted in my dad moving out and returning down south where he was originally from. I do remember being confused, and when friends asked where Dad had gone, through embarrassment I'd reply that he was working down south and when he found us a house we would all follow. Sometimes when I think about it all, it does seem strange that I would pursue such a life in sport, because I received absolutely no encouragement to do so. I don't wish to appear in any way remorseful, or badly done by, but as you will see shortly, if I wanted to go to the Harriers or anywhere else for that matter, I had to bus it (if we had the money) or bike it; if I was to wait for a lift, in truth, I'd wait forever! Years later when coming home on leave and getting off the last train into Newcastle, and the last bus gone, with no one to meet me, I'd hike the final 20 miles. Yet another good workout!

Although my dad sent money each week, it clearly wasn't enough as my mother very quickly started work again to make ends meet, initially as a house cleaner in a big house in Warkworth. The result of the latter was that Linda (who was now at grammar school) and I had to get ourselves up in the morning and rake up a bite to eat before leaving for school. Being totally undomesticated at the time, my breakfast was a handful of digestive biscuits and a slurp of milk, before legging it down the street. Returning from school a few hours later I would again grab a few digestives and have a slurp of tap water before commencing the energetic evening's activities.

My Mother!

My mother, who died in August 2014, was a very special person whom I loved so much, and I will always hold her in the highest of regards. She was a strong minded person with high moral standards, very loving as well as 'scatter brained' (her words). For the life of her she couldn't understand sport, she was always very forgetful, but oh so very funny.

In the latter few years of her life she suffered from Alzheimer's, and initially to a degree it wasn't exceptionally noticeable, again in her words, she'd say with a smile – 'Michael, I've always been like this' – and so she had! This tale will best describe her as she was when I was a young lad growing up.

Mother and Linda, 1952, recently back from Malta

Before leaving for work in the dark at about 6.30am, she would hover over me in my bed with a 'warning', which went along the following lines. 'I'm away, son, now listen, when I get in tonight, I want you in the house so I can see you, do you understand?' Burying my head beneath the sheets I'd reply exactly what she wanted to hear – 'Aye, man'!

Later in the day as soon as I got home from school, I'd do a very impressive quick change and whoosh, I was out, gone, oblivious to her warning. A while later of course in would walk Mother, and without even putting down her bag, would look at a 'sheepish' looking Linda –'where is he?' To which Linda who always did her best to protect her little brother would reply along the lines of 'Oh Mam, man, he won't be long, he'll be playing football!' Several hours later a very nervous, and very tired, Michael would return and be given a right old rollicking!

But that would only last till the next day when we'd go through the whole same scenario again. So she decided to act!

We had at the time a 'girls' bike in our coal house! Once in from school it would take me no longer than five minutes to wheel it out before sprinting along the street like Mark Cavendish – gone! As a means of curtailing my antics Mother thought it a great idea to let the tyres down! *'That'll fix him'* accompanied by a defiant nod of her head! But being my mother she left the pump on the frame, see what I mean about scatter brained? So I'd pump up the tyres and I'm off. Next night, the tyres are again flat, and this time the pump is gone! I walk across the yard to Ethel next door. *'Can I borrow your pump please, missus?'* Yes, son came the reply, and I'm off again! The next night, the tyres are flat, the pump is gone, she's had words with Ethel, AND the seat's missing. Not to be beat, I rode the bike standing up! It 'almost' ends there, because the bike is then removed and hidden, out of sight, out of mind. BUT!

A short while later, finding me gone as usual when she returns from work, she persuades my Uncle John to drive her around in an attempt to find me. Having been everywhere else, and tension building, they finally head to the beach three miles away. As they turn a corner and are facing a long straight road about a half mile in length, they are met by several of my mates on their bikes returning from the sea. *'You seen our Michael?'* she enquires! Looking over their shoulders my mates proceed to point *'that's him there, missus'* and looking down the road half a mile away, there I am, a lonesome little figure in the distance running up a local ascent called 'the lang Tommy'. You can imagine the next bit, however – so ashamed was she that I didn't have a bike, like my mates, that she went out and bought me a second hand red bike on hire purchase!! God bless her, she must have been frantic those years, all those hours at work, wondering continually where the hell I was and what I was up to.

For me 'looking out of the window in the house' was akin to a dog 'looking at a juicy bone'! For us both (the dog and me) there would always only be one outcome!

It is fair to say that once she had married, and Linda and I came along, my mother's entire life revolved around us; nothing else mattered, until that is, we had our own children then she had a few more to worry about. She had one fault as a mother – she simply cared too much!

Another school, more competition, and above all, 'musical revolution' that would change the world!

Up until around 1962 local pupils at Stobswood School would see out their entire education there, commencing at five years of age and terminating at 15. The only exception was if you passed the 11 plus exam, then you went on to a Grammar School where your academic superior ability was recognised and harnessed in expected preparation for a higher occupational status. However, around about 1962 the government of the day introduced what were referred to as Secondary Modern Schools, which meant from the age of 11 we all transferred to the closest Secondary Modern in our area; accordingly from Stobswood we all went to a school about four miles away at Broomhill, and for the first time we had to wear a school uniform and get a bus rather than walking. Once there we amalgamated with pupils from other schools in the area, in our case Red Row (pronounced locally as reed rare), and Broomhill. Apart from one or two early scuffles, as far as I can recall we all seemed to get along fine despite where we belonged. Clearly the school was a lot bigger than the family orientated little school we were at previously. This meant there would be much more competition to represent the school in sport! In brief as far as sport goes and for the short time I was there, I was a member of the school soccer team and won my first 1 mile race during the school sports day, and won a class cross-country race.

Music!

Perhaps my biggest memory of Broomhill was the huge cultural change taking place at that time in the early 1960s and at 11 years of age we were very quickly maturing and becoming much more aware and worldly wise!

Apart from my love of sport I have always had an equal passion for music, and the 1960s were an incredible period for just that, but not just music itself but also the characters and changing fashions that went with it. There was so much happening at that stage with new bands almost a weekly occurrence. Wow, what an era! Pop stars of the 1950s, such as Cliff Richard, Adam Faith, Marty Wilde, Billy Fury, Michael Holliday etc (an era I would describe as scented bubble gum, with the classic clean sounds of Wonderful Land and the Young Ones together with scented hair gel known as Brylcreem) were being rapidly replaced by groups such as The Beatles, the Rolling Stones, the Who, the Kinks, the Small Faces, the Searchers, the Yardbirds, the Pretty Things, the Animals, Them, Manfred Mann, The Beach Boys, The Byrds, Gerry and the Pacemakers, the Dave Clark Five, the Hollies, the Spencer Davis Group and a further abundance of Liverpudlian and Manchurian bands too many to mention here. Unlike today, where it seems success is largely dictated by good looks, the bands of the 1960s all played instruments and often wrote their own songs. Additionally, before attaining any musical success, they had done an apprenticeship for several years as they toured clubs and pubs, before appearing in the concert halls or on television. The Beatles were so different from anything seen or heard before, and other bands created raunchy sounds that even to this day still make the proverbial hairs stand on the back of my neck, 'You really got me' being a prime example. I was so lucky to be around at the beginning of that period and to witness the profound changes that would briskly follow. Now when I see an eleven year old (as I was then) I am immediately reminded how much they are open to influence at that age, noticing everything.

It's strange how much kids miss though while growing up. We were for the most part so interested in sport, music and the fashion that went with it, and the opposite sex for the first time, that we were for the most part oblivious of changing political scenes. Although, like countless others, I can remember coming in from school in 1963 and being told by Linda that JFK had been assassinated! In the 1960s there was a major potentially earth changing threat materialising between the USA and the Soviet Union, with nuclear war being a very real possibility – the 'Cuban missile crisis' – but most of us of a certain age back then couldn't have cared less! We saw what we wanted to see and disregarded the rest. As long as we caught sports report at 5 o'clock on Saturdays and 'Top *of the pops'! Or had the six shillings and nine pence needed to buy the next single on the Parlophone label we were happy!*

Boarding school and a coming of age! (The 1960s)

It's a pity Michael's ability does not match his efforts! (Comment on school report, Joe Lowe – form teacher)

After about a year or two at Broomhill Secondary Modern a school change was on the cards again and with the change, the start of an amazing two years away from the safety of home. A period never to be forgotten!

Our accomodation, 'just sheds in the snow'

For some reason Widdrington had a history of kids voluntarily going on to finish their education at a Boarding School in Bellingham, Northumberland. Bellingham is situated in the middle of some of the wildest, bleakest, yet most beautiful countryside in Northumberland. And all we needed to be accepted into this unique little school with its wooden accommodation, and classrooms was 'parental consent'.

Several older kids from Widdrington had gone to Bellingham before us and would return home at the end of term, with wonderful stories of their adventures and antics. With nothing other than a sense of adventure, Ossie, Ronnie, Alan, Boke and I packed our bags and headed for the hills; we couldn't wait. Two years later and the same principles would reoccur for me when I again left home and 'joined-up'! Education at Brown Rigg was delivered by live-in teachers, who slept at the end of our dormitories in their own tiny compact rooms. The education programme was the same as all Secondary Modern schools of that time, the only difference was that you slept at the school with your mates for several months at a time. Additionally it was a 'mixed gender' school with girls billeted just 50 yards away in identical dormitories to the lads. Oh what a school this turned out to be, phenomenal, wonderful, and looking back now I wouldn't have missed it for the world.

Strangely perhaps, you would think that children would have quite grave reservations about moving out of the stability and safety of their family house and with it all the home comforts with caring parents and close family members to look after them. As opposed to being many miles away and living in what amounted to 'wooden huts' with few mod cons. In many ways we were living in quite bleak conditions (winters in particular were very harsh), with only a small bed and a set of drawers to keep your few personal belongings in.

There is no doubt that being physically fit at Brown Rigg with a liking for the outdoor life was a real bonus as so much of our time, official and unofficial, was spent doing sport and other physical pursuits. It seems to me looking back that because we were all of a 'certain age', and the school was mixed gender, that the staff would attempt to wear us all out every day in an attempt to discourage 'mischief'!

You gotta laugh!

In the years I went to school, us pupils were occasionally, for want of another expression, 'belted' for perceived misdemeanours! I can well remember one such occasion at boarding school. On this day we were having an art class with a teacher we'd refer to (outside of his hearing range of course) as Little Stevie (after Stevie Wonder); I think his name was Stevenson. As usual for most of my lessons I was sitting next to Ronnie Gibbard. As we began adhering to Stevie's directive to draw 'something or other', Ronnie whispered *'Stevie's* looking *at you'.* It is fair to say that Stevie gained perverse pleasure from inflicting pain, generally on me, for some 'imagined offence'. He would hit me on the backside with a huge T Ruler, while giggling like a lunatic and saying at the same time, *'I'll show you, lad, mess with Sir and Sir will mess with you'!* Anyhow on this typical occasion, I ignored Ronnie's comment for as long as I could, and carried on drawing until curiosity got the better of me and I had a sly look up in Stevie's direction; much to my absolute horror, I was immediately met by his grinning bearded face accompanied by a *'get out here, lad, you'll never learn, will you'!* Although I was totally innocent of any wrong doing, I uttered, *'I'm sorry, sir, I didn't do anything wrong, sir.'* To which he'd reply, *'Nothing wrong you say, well why the hell are you apologising then, you'll never learn will you, lad, thick as two short planks!'* Much to the delight of everyone else in the class who were falling about laughing, he would then pick up this tree trunk of a ruler, before directing me to *'bend over that desk, lad, I'll give you sorry sir I didn't do anything'* at which point of course I would comply fully, bend over the desk before being struck as hard as you like on my tender, increasingly red arse! Bearing in mind my only offence had been to look at him (albeit with a rather pathetic smile) three or four of the best was a harsh penalty indeed. The daft thing was that the louder everybody laughed, including 'Sir', the more inclined I was to perversely join in laughing despite the quite considerable pain being inflicted on me. With a final swing of the 'weapon' I'd be directed to *'now go back to your seat and behave yourself, and I'll be watching you'!* To this day, I can remember leaving the room once the 'lesson' (if you could call it that) was over and Stevie giving me a smile followed with a *'now behave yourself or else'!* **Hells bells I'd only looked at him, prompted by 'Gibbard'!** In the current climate within schools and other training establishments, my 'beating' would make headlines all over our politically correct media! Needless to say, I never fancied Art College as a career move!

Apart from the usual educational lessons, there were additional prep classes in the evenings together with all manners of entertainment. We all had girlfriends, and although we were only 50 metres away we would write and send via 'internal post' soppy love letters to each other together with kisses on the envelopes and little endearing rhymes. During my first term there as a 13 year old, and despite being two years her junior, my regular girlfriend then was Betty Howie (the Head Girl!). A short while ago whilst looking through some old photos I came across one of Betty and flipping it over there was a hastily scribbled message on the back – *'playing football at Stobswood'*. Clearly intended for my mother, coming in from work! There were evening dances in the assembly hall, where we'd do a mixture of classical dances like the 'Dashing White Sergeant', the 'Valetta', or the 'Moonlight Saunter' (the latter being a smooch, but not being allowed to be quite as close to your partner as you'd like, ha!). But between the formal dances we'd attempt to copy the moves as seen on 'Top of the pops' while gyrating to the pop music of the day. These dances were both formal (educational I suppose) and informal. Acting on a formal announcement, *'will the gentlemen please take their partners for the ...'* we would sheepishly approach the girl in our sights and with a laddish grin, designed in part to make us look cool, say *'please may I have the pleasure of the next dance'*. We also went to the pictures in the village at weekends, and Sundays after church (compulsory) very lengthy hikes were arranged around Bellingham's wild terrain. Additionally on Sunday evenings each of the eight dormitories took turns in putting on concerts and plays etc. to entertain the rest of the school for a couple of hours. As mentioned, sport was highly encouraged; as such I gained school colours in everything available – Athletics, Cross Country, Football, Rugby and Cricket (never an avid cricketer, nevertheless I was selected to play for the adult village team) and was a member of the school gymnastics display team. I got my Duke of Edinburgh's award, and took part in swimming galas in the tiny freezing outdoor swimming pool adjacent to Tyne Dorm.

Michael's sportsmanship is of the highest quality, he puts tremendous effort and enthusiasm into everything he does (comment on School report – Alan Bradburn – PE/Games Teacher)

You now perhaps see the relevance of the title **'60 years an athlete'**! At this stage of my life I had already accrued 11 years of continued athleticism in some form or another, so just another 50 years to go before getting to where I am today.

Brown Rigg Boarding School Rugby team (I'm front right)

Just by chance!

At some point on a Saturday afternoon at Brown Rigg in 1965, a fleeting incident occurred which was to have quite a profound effect on my future life, particularly with reference to my ever developing athletic ambitions. As mentioned previously my only knowledge of the 'stars' of athletics was by reading the stories in the Christmas sporting almanacs I got as a child. However, on the occasion I now refer to, a local and therefore 'almost touchable' athlete came along who left me almost mesmerised.

On the Saturday afternoon in question I (with a mate called Ali Peak) was running around the vicinity of our dorm and surrounding area, fleeing the attentions of an older pupil called Albert Cairns, a guy from Berwick with a strong Scottish accent. Ali and I were scared to death of this guy, but rather than keep out of his way, we would antagonise him, name calling, that sort of thing, we'd get him suitably mad and worked up until he'd chase us whilst shouting obscenities in his Scottish twang. Anyhow as I ran into our dorm (there were two doors either end of the dorm, exits and entries) the television in the corner of the room caught my eye; seeing a running race on it I stopped dead in my tracks (I learned years later that it was the Inter Counties meeting from London's White City stadium). And for the first time as I stood rooted to the spot I heard the name of **Jim Alder of Morpeth Harriers!** Jim was winning this race and I learned a couple of years later that he went on to claim the then 6 mile Inter Counties title. Morpeth being mentioned on national television almost took away what little breath I had left from fleeing the irate Cairns!! Turning around and seeing the gruesome figure of Cairns coming in the far end door blowing like an 'owld broken doon cuddy' (an old donkey) and a face as mad as hell, in fear of my life I bolted out the nearest exit and continued with my desperate escape. However, once safe I told anybody and everybody within listening range repeatedly '**Morpeth on the telly, a guy from Morpeth was on the telly, hey there was a bloke from Morpeth winning a race on the telly, honest, from Morpeth, he was winning!!**'.

To be honest, following the race at that time I quickly forgot Jim's name, but not his win, nor the mention of Morpeth Harriers on national television. A little over a year later Jim's name would be forever embedded in my mind, due to his major successes in winning the Commonwealth Games Marathon title in Jamaica and gaining a Bronze medal at the same games in the 6 mile event! The first time a 'local' athlete had made the big time. A little more on Jim's effect on my entire sporting life later.

Did Albert ever catch me? Not a chance. As close as he'd get would be from 10 or so metres away whilst pointing his finger in my direction and glaring at me in the school canteen during meal times. Wonder where Albert is now?

At Brown Rigg, and apart from being a member of all the school's sporting teams, I also finished second to my best mate Ossie Moore in the school Cross Country, and won a one mile race during a school's athletic match between us and the Bellingham Village school. I placed well in the area championships and went on to represent West Tyne in the County – not much to brag about I suppose but times were different then with few opportunities to race. Our little wooden school in the hills was unique; it had everything young teenagers could possibly want: girls, fashion (we'd share each other's clothing if it fit), music, laughs, entertainment and a 'boat load' of sport. Due to the extremely close relationship we all shared living, learning and sleeping together there was a wonderful spirit amongst us all, a closeness and comradeship similar to being in the armed forces. We also had a little kind of conservatory at the end of each of the dorms which were labelled the 'day rooms', where there would be a record player, table tennis board, that sort of thing. But it was the records that caught my attention especially the more raunchy stuff like the Pretty Things (Roselyn, Don't bring me down) the Kinks, Them, The Yardbirds, and *the first LP by the 'Stones'* with, in particular, tracks like Mona, Route 66 and once I heard the harmonica on *'now I've got a witness'* wow – I was hooked, absolutely blown away (excuse the pun!).

Boarding school gave me an excellent apprenticeship in relation to living away from home and fighting my own battles. I would use the experience to good effect a few months later when I joined-up and started all over again creating a fresh identity whilst making my mark in Britain's Armed Forces.

Leaving School!

I left Boarding School in July of 1966, a few weeks prior to my 15th birthday. Strangely, despite my ability to remember so much of my life, I can't for the life of me remember anyone talking to me about taking exams at school, but they must have done, as several of my close mates stayed on and took exams, in the process gaining some valuable certification. But I left with nothing but a smile and a 'boat load of memories'. Despite my immense fondness of Brown Rigg School I 'jumped' as soon as possible whilst looking forward to life's next unpredictable chapter!

Strange really, when you think, it's logical to assume children including teenagers would relish 'home comforts' and living in an environment where they feel secure, loved, cared for, food on the table, surrounded by family and friends and protected from the hostilities and responsibilities of adult life. For me, going to boarding school, and then joining up was nothing other than a huge adventure. I can't remember at any time having any reservations about any of it, or feeling anxious, stressed, or in the slightest way worried, only excited about what unknowns waited for me around the next corner, and I

Me, Brown Rigg Boarding School, 14 years old

couldn't wait. But such is youth, and there is no doubt that I would feel somewhat different now as a 'very' mature man. Going on 'holiday' now is like going to war, and I'm only slightly exaggerating! Having it seems gone full circle, I now prefer my home comforts, music at the touch of a button, television, fridge, guitars and harmonicas, bikes, binoculars, and familiar bed!

Joining Morpeth Harriers and AC (The first time around)

On the 11th of August 1966, my 15th birthday, I received my first ever pair of proper running shoes, white Adidas with three black stripes! Chuffed to bits! Also by an amazing coincidence, that was the exact same day that Jim Alder won his Commonwealth Games Marathon Gold!

As you can imagine the local newspapers together with the local television stations covered Jim's heroics in detail. The win wasn't straightforward due to him approaching the stadium with a healthy lead, victorious, before being misdirected and missing the entrance to the stadium. Once the 'mistake' had been identified he was put back on course only to realise he was now in 2nd place with Bill Adcocks having taken the right entrance into the stadium and now leading Jim by 40 or 50 metres! However, Jim managed to make up the deficit during the final lap before crossing the finishing line first, and with the victory collecting the gold medal!

A short while later Jim returned home to Morpeth and was given a hero's welcome as the town turned out to honour him with a civic reception.

On hearing the news of the civic reception, I cycled the seven miles through to Morpeth and waited in the crowds to see him (and a handful of his Morpeth team mates escorting the car) pass by in an open top Rolls Royce type vehicle whilst waving to all his townsfolk. The stuff dreams are made of, local boy made good!

The next step for me, prompted by Jim's win, was to join Morpeth Harriers. Not having a clue how to go about it, I simply rode my trusty bike back through to Morpeth again and trailed the streets asking several people where Jim Alder lived. Strangely (bearing in mind his newfound celebrity status) no one seemed to know; as such I was totally unsuccessful until I ventured into Hardy's fruit shop on Newgate Street where I repeated the same question as to Jim's address and was informed that the best thing to do was to go direct to the Harriers who were known to meet every Monday evening for training on their Mitford Road site. I cycled home only to return a few days later on the Monday evening and head towards Mitford Road. Morpeth Harriers at the time was a very small athletics club; as such when I entered the 'hut' I was surprised to see how few people were actually there. I no doubt saw either Tommy Horne, Ernie Slaughter or Peter Carmichael, the three of them for many years wonderful stalwarts of the club. Anyhow I must have joined (I still have my membership card from 1966), although disappointed not to have seen Jim. Once the business was over I walked out and proceeded back up Mitford Road. As I approached Dogger Bank (a short sharp hill) who should be coming the other way but Jim Alder, eating an apple. I said 'hello, Jim', and he said 'Aye Aye'; star struck I carried on walking but glanced back several times in admiration!

Jim had a huge influence on me at that point in my life and for most of my years as an athlete, although it's true to say we were, and remain, like ships in the night, never being in each other's company for long. He was one of the lads, a plasterer by trade, there were no airs and graces, he was local, and he proved that with hard work and steely determination you were in with a shout. Unlike other North Eastern athletic 'stars' he remained a working amateur throughout his athletic career. I think it is fair to say he has had an up and down life but never changed as far as I can see. His autobiography says it all, and it is in my opinion criminal that he no longer receives the accolades that others have received due to their ever present limelight and media involvement.

On the eve of his 40th gold medal winning anniversary I humbly took him and his ever loyal wife Kathleen a card and bottle of wine, just a small token of continued admiration. He recently turned up as a spectator at a triathlon I did, standing all alone; as I ran past he gave me a shout, a proud moment for me even at 64, and I mean it! At the time of this event I had a chronic foot injury (should never have started) and the running was causing me massive pain with every foot plant. Right from exiting the water following the swim I was in immediate pain; as such I had been wondering whether to drop out of the event (I have never failed to finish any event in my life, except once in a triathlon where I had a double puncture) – however, his presence made my mind up for me! Even then at 64 I finished in the top 20 from over 200 but lame, the injury would end my racing season and result in 10 weeks of rest before I could even think of jogging again! Unbeknown to Jim, I hobbled around looking for him after the event, but to no avail. I was going to approach the event organisers and suggest they ask him to present the prizes. An opportunity missed – for them!

As from August 1966 I was a proud, paid-up member of Morpeth Harriers. For several months before leaving home to start my career in the Royal Navy, I raced for Morpeth on Saturdays and travelled through on my bike from Widdrington for the traditional Sunday morning long run with the seniors.

A typical Sunday as a 15 year old!

Out of bed early, biked (as we didn't have a car and buses didn't run before 10 or 11 in the morning) through to Morpeth (seven miles) followed by a 12-15 mile run with the Morpeth Seniors (slow pack) before cycling home. Home in time for Sunday lunch, followed immediately by a game of up to 15 or 20 a-side football, depending on how many turned up, on the 'bottom green' till it was too dark to play any longer. At the time I honestly felt nothing of it!

My first of many bike 'spills'

On one of these training runs I can remember leaving the Harrier changing rooms on my bike after the lengthy run, and at that time there was a cattle grid at the entrance. As I went over the grid the vibration resulted in my brake cable (which was wrapped around the handle bars, because it didn't work) dropping between my spokes, sending me crashing over the handle bars. Sprawled over the grid, I was conscious of several cars following me out, who all screeched to a halt and scrambled to my assistance. Embarrassed, hurt pride and with a few facial and head scrapes but nothing 'serious', I apologised before assuring all that I was ok, wrapped the brake cable once again around the bars, remounted my bike and continued on the homeward journey!

In Morpeth Harriers at the time as I recall there were three boys, Laurie Fogarty, Davey Moore and myself, a handful of youths including Dave Gray, Michael Whelan, Mick Watson, one or two Juniors including Maurice Brown and 'Appleby' and a bunch of Seniors including Jim, Tommy Horne, Peter Carmichael, Ernie Slaughter, Doug Cockburn and Bill Morrison. I can't recall any female athletes at all. How times have changed – mosey on down there now on a Monday evening and it's packed, great to see. Anyhow, I never won a race during the handful of months I was there before leaving to join-up, although I had some very encouraging performances and I did win six plastic cups once, having finished 3rd in a Harrier league event. As I remember a certain Mike McLeod won most of the boy's races. Mike went on a few years later to win Olympic silver, so I was definitely in good company. Some years later I went on to work with Mike's brothers in Northumbria Police, Paul and Tony.

Plucking turkeys for trainers

On the run up to Christmas, in order to pay for my second pair of proper running shoes (with the trade name Tiger, later to be renamed as Asics), I plucked turkeys on Jacky Herdman's farm. I sat on a stool in a small circle with four or five mature women and 'plucked away' while imagining how my new shoes would look! Once bought the shoes looked so good and smelled wonderful, I would take them out of the box, smell them and then replace them, always lovingly cleaning the muck off them with a damp cloth following each training run.

Shortly before I left home to join-up, I received a letter from Tommy Horne, which I've still got, wishing me *'all the best'*, and encouraging me to *'keep up with the running as you have real ability and the club is really sorry to lose you'*!

There is little doubt that the training and experience gained in racing with Morpeth would soon pay dividends!

Joining the armed forces (Royal Navy and Royal Marines!)

Leaving school I decided pretty quickly that I would join the Royal Navy, the navy being preferred to the other armed forces due to the perceived infantile notion that I'd get a free all expenses paid trip around the world. I was probably also influenced by my dad, a former Petty Officer, and my mother a former WREN. In fact most of my extended family have spent time in the armed forces: my grandads on both sides had been through two World Wars, and my three uncles had all been in the Army with my Uncle Robert having served in the RAF before transferring later to the Black Watch (so he could go with his mate Jim Taylor and fight in Korea and Kenya!).

Grandad Harris's walking stick!

A short while ago I was on my way out of my dad's house when he murmured something which stopped me dead in my tracks. Pointing at a walking stick in the corner, he said, *'Mind when I go, make sure you take good care of that walking stick, it was your Grandad's!'* My dad went on to explain that the stick would be at least 100 years old very shortly. Apparently in 1916, my grandad had been sent home from the trenches during the First World War. He'd been shot (we still have the removed bullets in a tin) and was being sent back for recuperation and to be 'patched up' properly. When he'd been operated on they gave him that walking stick to enable him to get around the hospital easier. Anyhow when he was deemed recovered, they sent him back to the trenches where he saw out the remainder of the war! The walking stick remained with my granny and was an ever present part of my grandad when the war was eventually over. My dad, who is currently 91 years old, told me that when he and his brothers were growing up, my grandad was never without this cane. When he died my dad took possession of it, and there it was lying there, and I had no idea of its history. Amazing little family story though!

End of school and old enough to take charge of my future!

It's hard to believe now but as a 15 year old (who'd have passed for 12 at the time!), having just left school, and with my dad away, and my mother at work, I simply got out of bed one day, and unaccompanied took the train from Widdrington to Newcastle, walked across the road from the Central Station and into a building appropriately called Gunner House, the recruitment offices of the Royal Navy and Royal Marines, walked up to the front desk in reception and declared bluntly that '**I have come to join-up**'!

Once again my memory serves me well. The guys looked at each other then with a smile and said, '*You'll have to come back when you're 15, son, and bring your mam and dad with you.*' 'I am 15,' said I, 'but my dad's away, doesn't live with us, and my mam's at work.' Assured from their assertion that they couldn't progress without my next of kin being present, I turned forlornly to make my exit, while wondering how the hell I would get my mother to accompany me and sign the required documents. Anyhow, all of a sudden one of the officers called me back, before explaining that there was no real reason why we couldn't carry out the entrance tests today simply because I was there, before reiterating that signatures would be needed before any completion could take place. Well, I did the Maths, English and General Knowledge tests and passed. I then recall doing press-ups and sit-ups on an office floor, together with a few step-ups on and off a chair, following which they gave me a brown sealed envelope, and some bus fare money, told me where to get the bus outside, and told me to attend the General Hospital for a medical, after which I was told to return. A while later I returned to Gunner House with the brown sealed envelope, grinning like the proverbial Cheshire Cat, having passed the medical as well. Having successfully gone through the preliminaries, I was then informed that they would write to my mother and confirm the process from this point onwards. Returning home, the wait for my mother to arrive home from work seemed to take forever. Eventually in she came to be greeted by – *'I've joined the Navy, you have to sign a form!'*

With a shake of her head my mother replied (knowing instinctively I think that this wasn't a wind-up) along the lines of *'don't be silly, you can't do that at your age'!* Following which she didn't dismiss the idea totally, but suggested that I took an apprenticeship first with the National Coal Board, *'something to fall back on you see'*, she said, which was pretty much the norm at the time when lads left school. Then she suggested maybe when I was a bit older I could think about the Navy again. *'No,'* said I, *'you don't understand; I've already done everything. Anyhow they will write to you soon and all you have to do is sign the forms, isn't it great!'*

True to their word, within a short while she received correspondence, and we went through to Newcastle and completed the forms – job done! I was given a start date of 9th January 1967; my first establishment was to be HMS Ganges at Ipswich, Suffolk. With approximately five months to wait, in the meantime I took a job on a local farm during the very busy harvesting period, which nearly killed me, lifting bales of hay all day for £5 10s a week (much more than I would receive in the navy). Mother got £5.00 for my board, and I got the remaining 10 bob! I was more than happy with that though, 10 shillings was much more than I had ever had! Apart from 'picking tetties' that is!

JUNIOR SEAMAN M R HARRIS R. N. soon to become JUNIOR ROYAL MARINE HARRIS M.R.!

A couple of days before the 9th January 1967, with my mother and luggage in tow I caught a morning bus from Widdrington to Newcastle. There was no fuss and no big send-off, just the two of us quietly leaving home. Throughout the hour-long journey I was aware of my mother's emotions as she tried her best to make conversation with me as I stared out of the window, probably mumbling incoherent replies whist deep in thought about my pending 'new life'. My mother (who I will love unreservedly forever) was the most caring and loving of parents, and a truly wonderful human being; on hindsight it must have been heartbreaking for her to escort her young son into another life far away from home – as mentioned in an earlier chapter, Linda and I were everything to her. In contrast, as far as I was concerned, I was brimming with excitement and couldn't wait to begin another chapter of my life!

In Newcastle, once we'd left the bus, the two of us struggled with the two bags down Northumberland Street on our way to the rendezvous point at the Central Station. As soon as we got within a few hundred yards of the station, I stopped and callously and bluntly asked her not to come any further, assuring her that I could manage from there! Stunned and no doubt shocked and disappointed, she put her bag down on the busy pavement as her eyes filled up and pleaded with me to let her come and see me off! I was adamant though, as I had these visions of loads of 'smirking sailors' standing on the concourse watching this new recruit approaching almost hand-in-hand with his mother, whist coming to serve his country with the Royal Navy – oh god, the thought filled me with dread!

I allowed her the quickest of 'pecks' on the cheek, before turning away and grabbing the two bags – and I was off! Approximately 20 or 30 metres down the path, my curiosity got the better of me and I stopped; turning around, I fully expected her to be right behind me. Much to my selfish relief Mother was still standing where I'd left her; looking at each other one last time she waved, I nodded, and I was gone. Much of my behaviour that morning could be attributed to the culture of my boarding school: parents were taboo, as were letters from them and I had much the same feelings that morning – after all as far as I was concerned I was an adult now!

A few minutes later I arrived at the station and was amazed to discover all the other soon-to-be junior servicemen had their families with them! Not just their families but it appeared all their relations and neighbours to boot. Soon I was approached by the recruiting officer I had last seen at Gunner House, looking over my shoulder as he looked for my parents. I made some excuse for their absence, at which point he escorted me over to the others, where I was invited to stand with another family and their son. The recruiting officer I fear must have thought I was an uncared for waif, whereas nothing could have been further from the truth!

As I recall we were all put up for a night (probably at the RN/RM reserve centre), before departing by train for Ipswich and HMS Ganges the next day.

On the train journey down to Ipswich, and purely by chance, I sat next to a guy called Roger Hugh (pronounced He-uff) only to discover he was a member of Gateshead Harriers. The two of us chatted at length about running and how much we were looking forward to all the promised sport in our new pending carriers. Ganges was a huge training establishment with literally thousands of personnel, both trainees and trainers. There were dozens of lengthy dormitories (each called a Mess) housing about 40 'nozzers' (as we were referred to) in each, with a couple of Petty Officers as Mess supervisors.

Initially for about three weeks the new arrivals were all put into an Annexe which was separated from the main camp by about 400 metres or so. Here we received all our uniforms and assorted kit and were given initial training in dress, marching, ironing, naval protocol etc, before being moved to the main training establishment. I can remember finding those first three weeks cold (it being early January), with dark mornings and austere buildings, lots of shouting and despite all the other recruits it was also a lonely time for me not knowing anyone except Roger. I also well remember missing the Harriers, and the Saturday racing with the smell of liniment in the changing rooms that was very prevalent in those days. Perhaps what was worst was that I had no personal identity, I was like the rest, a 'nobody', just a number (8158 I think?).

About a week into naval life as a junior seaman the first post arrived in huge sacks with literally hundreds of letters for our Mess. Names were read out by the POs at which point the individual walked up and collected their mail. There was none for me! *'What's the matter, George?'* (as I was initially referred to, a shortened term for Geordie) *'No one love you, lad, you're too ugly eh? Anybody got a spare letter George can have?'* The latter accompanied by much laughter all round! **I had told my mother that under no circumstances was she to write to me, under the premise that they'd all think I was soft!** The Boarding school having set the precedent. Anyhow I went full circle and very quickly put pen to paper imploring Mother, Nana and Linda to write me a letter each and pronto!

Me, HMS Ganges, 1967

Seems unbelievable now, however at some point in the next few days we were all seated in some sort of Lecture Theatre, an oath was read out, as I remember it, and one by one we were called out at which point (as 15 year olds) we marched up to a front table before signing a document confirming our allegiance to Queen and Country before saluting and returning to our seats! At the stroke of a pen we had all signed away nine years of our lives. It was to be several months later before I began to realise the enormity of what I'd done. Including three years mandatory in the reserves I had signed away 12 years of my young life.

Once in the main Ganges establishment, I was enrolled into 'Rodney' Division, and training and life in general became quite frantic; long days were spent learning all manners of general seamanship and specialising in a specific skill; I was to be a 'Gunner'. The latter was the only path to becoming a Physical Training Instructor; you had to be a seaman to specialise in physical training at a later date.

Within a couple of months I had been identified for my leadership potential and promoted to the position of 'Leading Junior'! My additional duties now included supervising the rest of the Mess (which amounted to 40 plus junior seamen), delegating duties while ensuring the Mess (sounds contradictory) was all sparkling clean and 'ship shape' as well as 'falling in' and marching the Mess everywhere to daily classes as an orderly body!

Captains march past, 1967
Me 'Leading Junior'
HMS Ganges – saluting at the front

Creating an identity! Before moving on again!

HMS Ganges, because of the thousands of personnel employed there, had a massive gymnasium complex with countless Physical Training Instructors running all over the place. There was also a superb 440yard running track. Seeing both of these facilities left me gleeful! I had never seen, let alone run, on a proper athletics track before and at every free-time opportunity I was down there, for the most part by myself 'getting the miles in'! In the gym I'd found my 'comfort zone' and was equally at home there, quickly catching the eye of all the supervising PTIs, **and one in particular would be responsible for a massive forthcoming change in my future years in the military!**

Sport has always given me the means to create a personal identity. Not because I was/am supremely talented but because the effort I gave was always nothing other than total! During this period of my youth (still 15) I was beginning to mature as well, growing, getting stronger and with the strength came additional speed. I was no longer one of the youngest in the year group and even if I had been it didn't seem to matter now. The work done at Boarding school together with the training and racing with Morpeth Harriers was coming to fruition.

HMS Ganges, 1967
Cross country champs – 1st

At Ganges I became *'a name'*! People recognised me because of sporting successes. I had won a mile race in the Inter Divisional Championships in 4m 48s and then won the 2000yards steeplechase a while later on the same day. I also won the Ganges Cross Country Championships following which when I entered the canteen they all stood up and clapped, 'almost' bringing a tear to my eye. I was a capable boxer, a decent swimmer in the inter-divisional swimming gala, never afraid to swim whatever event was on offer and void of an entrant, and I was also 'earmarked' for a place in the gymnastic display team. Above all because of my recent promotion and my sporting successes I had become a valued member of my division, gaining welcome respect from both my 'ship mates' and the training staff. I had created an identity different from others and I was as proud as punch. As with my previous life and with my future endeavours – no one had 'given' me anything, I took it, by working harder than the others – certainly not because I was 'a talent'! I would love to have said I was born talented, but in truth I don't think I was special at all, **just a 'dreamer' and a 'grafter' and the two are sound and amicable partners!**

HMS Ganges athletics champs, 1967
One mile – 1st – 4m 48s

Navy PTIs were recognisable by their white vests and blue tape around the periphery, very smart! However within the PTI team there was one who stood out from the others; he was different. First of all he appeared a loner not really engaging, as far as I could see, with the other PTIs, nor did he shout so much, rather using encouraging tones, without the screaming! But the other noticeable difference was that as opposed to 'blue' ribbon on the vests of the Navy PTIs he had 'red', identifying him as a Royal Marine Commando! If I'm honest I had at the time little knowledge, if any, regarding the role Marines had within the Admiralty, nevertheless this guy stood apart.

Much to my surprise the Marine PTI (unfortunately and for me unusually I really can't remember his name) approached me one day and asked for a word. We walked around a corner from the gym, and he bluntly told me *I was in the wrong outfit,* and *'you should be with us'!* All the PTIs to me were gods, this guy even more so. Not knowing how to respond or fully comprehending what he meant, I can remember just standing there to attention and nodding. He followed up his observation with *'I can maybe fix it! What do you think?'* I just nodded and said yes Sir! He then bollocked me for calling him Sir, saying I should refer to him as Corporal. At Ganges we called 'everybody' Sir; this I suppose was a refreshing change. With an *'I'll be in touch'* comment he was gone.

The latter didn't go unnoticed, and once the session was over some of the lads came around asking what he had wanted. I informed them of the brief meeting and his suggestion, but I was totally puzzled! Some of the guys had knowledge of the Marines and spoke in awe of their role and reputation. Within a short time I was excited and waited eagerly for further contact.

A short while later I was called in to see our Divisional Commander who said words to the effect of, *'so, Harris you want to join the Marines eh?'.* Following which, he got up from his desk, tapped his knuckles on my head (like knocking on a door) before saying, 'W*ell you've got the credentials, son!'* He then informed me that before finalising a transfer he would arrange a visit to The Royal Marine Training Depot at Deal in Kent. This all went so fast, unbelievable! Before I knew it I had taken the train from Ipswich to London then on to Deal. Having to travel as a 15 year old in full naval uniform, I must have been a strange sight which I'm sure prompted some smiles!

Arriving at Deal and being picked up from the station, I was almost immediately ushered into the dining room as dinner was in full swing. The noise that greeted me as I entered in 'naval' uniform was like a Shearer goal at St James' Park! The recruits were banging on tables with all their cutlery whilst shouting inaudible (no doubt obscene) comments!

To cut a long story short, what I saw in the day or so that I was there blew my mind. The dress sense with the putties, rifles, webbing, uniforms, boots, attitude, the marching and running around quickly made my mind up. Also it seemed in the short time I was there that Marine recruits were treated more like adults regardless of age. NCOs were referred to by their rank, as such I had to be told several times to stop referring to everyone as Sir. My mind made up, I returned to Ganges and confirmed I'd like the transfer 'thank you very much!'. None of this would have happened without the intervention of the PTI corporal, and sadly once I left Ganges our paths would never cross again. Over the coming years I occasionally appeared in the Royal Marine quarterly Magazine (the Globe and Laurel) for sporting reasons and I have wondered whether he ever saw those articles and photos. If so he would be well entitled to a satisfied smile, as without his intervention who knows how my life would have turned out!

A short while later I handed in my kit, packed a small bag and was ready to leave. But not before the whole Mess were mustered outside where I was given a standing ovation, Hip Hip Hooray, loads of cheers, good wishes, handshakes, and with a tear in my eye, totally overcome, I jumped into a Land Rover and was taken again to Ipswich station, but this time I wouldn't be returning!

22nd October 1967 a Junior Seaman becomes a Junior Royal Marine!

GPMG Gunner, Deal, Kent
The depot

I arrived at Deal in October 1967 having transferred from Junior Seaman to Junior Royal Marine with a new intake of 44 other 16 year olds. Now a seasoned (almost!) serviceman, although I'd only recently turned 16, I watched with a degree of amusement as the other lads entered into a life totally different from anything they'd known previously. Just like Ganges we all eyed each other up, all of us so different. I was lucky this time, I already knew how to bull boots, make my bed, iron and fold my clothes to the precise size of a Globe and Laurel Magazine. I knew how to stand to attention ('and face the front') and how to march in step! Having said all that, life here was so much more demanding than Ganges, few smiled at Deal (smiling didn't seem to fit somehow), there was a real fear and trepidation element attached to all the trainers and as recruits we had an innate massive degree of respect for our trainers and anyone who had earned the coveted 'Green Beret'!

Receiving 'Patrick Wall' Trophy for Junior Marine
showing most initiative in expedition training

Everywhere you looked at the depot there were recruits marching and running around. Even off duty you were required to march in step to the canteen, on site pictures, gymnasium, or NAFFI. As such in many respects you were never off duty. I can clearly recall on one occasion being called with haste to see the camp Adjutant. Having recently won a cross country race while representing Junior Wing, I assumed somewhat naively that I was about to be congratulated. However, I was very swiftly brought down to earth, and severely chastised for not having 'eyes righted' him (a form of salute) as I passed him 'during the race'! The latter in some respects would be the same as winning a 100 metres race in the Olympics but losing out on the medal for failing to salute the Queen as you sprinted past the royal box! But correct military protocol was everything, we wouldn't dream of questioning anything – *'know your place, Harris'!* *'Yes Sir, sorry sir'!* I was then 'about turned' and marched out in apparent disgrace.

I spent 32 weeks of basic training at Deal. Marching and drill, weapon training, much gymnasium work, education, religious instruction, spit and polish, route marches, speed marches, map reading, expedition training, seamanship. I was also awarded the Patrick Wall trophy (which I've still got) for the Junior Marine showing the most initiative in expedition training, the latter during a two week outward bound course in the Inverness area of Scotland. Throughout the 32 weeks at Deal as I recall we weren't allowed to leave the barracks unless it was on a training exercise, so no need for civvies!

Being presented with a diamond by CO Colonel JAC Uniach

Sport was encouraged and representing Junior Wing was greeted with acclaim. As with Ganges I had representative honours in athletics, cross country, boxing, football as well as discovering a talent for Hockey which I'd never played previously. I now had an uncomfortable dilemma. Each sporting section was supervised by a particular PTI. As such a decision had to be made in relation to which sport/s would I favour? Representation in one sport would often clash with competing in another if as happened regularly they were held on the same day. One preference would lead to neglect of another. Each PTI had words with me clearly indicating a preference for their own sporting section, but the decision could only be mine. I was keen to please them all, but clearly this wouldn't be possible and much soul searching would be done as competition days approached!

I must have once again impressed during this period as I was soon (similar to HMS Ganges) promoted to 'Section Commander', with similar responsibilities to Leading Junior at Ganges. Then later on I was promoted another step up to a 'Diamond', the latter along with another three of my colleagues. We took the 'rank' down to 16 weeks of Commando training in Lympstone, Devon. Of the 44 who started in October only 21 of us would leave for Devon, the others were absent, for various reasons.

As mentioned we had 32 weeks of 'basic' training at Deal, and condensing 32 weeks into some sort of readable literacy is very difficult, I mean 'what do you include? and what do you leave out'? There was a lot of pressure put on us 16 year olds, and although we didn't smile much, we did have loads of laughs. I worked with some wonderful 'boot necks' and entered into terrific friendships, the camaraderie was something very special.

An example of how we operated is as follows: Our inspections on parade were so incredibly strict and in-depth, that no stone was left unturned. Your face was lifted up skyward (to inspect your shaving efficiency) so the sun shone on it, identifying any hint of 'bum fluff' or a missed solitary hair or spot of stubble. Weapons were stripped, bayonets had to be gleaming, and boots were perfect; webbing the same. We even had to drop our trousers – by numbers – to ensure our 'pusser' long white baggy underpants were clean. In order to inspect the latter, underpants were lowered to the ground, at which point whilst 'standing at ease' a 'pace stick' would be placed between your legs and your 'bollocks' somewhat harshly moved from side to side, all whilst we stood on parade, with not a hint of emotion while the whole exercise continued. *Attention to detail* was absolute paramount and the real issue. The theory was that if you hadn't shaved with precise attention to detail, or god forbid your underwear was in the slightest bit 'shabby' then your rifle (your best pal and your lifeline) may well be the same! We questioned absolutely nothing!

I doubt whether many of these practices would be acceptable now, they'd fall into the category of an infringement of one of the Human Rights articles, such as 'Inhuman and Degrading Behaviour'. Also (although the word is open to interpretation) 'bullying' was rife then. For me it was all acceptable then and remains so now. The concept was simple: in the heat of battle, there will be little, if any, time for hesitation, when a command is issued there must be an immediate response. There will be little time for deliberation, in other words you do as ordered – *do or die* being the principle!

I have mentioned previously how I have always tried to achieve a 'personal identity'. Initially as a Junior Royal Marine once again thrown in the mix with 44 others all wearing the identical same uniforms, and as one of the smaller guys at 5'8" tall, I was quickly lost amid the mass. Larger guys stood out like a sore thumb, until that is we were allowed to express ourselves through the 'effort' we gave during physical activity. Discipline, guts, willpower, pride, and pain tolerance are higher credentials than dressed appearance!

Many years later as a Physical Training Instructor with Northumbria Police I regularly supervised physical fitness tests and took countless training sessions. I held the view then as I do now, that you can learn more about a person's character in a gymnasium situation than you ever discover by putting a pen in their hand in the stress-free serenity of a warm classroom. I would quickly add, having said that, that I am not referring to 'physical prowess' or 'talented' athletic types, but rather the *effort* given! Our fitness tests were described as 'Maximum and Progressive', simply meaning that the student does as much as possible. The principles were the same as any other interview type situation: you do your absolute best, the reward at the end could well be a job. Within a very short space of time whilst conducting these sessions I could tell who I would prefer to work with on the streets had I been an operational cop. The guy or girl who would die 'trying' **or** the girl or guy who was clearly blessed with a higher degree of physical fitness BUT would stop simply because they were becoming 'physically uncomfortable'? I truly believe that the effort given in a gymnasium type situation is transferable to other elements in life including police work, and therefore predicable as a character indicator. Whilst it is contested these days in certain quarters, I believe in principle that 'we are what we are' and personal pride in my opinion an ever present motivator, and in the gym or on the sports field the effort given is often a portrayal of the individual's character. On a personal basis, I lost many competitions because I wasn't good enough to win on the day, but in another sense I also won them all as well simply because doing my best was an irrefutable victory!

At Deal we spent a lot of time doing weapon training becoming expert practitioners in an array of weaponry, stripping them, keeping them immaculately clean regardless of conditions, putting them back together and firing them on the range. GPMGs, SMGs, SLRs, Mortars and Grenades being the most frequently used. Forty years later and the procedures are as clear now as they were then – 'cock, hook and look', or 'safety catch, pouch, off magazine'. A bit like primary school with 'times tables' – repetition works, maths was never my favourite or best subject by any means, but even now if you were to ask me any times table question as quick as a flash I'd respond with the right answer – 7 x 8, 4 x 9, 6 x8, 9 x 5, 12 x 7? Go on ask me!

At certain times in training we would encounter a trainer who had acquired, for want of another word, a 'reputation'! On one such occasion we were assigned to one such guy who would take us for a one-off weapon training session. The guy in question had been a sniper in Aden, and by all accounts a successful one at that, having shot and killed several 'baddies'. The training session was unusually quiet, until one brave soul addressed him with a question, *'Corporal, what is it like to kill someone?'* With our hearts in our mouths, amazed at 'Smudge's' nerve, in absolute silence we waited for an answer! Without even looking up, the corporal replied – *'what was your first w..k like?'* and so ends the lesson, as we looked at each other out of the corner of our eyes, while quietly going about stripping our weapons!

Repetitions are not always positive (because they can reinforce bad practices as well) but learning by continuous rehearsal results in instinctive behaviour, and with instinctive behaviour you don't engage the brain – as such, useful when under pressure. Certainly 40 years later and those endless repetitions are still embedded in my long term memory store.

The gymnasium was a place of absolute frenzy. From the moment we entered till the moment we left we 'doubled' (jogged), even when getting changed or showering. Standing still was taboo. We would march to the gym in Lovats or whatever else was the 'dress of the day' and for the most part wearing ties. Imagine for a moment the steam, the extreme heat, the profuse sweat, the continuous shouting from several PTIs which would echo off the tiled walls, and all the while we would be jogging on the spot while undressing and dressing. Once ready we jogged with absolute haste into the sports hall, for a 'beasting'. Great stuff!

The gym work was a mixture of highly energetic activities using boxes and horses for vaulting together with strength exercises such as fireman's carry, press-ups, dips, burpees, sit-ups, astride jumps, tuck jumps, sprints; and many hours were spent on *rope climbing*, whereby we would climb to the top of the rope, hang a while before obeying commands to 'bend ... And ... stretch' and 'bend ... And ... stretch, bending our arms before stretching to achieve a full range of movement using body weight as resistance! We would hang upside down from the top of the rope, head facing the floor, fearlessly showing our mastery of the ropes before climbing down under control, and then standing to attention, chest heaving before repeating the same exercises. The bigger guys often struggled particularly with rope work because of their weight, whereas the smaller types such as myself were 'quids in' with impressive weight to strength ratios. Strange how you can find pleasure in so much pain; maybe helps if you're a bit thick!

Rope climbing again, 30 years on!

Entering the gym one morning at Force HQ and some 30 years after my initial Marine training, a group of Trainers were looking perplexed while staring skywards at the top of our climbing ropes. 'What's up?' said I. 'We'll have to get some scaffold out, Mike – the ropes are tangled at the top, we can't pull them away!' Without a thought, I put my bag down, climbed to the top of the ropes in a couple of seconds, and held on to the rope with one hand before untangling the others with my free hand. All done in a handful of seconds. Who says the Marines don't prepare you for 'Civvy Street'? Clever sod eh?

Anyhow the 21 of us eventually left, passed out, had our photos taken with all the sporting trophies we'd won, went home for a couple of weeks' welcome leave before we returned, not to Deal this time, but to Lympstone in Devon for 16 weeks of *Commando training*, culminating if all went well in being awarded with the coveted 'Green Beret'! As mentioned in an earlier chapter, although still 16 years of age, I don't recall any dread or foreboding in relation to the pending move, only a sense of adventure with perhaps some nervousness and maybe a little fear, due to the phenomenal reputation of Lympstone.

For the most part whenever I went on annual leave, I'd arrive by the last train into Newcastle, generally around 22.30hrs. This meant I'd missed the last bus to Widdrington and with no one able to meet me I was faced with a lengthy 20 mile 'yomp' to get home. A taxi was out of the question, so I'd pick up whatever bag/s I had at the time, walk a mile or two up to the A1 where I'd optimistically stick out my thumb and hope for the best. I often got home at 4, 5, or even 6am, having decided on a brief kip on the way occasionally, home from home, even on leave. Nothing was easy or straightforward even on leave, for me at least. **All part of '60 years an athlete'!**

Commando Training!

At Lympstone life was hectic (an understatement!). I could write a separate lengthy book about this spell alone, as most ex 'booties' could, but I am sure that has already been done by others and this book is entitled **60 years an athlete,** therefore this period is only a part of the story, as such reduced to fit the title. On hindsight, and bearing in mind our age when going through all this, *we were incredible*! At that time I wouldn't have thought that we were incredible, we just accepted it for what it was and got on with it. Now in hindsight looking back, the stuff we did as 16 year olds (kids) was nothing short of amazing.

Endurance course, Lympstone, I'm up front

Condensing it down is difficult, however, for those who haven't been there! Consider yourself as a 16 or 17 year old in the harshest winter weather of January, February and March going through the following: Battle PT, Assault courses, Tarzan courses, Endurance courses, 9 mile speed marches, 30 mile timed route marches together with exercises on both Woodbury Common and Dartmoor. Then you had the drill, continuous personal and room inspections, weapon training etc.

An early example of the Endurance Course was as follows: For our first one (one of several) we were ordered to be at the start of the endurance course, ready to go (which was on Woodbury Common, approximately four miles from camp) for a 7am inspection. However, we weren't given any directive as to 'how' to get to the common. We learned a short time later that it was taken as read that we would walk or jog there, while carrying all our webbing and rifles. However, we thought (as always encouraged to) that we would simply use our initiative – we ordered taxis! Unbelievable when I think back. Anyhow we got into the taxis outside the main gate and proceeded to Woodbury Common. Once there, in the semi darkness and the frosted heather, we were met by several Training Staff, a mixture of Corporals and Sergeants, unwilling or unable to believe what they were seeing, spitting hell fire, incredulous at the audacity in us new entrants to Lympstone having the gall to 'cheat' with so much apparent nonchalance; it must have resembled a 'Carry On film'! For us of course we would never have had the nerve to 'cheat'. But in the absence of any directive as to how to get to Woodbury at that time in the morning with no transport, we simply used our initiative. To say the next few days were difficult is an absolute understatement. But back to this *Endurance Course...*

The course itself was a mixture of freezing cold pools of water, neck high, mountains of mud, dark tunnels where we had to crawl belly down for extended distances over rocks and shingle, plus a water tunnel where we were totally submerged, all done at the 'double' (running in full kit with weapons). In order to complete the course we were all placed in teams of three and regardless of any variation in fitness levels we were to stay together throughout as a team. Once the endurance course was complete we would then run the four miles or so back to camp, soaking wet and with webbing causing major discomfort whilst rubbing on our lower back and shoulders. Once back to camp, we were required to immediately fire off ten 7.62m rounds into targets, firstly to ensure we had looked after our weapons and that they were still capable of operating despite the water, mud, and dirt, and secondly to ensure we were still able to hit the target. Failures to complete all elements resulted in re-runs.

Military exercises on Dartmoor were commonplace. We would leave barracks on a freezing cold Sunday evening, and sit in the back of a 'three ton' truck for three hours with our rifles housed between our knees and our faces 'cammed out' before disembarking with all our kit, receiving a 'brief' in the dark, given map references and rendezvous points before heading out into the darkness and the most hostile of landscapes for several days, with maps and compasses and no immediate 'adult' supervision. As mentioned previously I was a Diamond through all of this, and as such would act out the role of an NCO with the additional responsibility of leading a section of around 10 marines with all the welfare issues, map reading and general leadership duties. We slept out in snow, wind and ice with little in the way of protection, snuggled up close for additional heat. Often enough in our haste to find shelter from the wind, we would find a sheltered spot, only to discover at first light that we were sleeping in a small stream and soaked! We'd rouse, clean our rifles, have a quick bite to eat, and briskly set off again with map references to an RV point several miles away, to be met by a Corporal or Sergeant, who would give me further orders, and woe betide if we arrived late – we were kids, but must have already been some of the toughest soldiers in the world. Dartmoor seemed like another planet – you could be there for days and never see another living soul except for the occasional donkey who would stand motionless like a bush in the dark until you got within a metre or so before letting out a 'snort' and scare the shit out of us.

During one of these exercises I well remember leading the section on a pitch black night when you couldn't see but a metre or two in front of you, when all of a sudden I cascaded down an incredibly steep ravine. Arse over tit as the saying goes, I tumbled for what seemed like forever, banging my body off trees and boulders before lying in a heap in a torrent of rapid water at the bottom. Stretched out almost motionless I lay in this 'stream' trying to get my bearings, when I heard *'Hey Mick, where are you? Do you want us to come down that way?'* The lads hadn't a clue of my predicament and I certainly wasn't going to tell them! *'Stay where you are,'* I shouted, and scrambled my way back to the top – stirred and shaken somewhat! To this day I remember my outstanding concern while 'bathing' in that freezing stream was not broken bones or concussion but the location and wellbeing of my rifle and compass! I said little afterwards, pride severely hurt, the less said the better!

If you are still in any doubt about our general resolve and strength, mental as well as physical, imagine this, whilst remembering we were at the time barely 16 years of age, several of us like me looking no older than perhaps 13 or 14 years. The next time we have a bitter cold January night, maybe -7 degrees with frost on top of frost, look out your bedroom window before you jump into your warm little bed and pull the covers up to your chin, and think instead about climbing into the back of a canvas covered 3 ton truck where we'd sit for the next two or three hours. Once on Dartmoor, we'd jump out and 'fall in', very little being said! As the section commander (Diamond) I would then gather around the smallest of lights and be given my RV points together with a final brief, relating to where and when my section was to be in the coming days. Moving back to my section I'd give them the briefest of info before glancing at my map, setting my compass in the dark and heading out into the bleakest of terrain. For the following few days this 16 year old (and I wasn't alone) would have total responsibility for the 8 or 10 junior marines in my section. There was no Helly Hansen or proper 'thermals' those days and no Goretex; we had heavy woollen clothing and even heavier boots, and of course we had our ever present weapons which we treated like newborn babies, we cuddled them, kept them dry, fed them (with copious amounts of oil) stripped them and cleaned them all with loving care. As you read through my 'journal' you will readily see how much discomfort I have endured during physical pursuits over many years. These months, all things considered, were as tough as any I have encountered. At the risk of over repetition, I'll say it again: we were barely 16 and these 'exercises' were just a small although essential part of our commando training, jammed into our 16 weeks. Yes we were tough, that's for sure.

A regular occurrence for me during speed marches (normally between six and nine miles with all your kit), being noted as one of the fittest in the Squad, was to be given the onerous task of 'traffic control'. This meant you had to run on in front of the squad and inform the Sergeant of the state of traffic movement as we approached crossroads etc. e.g. 'all clear Sgt' or 'traffic Sgt'; once the squad was past I would sprint once again up to the front of the squad and onwards for another 40 or 50 metres until the next junction before repeating the same process.

This would continue till the end or until someone was struggling to carry their weapon, or just becoming fatigued, at which point I would get the call 'George, get your f..king arse back here and take charge of his f..king weapon!'. I would then be relieved of traffic control only to be lumbered with another rifle to carry apart from my own.

For the 'extra duties' I had somehow accumulated there was never a hint of gratitude, although I've no doubt it would have been noted, somewhere. I say this as I can clearly recall one Saturday evening (unlike Deal we were 'let out' on weekends) down in Exmouth with the guys at a place we frequented called the 'Pavilion' where bands would play, girls would gather and alcohol would flow. The Pavilion was where I first heard the name of a 'blues icon' called Sonny Boy Williamson! His name would often crop up when a singing harmonica playing front man would introduce his next number 'as another Sonny Boy Williamson song', a name not easy to forget!

Normally we would never dream of being in the company of our training staff (they were like gods to us) and socialising with them was out of the question, but on this one occasion, a corporal was leaning on the bar a few feet from me as I got the round in. As I looked in his direction he summoned me over via a nod. As I got there (and he wasn't alone) he asked what I was drinking; stunned, I replied that I was in a round with the lads. He nodded before, almost in a whisper, said, *'You're f..king alright you are, George, you know we think the world of you, don't you?'* Totally shocked, and not knowing how to react, I sheepishly nodded before being told *'go on then, f..k off!'*. As mentioned during training, we rarely if ever received positive comments, at least not of a personal nature like this. Tell you what though, on this occasion, and I mean this, I could have shed a tear or two! *Mind games!* But it's an example of how much in awe we were of these people who beasted us up, glared, shouted, even physically manhandled us (for want of another expression); our respect was total and un-conditional!

As a Diamond, and along with two others, Tommy Gunning and Phil Catheral (great mates of mine), whilst coming to the end of our training, we were interviewed by three officers for the accolade of 'Kings Badge'! A monumental award which was 'sometimes' but not always given to the best all round recruit. All your qualities were considered before a final interview was completed; during this interview you were asked certain questions on various topics. At the time I thought my interview was going really well until I was asked a question along the lines of 'what are your views on Enoch Powell?'. Clearly a political question. At Lympstone reading newspapers or even watching television wasn't high on our must do list! The question stunned me into silence. Whilst I'd heard his name of course, I truly had little idea about him, nor his comments or actions. As such I conceded defeat with an adolescent and pathetic silence, followed by an apology 'I didn't know much about him, Sir'! As the three officers stared at me, I can recall the thought that if indeed I was in with a shout of the Kings Badge – it had just disappeared! As luck would have it, none of the three of us received the award; I just wonder now whether that was due to our lack of political awareness of the country at that time, and how politics and foreign policy may affect our future military roles. But hey, you know we were at that time 16 or 17 years old and had been inadvertently sheltered from all things in life for 18 months, except military expertise, so no shame in our ineptitude regarding political awareness!

Anyhow, a short while later most of us passed out and received the iconic Green Beret.

The negative side of my early 'promotions' (which I'd never sort) all the way through training including HMS Ganges, left a longing in me just to be normal in terms of duties, without having the quite considerable responsibilities I had somehow inherited and been designated which led to the supervision and leadership of others. Once finished with training it felt like a huge load had been taken off my shoulders – now I was just a fighting soldier as opposed to a fighting soldier with responsibilities for many others. Those initial early leadership duties throughout training would result negatively on any future promotion ambitions as a Royal Marine – I wasn't interested!

A serving Royal Marine Commando!

Following the phenomenal in-depth training I had received over the previous 18 months as a junior marine, the next few years were spent serving in three different Commando Units: 45 Commando, 40 Commando, and 41 Commando.

45 Commando!

My first draft was to 45 Commando, at the time housed at Stonehouse Barracks in Plymouth. Immediately accepted by my comrades as an equal (well, almost!) despite my youth, I once again subconsciously forged my own personal identity, and once again it was mainly through sport that I was to stand out and obtain additional respect. I took part in everything physical not as a duty but rather as a vocation. All the incredible exercise I'd done in training in all its varying forms had not dampened my enthusiasm one iota. I was never a talented prima donna type, rather a grafter whose effort in sporting competition has never changed from four years of age and onward. I won races and played football for the unit. But I wasn't alone in my physical endeavours – clearly there were others.

Although this was over 45 years ago there are people even from this long ago period that I will never forget (although names are occasionally elusive) for many reasons. It is fair to say, the Royal Marine Commandos attracted a certain type. Personalities in the ranks were many, ranging from funny devil-may-care people who found 'everything' a laugh, to adventurers always looking for something different; and also there was no shortage of hard, hard people – the latter came in every shape and size imaginable, not the perceived Arnold Schwarzenegger, Vinnie Jones, or other modern silver screen hero types. I often found these people to be loners; the few guys I knew in this category weren't brash or in any way loud, they didn't need to be, there was an aura present that is hard to describe, and there was always a certain calmness that surrounded these guys. They didn't feel it necessary to tow the party line, in a nut shell; they stood out because they were different! I would start out initially by looking at these types, not directly, but from a distance and more from the corner of my eye. In my first fighting unit, one such guy never spoke to me for weeks – 'Sox Arnell' (as I remember he had black sleeked back curly hair and a facial scar) – he wasn't offensive, just never seemed to notice me and certainly I wasn't about to approach him! In the NAFFI he would arrive alone, down four or five pints in quick succession and leave as quietly as he had arrived. Anyhow, one day we had a cross country race; I had already 'shone' in similar events, but on this day as we lined up I was aware of Sox standing next to me. As I had never considered him an 'athlete' as such I took little notice – until, that is, we set off. I went straight into the lead, pushing on as one by one the others began to fall off the pace. After a while I was aware of heavy breathing on my shoulder accompanied by fairly regular 'grunts'. Eventually slightly concerned about the competition I took a quick glance backwards to be met by Sox's sweat covered and contorted glare as he tried desperately to hang on to this young 'whippersnapper'! I surged on surprised and a bit scared; I say scared because there was a part of me that wanted to hand over the lead to him as a token of my respect. However, this wasn't in my nature, and I guess he wouldn't have taken it on those grounds either, so I raced on to the finish. Once over the line several others followed me in, before Sox had crossed the line. Staggering up to me with an outstretched muddy wet hand, we shook hands as our eyes briefly met; he said nothing, just simply nodded, and turned away! There can be little doubt that the pain Sox endured that day far exceeded the discomfort I tolerated. At least I was now assured that despite his nonchalant manner, he knew who I was – not as a talented athlete I hasten to add, but rather another 'bootie' who could cope equally as well as himself with pain!

There would be certain times in the future when I would be under duress; at such times, for guidance, I would contemplate how Sox and one or two others would operate in a similar situation.

My basic philosophy on sport has never changed. Winning or losing doesn't matter – there are more important aspects relating to performance. Physical pursuit allows us all the opportunity to obtain an identity. Your character is laid bare during competition, but not by winning, for winning is only a bonus, and there can only be one outright winner; however, the latter doesn't mean all others are losers. But winning comes a long way second to the effort given. Pride, perseverance, will-power, guts, honesty, pain tolerance – and I could go on – are all fundamentals within the realms of sport. What you see is what you get; there's no hiding place! As for Sox? At that time he would have been the first person I would have selected to operate with, had the opportunity ever arisen, even though on this occasion he ended the race as an also ran, but only in terms of position!

I do despair these days though, especially when a prominent sports person has their autobiography serialised in a daily newspaper. None of the above seems to matter one jot. The book apparently becomes interesting not because of the sporting success – rather how often they have been out of their heads on alcohol and/or drugs. How many affairs they have had, how many psychologists they've seen, or how much money they've wasted on the horses etc. The accompanying photos show not what you'd envisage – action sporting shots – but photos depicting a drunken night on the tiles. And these are supposed to be our children's sporting role models! Very sad, and a far cry from my heroes of yesterday!

In typical marine type humour a strange 'occurrence' happened to me in my early days at 45! I'd gone out with a few mates one night down Union Street and when we returned later in the night, as we walked over the parade ground, our attention was directed to the drill shed roof where it appeared in the dark that some poor bugger's bed was on the 'roof' (a quite considerable height) with sheets blowing in the wind! Laughing fit to kill ourselves we went to our various rooms, only to find it was 'me' who had no bloody bed. Of course entering the room no one let on and I slept on a chair in the television lounge. When I came back from breakfast the next morning my bed was all back to normal; looking around the guys there wasn't the slightest hint that I'd been the source of the joke, it was just never mentioned, apart from a comment of *'you get lucky last night, George? You dirty Bas....d'!*

At 45 Commando I also got my first taste of 'sea sickness' as Yankee Company embarked on a three month tour of the Mediterranean, in a flat bottomed ship called HMS Fearless. Spike Milligan once said 'the best cure for sea sickness is to sit under a tree'! Oh what I would have given for a tree!

Our journey across the Bay of Biscay in a flat bottomed ship will stay with me forever; sea sickness lasting several days is truly the most horrendous of experiences. Always made worse by seasoned 'old sweats' who would make life as intolerable as possible for those who were endlessly spewing vomit all over the place. Bacon sandwiches and black pudding were 'generously' brought back for us from the galley, ugh! Tots of rum were all of a sudden made available by the bottle – recommended by all accounts to sooth your aching stomach – Ha!

Once into the Mediterranean, we would be helicoptered off to begin our NATO exercises in various countries. Once the task had been accomplished we would be picked up and returned back to ship. On deck before we were allowed below we would stand to attention while being hosed down by high pressure hoses head to toe until we were free from all surplus dirt.

Once exercises were complete we would sail into a port such as Malta to begin a few days' rest and recuperation, also known as getting bladdered! During one such visit I won a race up to the top of Gibraltar's highest point and back down; I still have the trophy! (In the loft with the rest, of course.)

Having been with 45 for about a year, I was informed by one of my room buddies that I was about to be drafted and I'd best take a look on the company notice board. Sprinting down the stairs with absolute haste I discovered I would be joining 40 Commando Unit in Singapore, for an 18 month tour of duty training for jungle warfare!

Singapore had an awesome reputation. A den of iniquity, much loved by 'royals' for its array of dubious off duty 'activities'! Apparently on offer would be a very diverse menu of everything we would find 'attractive' and 'appealing'. I couldn't believe my luck!

Within a short while I was leaving Plymouth and heading for Singapore to join 'A' Company, Royal Marines. Additionally I would be having a much welcomed reunion with some of my mates whom I hadn't seen since leaving training. Apart from 40 Commando there was, across the air field, 42 Commando, another identical fighting unit with the same jungle warfare remit.

In 1969, as an 18 year old from Widdrington, Singapore was to open my eyes like never before and maybe even since. From the beginning, in Singas as it was known to us, life was so different. Our daily uniform when not engaged in jungle warfare was shorts and shirt as opposed to general uniform in other parts of the world. Our general issue firearm changed from SLR to an Armalite, which was lighter, therefore more manoeuvrable and especially suited to moving through the intense undergrowth of the Malaysian jungle.

Two man mile 'Feb Sport' Singapore – 1st
45 minutes after boxing hence swollen face

Sport in particular was very high on the agenda in Singapore. As such I was in my element. Such was the spirit of competition that whenever we got a break in training, rather than relax or lie down out of the sun, games of volleyball were hastily arranged and played with real passion between sections and companies. Once a year in Singapore there was a full month set aside for a continuous succession of sporting competitions; that month was February, therefore the sport was referred to as Feb Sport. As well as 40 Commando, 42 Commando, and Brigade, an armada of Royal Navy ships would head for Singapore for 'R and R' and full participation in every conceivable sport on the programme. At the time I was 40 Commando cross country champion, as well as winner of both the 1,500 metres and the 5,000 metres in the unit athletics championships. I boxed, played football, took part in swimming galas and was a key player in the unit's hockey team. All of those were included in the Feb Sport programme, so I would be fully employed going from one tournament or competition to another. I actually have a photograph of me running in a two man mile event for the unit, and with the 'eye of an eagle' you can just about see how swollen my face was during the race, having finished a boxing bout just 45 minutes previous to the race. With Tommy Gunning we won the two man mile, but I got beaten in the boxing on points to an Irish seaman!

Me (front left) 40 Commando Singapore, 1st Team – 1st Individual
I am rolling money around in my fingers – having made
money for the Sgt Major – my earnings!

The Royal Navy Cross Country Championships took place during this spell, which I won. Immediately following the race I was approached by a Lt/Commander called Ian Teesdale who, following a quick congratulatory hand shake, asked me whether I would be interested in running a Marathon. I was 18 at the time and although I was superbly fit, running 26 miles didn't appeal so I respectfully declined. As I turned to walk away he muttered something about 'well that's a pity, Hong Kong is nice this time of year'! Turning on a sixpence we were immediately back face to face, with a *'how long have I got, Sir?'* followed by *'can you arrange the time off?'*. Anyhow a short while later I and three other Naval Officers caught a flight to Hong Kong to take part in the first ever Hong Kong International marathon. We were well catered for, good hotel, great food etc. – not what I was used to. The

Just before Hong Kong
International Marathon, 1969

food was too good to ignore and I started the marathon with a belly full of bacon, eggs, sausages, fried bread and beans! Hard to believe! Anyhow, I finished 17th and ran 3hrs and 10mins, which, looking back and considering my age as the youngest person by far in the race, a lack of appropriate and specific training, the heat, plus my inappropriate diet, was pretty commendable. I had also 'hit the wall' for the first time in my life, at around the 22 mile marker, a horrible feeling whereby you are literally operating on nothing, so your pace slows considerably and only your determination would see you through the remainder of the event. Thousands of people had lined the route to support this inaugural event and I remember well being embarrassed by my 'oh so slow jog' for the remaining four miles. Once across the finish line I had such an incredible craving for food and water that despite my love of animals I could have eaten a scabby horse – twice! I wouldn't run another marathon for another 10 years.

A bronze medal in the Singapore National Road Walking Championships!

There was one other notable sporting event which I was directed to compete in, the Singapore National Road Walking Championships! Out of the blue one day I was informed that I had an entry in the above event and was 'ordered' to go down to the city and represent the corps in the National Championships. Bloody walking – couldn't believe it, why me? The exact distance I really can't recall, but looking back now it was probably eight or 10 miles. To cut a long story short, we started (hundreds of us) in a stadium with a lap of the track before heading out into the traffic-laden, poisoned smoke-filled streets, inexplicably I finished 3rd! I was in major pain though, due to the totally abnormal way the body moves when walking as fast as you possibly can while keeping at least one foot in touch with the concrete for 90 minutes or so. My memory of the finish still makes me laugh 45 years later. As I entered the stadium a bunch of my mates who had come down to spectate and no doubt take the piss, started wolf whistling, blowing kisses, accompanied by obscene offers of a sexual nature; being totally distracted and laughing uncontrollably I was in major risk of being disqualified as my walking action crumbled into even further farce. Regaining my posture I struggled on to pick up my first and definitely my last race walking plaque! I've still got it!

The off duty lifestyle in Singapore at that time for a young lad of 18 was incredible. We worked hard, especially if we were up country in the Malaysian jungle, but we played even harder. Often we would leave camp around 22.00hrs on a Friday night with a healthy roll of 'bucks' in our pockets, grab a pick-up Taxi outside the gate and head for the city, often wearing no more than a pair of baggy shorts and a t-shirt. Not returning till late on Sunday evening, slightly the worse for wear! I'll not go too much into detail, but if you ever attended sick bay (which was shared between us and 42 Commando) there were two lines of benches (so I was told!) situated opposite each other. On one line would be those who had basic sickness issues, and on the other were those who had caught 'something'. The latter 'disease' was a 'chargeable offence' and classed as a self-inflicted illness!

We had only four to a room in our barracks (called Dieppe) which made life pretty comfortable, and all of us had various mod-cons such as record players and top of the range tape recorders, expensive cameras etc., all at knock down prices. Part of the buying was the entertainment you would encounter as you went to purchase your item. In one shop an item may cost 50 bucks, in the next 45 bucks and the next 35 until you went back to the initial shop, reported your progress and then got it for almost half the original price.

A little dog called 'A'

Another accepted 'tradition' was that most of the rooms had a rescued dog. The dog was simply acquired on a trip to one of the many small villages dotted around. We would carefully select the most flea ridden, starving little guy we would see – and 'nick him', pick him/her up and bring him/her back to camp and have him/her adopted. How this was tolerated by our officers still amazes me. The only stipulation was that you had to register the dog at Security at the main gate. Once along there, you'd give the dog a name (normally an 'obscene' one) and identify ourselves as the legal owner/s then put a collar on with its name; finally you'd give your room number and that was it. The dog in the room next to us was called 'clitoris' and that was one of the milder names – many others had four letter names, if you get my drift. We were a bit lazy in my room and christened ours simply 'a'. During the course of a conversation his little head would turn a million times!! The dogs were treated like the Queen's Corgis, loved and well fed; they couldn't have believed their luck. As one of us left the unit to return to the UK, our bed was immediately replaced by another 'Booty' who would then take over responsibility for the hound!

Jungle warfare was 'uncomfortable', as the terrain and climate was so hostile and unforgiving, you'd go from extreme humid heat to thunderous rain, whereby the noise from the downpours onto the leaves was almost deafening. We wore the same clothing for a week, never took our jungle boots off, and weren't allowed soap because of the scent it would give off. Moving through the undergrowth for hours with no tracks to follow was exhausting, and you quickly became dehydrated due to sweating so profusely. There were a million creatures of every type who would generate a phenomenal amount of noise especially as the sun came up first thing – the dawn chorus never sounded like that in Widdrington. Amazing how quickly you'd adapt though. Initially leeches were abhorrent; however, within a short period of time you just ignored them as they'd hungrily feast on your blood before dropping off, fat and satisfied and no doubt well nourished, but possibly also suffering from VD or something! Serves em right, eh? Water was a huge problem for us, as Second in Command of a section I was regularly sent out with map and compass to find a water hole. Incredible how resilient the human body is in relation to diseases – we drank anything and everything, rarely used our pills to 'cleanse' the water, and never syphoned the water through our water bags, we were for the most part just too desperate. Some of the water pools we came across were very small and infested with flies and mosquitoes, often with the footmarks of small animals on the periphery. Yet despite the filth, we caught nothing as far as illnesses go!

The nights were absolutely pitch black, you couldn't see your hand an inch from your face, and it was a regular occurrence to be woken by a moving ground sheet you were lying on, the movement due to the world's biggest rat, no doubt seeking a bit of warmth and comfort during the cooler temperature of the night!

Once the exercise was complete at the end of the week we'd sit in the back of a three ton truck for a few hours and return back to camp. *It wasn't unusual for me to race successfully the day after representing 40 Commando, and I still have various trophies – in the loft of course!*

Singapore was an incredible draft (I was also lucky enough to see Hong Kong on three different occasions) and I may well have stayed given the opportunity. However, my 18 months were up, and I flew back in January 1971, this time to join up with another fighting unit at 41 Commando in England. Apart from the freezing temperatures which greeted me – which had become a distant memory whilst in the heat and humidity of the Far East – there had also been a cultural change in the UK, which was to profoundly affect me!

Back home and oh what a change!

The journey back from Singapore with three hefty bags was at best laborious, at worst horrendous. A lengthy 18 hour or so plane journey on a VC 10 was followed by an assault course while overcoming all the obstacles on London's streets and Underground. I would place one bag down whilst I'd move the other two, then go back for the one I'd left. Eventually I got to Kings Cross and as was the norm I arrived in Newcastle very late at night, tired out and freezing. As usual, with no one to meet me, I taxied up to the Haymarket before making my weary way onto the A1 to begin the now familiar action of 'thumbing it' the 20 miles to Widdrington. On this occasion I eventually got a lift in a lorry before falling asleep in the cab, missed my preferred drop off point and staggered into Morpeth. There I sat in the square opposite the Town Hall too knackered to go further. I decided to wait a few hours on a bench and get the first morning bus back 'home'. However, by a stroke of good fortune, a police car pulled up. The officer, a Sgt, came over and questioned me, at which point I produced my ID card and explained my predicament. Taking pity on me he gave me a lift in his Panda car the seven miles to Widdrington. I had to knock several times to wake up my mother, whose face I'll never forget after she'd shouted her customary 'who is it?' Before opening the door with the most beautiful Mother-to-son smile as I stood on the step, followed by 'ee you've changed!'. The next few weeks I was well and truly spoilt, although she gave me a rollicking twice or thrice, for coming in at three or four in the morning, with a *'you can't be up to much good coming in at this time mind, Michael'* – and she was right! But I was young, free and healthy! Say no more!

My mother was the sweetest and most loving person in the world, but she had a temper. To this day I can remember, while being on annual leave, on many occasions returning home full of trepidation in the early hours after a night out, to be greeted by her (unable to sleep while I was out) sitting in an armchair, legs crossed, with a *'what time do you call this?'*! Although I was now in my twenties, there was no change at all in her attitude from the time that I was a lad, only now of course she couldn't let my bike tyres down as she used to keep me in! On one occasion I remember going to Sunderland's Majestic nightclub on an organised bus trip from Widdrington, some 30 miles away. I got wonderfully drunk; fell asleep in the cleaner's cupboard (without a cleaner I hasten to add), and with the place now empty, I was woken in the early hours by the cleaners who summoned 'someone' to 'help me'. Ha! At which point the bruiser 'escorted' me roughly to the doors before bundling me down the steps. At this time I became aware that my leather Jacket was missing, and with it my ID card. I shouted back up to the guy, 'Which way is it to Newcastle?'; he pointed, told me to 'now f..k off', at which point I set off for another training jog into the early morning light. I was now desperate to get home as quickly as possible as I was due to travel back to my unit in a handful of hours. But what troubled me most wasn't the lengthy run home, or the loss of my jacket, but rather the loss of my ID card (a hanging offence!). I got a couple of lifts and arrived home about 8ish with a couple of hours to spare before my 10.00am bus to the 'Toon'. Well, you can imagine the reception I got from Mother (I'd sooner have dealt with a Sgt/ Major, and I'm not joking!). *'Where's your jacket?'* she said. *'Alan's got it,'* came my reply. *'Well you'd better get down there and seek it then, hadn't you, then get back here and pack or you'll miss your bus and train, then what?'* I had as much hope of Alan having my Jacket and ID card as Newcastle winning the league! But oh what joy, Alan came to the door, with a *'where the hell were you'* comment, BUT clutching my jacket and within it was my 'oh so important' ID card. Grabbing the jacket I said *'see you in a few months'* and legged it back up home, none the worse for wear, just a bit 'tired', but I'd been worse! Even when I left the Marines and returned home to civvy street, my mother would never get used to my often 'unsociable hours'. Despite my age, she always worried; she simply cared a little too much.

January wasn't a great time to leave Singapore. The climatic difference between the Far East in Malaya and the North East in Rural Northumberland in January couldn't have been more of a contrast. I shook and shivered for my extended 6 week leave whilst subconsciously trying to adapt and acclimatise to the sub-freezing temperatures. But there was, at least for me, another climate change apart from the weather.

George Harrison had always been my favourite Beatle and at this time he had a single out which seemed to me to aptly reflect the social environment hovering over the UK; the single was *'My Sweet Lord'*. I loved it, it was beautiful and seemed to go hand in hand with the era, very gentle (as George was judged to be) and seemed to express hope and trust in his god; it was also different from the boy meets girl, lovey-dovey type pop music scenario. Throughout my life when particular records are played (and there are many) they can immediately take me back to where I was at that time in my life. Whenever I hear 'My Sweet Lord' it reminds me immediately of those freezing cold days I spent at bus stops and elsewhere whilst moving around what seemed to me at that time the harshest of English winters. Even now listening to 'my sweet lord' makes me feel so good, and when alone in my car I occasionally divert from my beloved blues and put that track on full blast and shout the lyrics out, lost in the moment! As good as five pints of Guinness, only a hell of a lot cheaper!

In Singapore we had become almost totally detached from life in the UK – everything we got out there such as newspapers, films, music etc was several days and occasionally weeks late. When I left England, most of the guys had relatively short hair, but when I returned without exception they now all had the fashionable long hair! New bands which we had heard in Singapore, but rarely seen, were having a huge impact on the younger generation. Led Zeppelin, Deep Purple, Ten Years After, Black Sabbath, Rory Gallagher and so many more, as well as the huge festivals of Woodstock and the Isle of Wight announced a new era of 'love and peace' and 'flowers in your hair' and the contraceptive pill, all of which encouraged liberation and freedom. All of a sudden, due to all the changes, I had noticeably become 'unfashionable', mainly due to the incredibly short hair forced on us. While most of the young extolled the virtues of peace and love, in total contrast I was a Royal Marine Commando with a skinhead haircut who was primarily trained to kill! I found out pretty quickly that girls weren't even slightly interested!

Following my extended leave I travelled as directed to Bickleigh to join my third Commando Unit – this time 41 Commando.

My company didn't hang around long in England before we travelled on HMS Bulwark, a huge Commando carrier, back out to the Mediterranean before disembarking in Malta for a six month or so stay (my place of birth). Life in Malta was quiet, nothing of real interest happening, but the weather was superb, and for the most part this period was an extended holiday. Talking of holidays! At some point whilst in Malta we were given a two week period of annual leave. Together with two of my mates we decided we would get a ferry across to Sicily, and travel from there up through Italy to Rome. However, it transpired that a woman had been murdered in a notorious street in Malta called the 'Gut'. This was a long street consisting of drinking bars. The Gut was a regular haunt of squaddies, and once the murder had happened, it was put immediately out of bounds to us all. My two mates, whom I was to travel to Italy with, decided to ignore the ban and went anyhow. They were caught and put inside a military jail for a short time, which coincided with our intended trip to Italy. Anyhow to cut the story short, I went to Italy by myself. Landed in Sicily, and proceeded to hitchhike up through Italy to Naples and on to Rome; the later part I took a train. This all turned out to be the trip of a lifetime, the weather was wonderful and I slept under the stars, booking once or twice into a cheap back street hotel just to get a shower and cleaned up. Purely by chance I had my 21st birthday in Rome, although I only became aware that it was my birthday simply by chance. Sitting on a bench in the vicinity of the Colosseum, there was a guy sitting next to me reading an American paper. Glancing over, I first noted the English text, then the date on the top of the page! On that sunny day in 1971 I bought a blues compilation LP simply because there was a mention of Sonny Boy Williamson on the cover, the name I had first heard in the Pavilion drinking den in Exmouth, while completing Commando training a few years earlier. Following my purchase I went on to buy a harmonica, and develop a loving partnership as a blues-loving harmonica player. My passion for blues music was probably nurtured a few years previously while listening to the 'Stones' and 'Pretty Things' at Boarding school, but that fortuitous trip to, of all places, Rome, would lead to a phenomenal passion that goes on even today, 43 years later, and invariably will accompany me to my grave! Whilst it might sound strange, I do believe there is a very real connection or correlation between blues music and sporting ambition, because whilst there are many highs, there are probably many more 'lows' associated with the life of an ambitious athlete! More later on that view!

A strange thing happened while serving in Malta. One day I was playing football against the Royal Artillery, when I became aware of a guy being referred to by his team mates as 'Geordie'. Once the game was over, as was the custom, we all went for a drink in the NAFFI. At some point I went across to 'Geordie' and asked where he was from. He was reluctant to say as in his words 'I would never have heard of the place'. Coaxing him a bit further he said, much to my amazement, he was from a tiny little place called Stobswood. Totally shocked, I replied, *'That's where I went to school!'* The two of us looked at each other in amazement, before learning that both of us had attended that small little school in the woods, but were separated by a couple of years, he being my senior by a few years. The guy's name was Johnny Wharton and many years later he was back home visiting and again simply by chance he was having a pint in the local Cricket Club at Stobswood. Although he now didn't recognise me with my long hair, I immediately remembered him, went across and we had a good night reminiscing.

Anyhow back to 41 Commando in Malta. Another bit of good fortune was to follow and we were informed we would be leaving, once again on Bulwark, for exercises in the Caribbean, before anchoring in Jacksonville, Florida!

Our two or three weeks in Jacksonville were terrific. The Americans were the most generous and hospitable people I'd ever known. We would be below deck, when a message would be transmitted over the tannoy system, which would go along the lines of 'two marines and one seaman required for tour of Jacksonville', or words to that effect, and the first three up there would be whisked off in a limo for a period of American hospitality. A few hours later, suitably entertained, well fed and watered, we would be dropped off back at the ship with handshakes and pleasantries, while thanking 'us' for our time. One of the stipulations whilst in the States was that for some reason we had to wear uniforms at all times whilst 'ashore'! This led to a pretty hairy incident on one occasion, The main reason was that the Vietnam War was in full swing during this period, with many Americans being totally against America's stance, particularly the younger generation, and although we weren't engaged in the war, our uniforms caused some regular consternation while in Jacksonville, in the form of dirty looks, but nothing really serious.

On one occasion, having very recently arrived in Jacksonville, and whilst leaving the dockland area, a black limo pulled up, a window was lowered and a guy shouted out *'Get out of Ireland, you Bastards'!* We stood there a little taken aback, before one of our guys as quick as you like replied – *'Ireland, the gits, they told us we were in America!'* At which point the car pulled away with a screech of tyres.

On another occasion whilst in Jacksonville, with a couple of my mates we went to see three rock bands performing, The Edgar Winter Band, Black Oak Arkansas, and our own British trio – the Groundhogs. In the massive auditorium, as drink flowed, I became acutely aware of a strange aroma circulating around the place. A smell I'd never encountered previously, which on investigation we discovered was drugs. Anyhow as the night progressed the behaviour of the people in there, and this included many 'hippy' types, became increasingly volatile and unpredictable. Fights broke out in various quarters, and with an air of 'anti-establishment' about the place and with us standing out in military uniforms, we decided to hastily leave the building. Outside there was pandemonium, cars were up-turned, police sirens were going off left, right, and centre – in fact it turned into a mini war zone, and there were the three of us standing there in Royal Marine Lovat uniforms, complete with Green Berets! We began to leg it through the back streets, before becoming separated in the mayhem taking place. Eventually more by good fortune than our advanced map reading skills we all safely made it back to the sanctuary of our very welcome 'battleship grey' ship. Having been in several dubious and hostile environments in recent years, this compared well with any of them, that's for sure!

Taff's underpants – ugh!

Once finished on our tour of the Caribbean and the States we would return back to the UK. But not before in typical Marine type humour an incident occurred, that I still to this day laugh about. Whilst in Florida a few of us took a coach trip on a Greyhound bus for a couple of days to see The Kennedy Space Centre, Disneyland, and a Marineland-type place (dolphins etc.) Anyhow the trip included an overnight stay in a plush Motel. I shared a room with Taff Mathoulin and a little guy known as 'Maggot'. There were only two beds in the room, a double and a single; Taff and Maggot shared the double and I had fortuitously got the single. Anyhow, we all got very drunk that night and returned to our room well happy with the night's entertainment. A couple of hours later I woke up whilst being horribly sick; I couldn't quite make the toilet and was sick all over the beautiful fitted carpets, while the two lads slept on oblivious to it all. In my drunken stupor I searched franticly for something to clean up the slimy vomit, coming across a pair of someone's (not mine I hasten to add) underpants. I gathered as much of the mess up as I could before rinsing the pants under the tap and replacing them where I'd found them. Come the morning as the three of us woke, Taff let out a muffled *'ugh! F..k..g h..l '* followed by *'what a night'!* I kept a low profile, squinting half underneath the bed covers, as Taff struggled to put on his horribly soiled underpants, which were not only sopping wet, but also had all sorts of food-like attachments hanging from them. *'You dirty bastard,'* I commented from my little dry bed, as Maggot quickly ran to the bog to 'also' be sick. We couldn't wait to meet the others and tell them how repulsive Taff was, as he continued throughout the day to wear his vegetable carrying, 'damp' putrid underpants whilst completing our tour of the famed Kennedy Space Centre. Happy days!

I left 41 Commando for an unusual (for me anyhow) draft and went to Poole in Dorset, our amphibious training centre, for what would be my last posting before leaving the Services for good. Poole for me was an anti-climax, apart from continued participation in all things sporting, and I began to give a lot of thought to my future. I had no interest in promotion, and apart from the troubles in Northern Ireland, which strangely I had somehow missed (not on purpose I hasten to add), there was little going on. In fact such was the remit of the Royal Marines as the finest fighting force in the country and probably the world, that we had little if any choice as to where we would serve, we travelled as individuals as directed, unlike many of the army regiments who travelled as huge bodies all their service life. The oft referred to *'first in – last out'* speaks volumes about how we were expected to operate!

Paddy's Ginger Wig!

The good thing about Poole was the social life. I met up again with an acquaintance from 41 Commando, Paddy Anderson. Paddy was a tall, ginger haired Irishman who cared little about anything; in fact everything about Paddy appealed to me. Above all he made me laugh, without trying and even without knowing it! At weekends Paddy and I would often jump on a train and travel up to Southampton, watch a match, get a B and B, and go clubbing. Due to our ultra-short hair, a rarity in these times, Paddy used to carry a horrible, ginger, unruly wig in an ill-advised attempt to look normal (in truth it made him look like 'Dennis the Menace'), in a plastic carrier bag, so designed so that at a minute's notice he could get it out and place it on his ugly head, thereby – or so he thought – becoming instantly 'attractive' to the ladies. No sooner would we be leaving the train station than in full view of everyone, without any hint of humour, he'd rummage around in the bag and remove the wig, look at his reflection in the window, and place the wig skew-whiff on his head. He'd then look at me as others looked on, and I would nod my approval. But better was to come. When we went clubbing Paddy used to wear the wig, but half way through a dance he would take off his wig, wipe the sweat from his forehead before placing it back on like an ill-fitting cap. Of course the girls we would be dancing with would grab their handbags from the floor and make a hasty, desperate retreat. At which point Paddy would turn and say to me, *'You gotta get a wig, George, or me and you are going nowhere, with you looking like a bloody squaddie!'* Paddy introduced me to a lifelong liking for Guinness; as such when I'm drinking the 'black-stuff', I often find myself smiling affectionately as I recall those lunatic outings!

A wedding prank!

Around about this time, whilst Paddy and I seemed to be almost joined at the hip, the two of us, unbelievably (I mean who in their right mind would invite us two to their wedding?), and two others, were invited to a mate's wedding in Gillingham. The problem was that Paddy and I didn't have 'wheels' for the fairly lengthy journey, and just as we were about to decline the offer, Paddy, from god knows where, 'acquired' in his words a 'sports car'! *'Come and have a look!' he* says. We go outside to the car park adjoining our room, and as I cast my eyes around looking for a Triumph Spitfire or an MG Midget or something equally exotic, Paddy shatters my expectations and points over yonder to a car standing all by itself – an antiquated Morris Minor with what you'd describe as half a roof on, simply because, the soft top roof (a onetime 'convertible') was stuck half open or I suppose half closed depending on your outlook. In Paddy's books, however, any car, which let both the rain and the sun in through the roof, was definitely a 'sports car'!

Anyhow a few days later the two of us headed for the open road, full of optimism, away to the wedding. The car shuddered somewhat if you exceeded 40mph, so we 'cruised' the journey at 40! My memory of this journey without a radio is vague apart from Paddy regularly breaking into song, and the song he sang was Olivia Newton-John's 'country road'! over and over and over again! Funny how you remember these meaningless little things. All this time later, I still detest that bloody song!

To cut a long story very short, once we arrived and with the other two (who didn't travel with us – 'for some reason'?) we decided we'd play a prank at the ceremony on Pebs and his unsuspecting wife to be, which went along the lines of: When the vicar said words to the effect of 'if anyone present has any just reason why 'Pebs' and his wife should not be joined in holy matrimony speak now or ....'! At which point the four of us would stand-up and utter 'EM'! Before sitting back down again. We changed our minds, BUT, didn't tell Paddy! So there we were, sitting like 'normal people' when all of a sudden I gets a reminder via an elbow in the ribs together with a wink and a nod from Paddy, whereupon right on queue, and in total isolation, Paddy (at 6'4") briskly stands up and comes to 'attention' before shouting from the back of the church 'EM'!! Everybody from this sizable family wedding (including us) turn and look directly at Paddy, as he stands there all alone, now stunned and in denial at his abhorrent childish prank! Not knowing what to do next he lingers for a few seconds whilst returning all the worried looks, before proceeding to quietly sit back down with his head bowed looking at the church floor, at which point the three of us totally blank him out! For the next few seconds he pathetically looks at me several times for some sort of supporting acknowledgement as I do my best to mimic a 'grown-up'!

What I remember now about this childish little escapade is a total lack of any acknowledgement from Pad, he simply behaved as if nothing had happened, didn't question or 'threaten' us. After the ceremony, we all filed outside for the customary photos, and somewhat strangely Paddy simply stood outside smiling pleasantly at the other 'guests' while nodding and having a smoke. Of course no one in their right mind was about to challenge him, not even Pebs. To this day I remember going round the corner of the church with my two 'colleagues' and laughing fit to kill ourselves, before 'cruising' back to Poole in our 'sports car' – with another bloody sing song!

A bit of part time work!

Although it was taboo to have any sort of 'outside work', while being deployed at Poole Paddy and I quietly got another part time job in an attempt to make some additional pocket money. The job was in a sausage making factory and the hours were hostile. We'd climb a wall at midnight and head down to Poole to put in four or five hours of sausage making work in this factory till about 5am, following which we'd climb the wall again so to speak and return to barracks. In the factory we'd be given big white hats and white overalls and even a pair of wellies each. We'd then spend the hours, putting sausages into cartons at a rapid rate of knots on this conveyer belt. Or pulling row after row of sausages out of freezing cold tanks, or sweeping the floors while shovelling the excess meat that had fallen onto the floor straight back into the sausage making machines. Within no time at all we were both bored rigid, and that's where the fun began with Paddy doing all sorts of obscenities (while all the sane people watched on) with the sausages while laughing like a bloody maniac. He'd have the sausages protruding from his hat or his collar and dangling down his back, or hanging from his wellies and of course sticking out from his trouser zip etc. Because everyone thought we were mad, or at least 'a little unhinged', nothing was said. Until the manager came up one night and said there had been a downturn in sausage meat popularity and sorry but the two of us were surplus to requirements. He did say that if there was an upturn he would be back in touch, ha, I bet!

It appeared to me at the time that there was a very exciting world materialising outside of the military. Above all freedom seemed a very attractive proposition. To go where I wanted, when I wanted, wear what I wanted, and grow my hair long like my mates in Civvy Street, to chase lasses – and 'be in with a shout' – and follow the music scene and go to concerts and music festivals all sounded very appealing. With my time at Boarding School where I'd been for two years prior to joining-up I had never had freedom, so perhaps it was a good time for a change, and I relished the thought. Shortly afterwards I was to leave and become 'almost' normal!

Always described as a very professional and reliable Royal Marine, I served in many countries, including Malta, Gibraltar, parts of Italy, Cyprus, Sardinia, Crete, Singapore (for 18 months), Hong Kong, USA, and the Caribbean, but never saw active service; there was little happening around the world during my years, and having been for most of my service in fighting units I was lucky! People clearly join the armed forces for a variety of reasons – for me, being so young, the attraction was only ever intended as an adventure, a way of seeing the world. Certainly as a young man, as ridiculous as it must sound, I'd never envisaged killing people (despite the latter being part of my job) and that must appear incredibly naïve now considering how dangerous the world has become over the last few years.

So, having been given my demob date, I simply went onto a Garage forecourt at Parkstone, paid £80 for a mini (although I didn't have a licence at the time), went back to Barracks, handed in all my kit, packed my bags, put them into the back of the car and drove 400 or so miles 'home', to begin a new life!

A few months prior to me leaving the marines, I found out my best mates from Widdrington who I'd grown up with had all emigrated to Australia – Ossie, Johnny, Trevor, Jimmy, Franky and Tony – leaving a huge hole to fill. Strange how things work out though, I have absolutely no doubt whatsoever that had I been free at the time I would have been part of this exodus; it would have appealed totally to me. The guys come back occasionally, but they've all carved a good living for themselves and I do miss them terribly! Such is life. Had we been around some years earlier we would have probably gone off to war together; as it stands the way I look at it now, we are simply a flight apart! Strangely, despite living on the Gold Coast, they all miss Widdrington with its diverse climate and unique English countryside, far removed from the sun and surf they are now accustomed to. My roots are here now for sure and as mentioned previously, I wouldn't want to live anywhere else!

Bellingham reunion, L-R Johnny, me, Ossie, Alan, Trevor, and Keith

Back to Civvy Street, freedom, and a new life beckons!

Having bought my first car (an old mini, for £80), I shared the journey up from Poole in Dorset with a friend, John Ashby, who was now also a 'former' Royal Marine. John needed a lift; as such I would drop him off in Hull, before continuing my journey up to Northumberland. Although I now had wheels, I had no licence and no insurance, which of course sounds callous now, but at the time those two issues weren't a priority for me at all.

Although I'd spent several years in the services I now realise that I'd been sheltered from the realities of 'ordinary' everyday life. Service life does that to you, although you are oblivious to that fact at the time. In the forces you dress as you're told, you attend and depart where and when you are told, you don't have to buy groceries or pay rent, and you have in many respects far fewer general responsibilities than other people in society. In the services you are in fact to a degree cocooned inside a very powerful organisation which takes care of you and almost totally controls all your activities. I accept fully now that despite my age in the latter few years of my military service, being well into my twenties, that there was undoubtedly an immaturity about me at that time, and even a naivety about life's responsibilities which would continue for a while yet. Also I wasn't married nor had children then – so very few responsibilities!

When leaving the Marines I had a certain feeling at that time which I find difficult to explain now. But remembering that I had been to Boarding School for adventure and a lifestyle different from others, and then quickly enlisted into the British Armed Forces for the same reason, and here I was several years later, as an adult still looking for the same adventure but this time with a different take on the subject due to my newly acquired 'freedom'!

I felt at the time an overwhelming sense of *euphoria* (honestly, I still occasionally have that same feeling even now, 40 years later) based around the fact that I was now free to do literally anything which took my fancy. Absolutely fantastic! Reflecting back now on my thoughts then, I could and did consider myself a 'free agent' for the first time as an adult. I didn't have to go home, nor did I need to work; in fact, on paper at least, I didn't have to do anything I didn't want to. I could dress as I pleased, grow my hair long and have a beard if the notion took me. I didn't have to carry an ID card and wear dog tags, and was free of any type of authority except the law of the land. I could emigrate or work abroad, have a lie-in in my own little room, in my own soft bed (with a hot water bottle if it took my fancy). I could start a job one week and finish it the next if it didn't suit! Ok, I accept that I may have laboured the last paragraph and elaborated perhaps a little too much, but honestly driving up home from Poole, every time I thought of those things mentioned above, I smiled!

Few in our society ever think about freedom; it's taken for granted, primarily because it is engrained into our 'oh so liberal and democratic society'. We all have much to thank our forefathers for, fighting as they did to ensure our continued freedom.

Back home!

Within a few hours of arriving home, a friend, Johnny Morton, was knocking on our door, firstly confirming that I was indeed 'out', before the inevitable *what was I going to do now? 'Because there's no work, Mikey'!* My mother was so pleased to have me home and I remained absolutely pampered for a short while. She encouraged me to have a few weeks off, saying there was no rush to find work – have a holiday – put your feet up, son, you've earned it!

Despite my mother's attractive offer, and Johnny's remark about there being no work, I was working full time within a week; it just happened. After about three days at home I had gone into Morpeth and visited what was known then as the 'Labour Exchange'. I explained my situation, told the lady I was looking for work, she asked me about what I wanted to do, and I replied anything to do with sport would be great, failing that my only stipulation was that I insisted it would have to be something physically active and preferably outside, but apart from that, I really didn't mind! Within a few minutes after confirming that although there were Sports Centres being built in Ashington and Newbiggin, it would be some time before they were fully functional, she then smiled and said, *'but I may have something right up your street',* literally. There was a vacancy for a forestry worker operating from Ulgham, only two miles from home! I couldn't believe my luck. I attended a very ad hoc interview in the front seat of a Land Rover with a guy called Tom Oliver (who was at least impressed that I had been in the Marines) and offered a start within a small 'gang' on the following Monday, starting at 7.30am.

Nature, and living at Widdrington!

For the next two years or so I would work as a forestry labourer, for the 'Forestry Branch' of the Coal Industry Estates. With few responsibilities, my wages were used for little more than 'beer money' once I'd paid my board. Duties were all physically orientated, felling, digging, planting, fencing etc. and all facilitated within a ten to fifteen mile radius of Widdrington. I have an enormous passion for everything countrified; always have had, harnessed presumably right from my early school days while walking and running through the woods and fields back and forwards on my way to school. The different smells of autumn with the earthy smell of decaying leaves and the striking show of ruby red rosehips, and then the frost, ice and snow of winter, before entering into the absolute joy of an English spring with the scent of wild garlic, bracken and bluebells, and then the summer months with the white and pink dog roses and honeysuckle in the hedges. I have begun to realise over the years how much I love Widdrington and the surrounding area. When I was young I didn't realise it, I wanted to be away to more exotic climes; but this is where I belong. I feel sad for people who are surrounded by everything I have, yet fail to see or hear any of it. So many are obsessed with material things, whilst bemoaning the fact that *'we've nowt here, no amenities, nowt'!* But I tell you, it's great around here, and even more so if you're an athlete. Wonderful for cycling, there are no traffic lights around here; if you want hills, there's an abundance of them waiting for you if you go inland; if you want flat terrain, then keep on the coastal roads. You have the best beach in the world with a huge expanse of golden sands less than three miles away, then there are several country parks to run around, as well as several lakes available to swim in, yes absolutely terrific! All the latter, of course, despite the weather being somewhat inclement with rarely two days the same. All in all though, I need little else and I consider myself very fortunate to live here.

My sporting life during this period revolved around occasional games of 5-a-side with the lads at Ponteland, Gary, Alec, Henna etc and running 'for fun', after a hard day's work, followed by the obligatory press-ups, dips and sit-ups. At weekends I'd run at the beach, often with Ian Wright and Willy Douglas (a very close friend of mine since my first day at school). In the fairly near future the triviality of my training at this time would change considerably, but more on that soon! Still, as the title of my book states, *'60 years an athlete',* I never stopped training, even in this transitionary phase of my life. Also my job guaranteed some real strength conditioning, in the purest of air, well away from the smoke!

My social life at this time was wonderful. I was free, and once I'd paid my board, I had money to spend and I was generous with it; I had long hair, and as many of my mates regularly remind me – was daft as a brush! On a Friday night after work and a bath, we'd all meet at Widdrington Club and have a pint or two before heading off to more entertaining venues. The disco years were in full swing, and with so many venues we were all spoilt for choice. We'd often return to Widdrington for the last drinks though, mainly because there were always invites to house parties, where we'd pay a 'quid' and spend the wee small hours in someone's house having a whale of a time, before staggering home.

A trip to the Races! Just like a script from 'one flew over the cuckoo's nest'!

Apart from those normal weekends out there were occasional coach trips to 'the races', Redcar, York, and Ayr being the regular haunts. I have very clear memories of a trip to Redcar races during this spell. We'd meet at the club as early as 6.30am, have a pint or two, climb aboard the coach, and have another drink or two during the journey before arriving at Redcar mid-morning. We'd head for the boating lake, before behaving like the lost souls in 'one flew over the cuckoo's nest', race each other in the boats, fall in the water, get covered in

Lester Piggott and Edward Hide

slime and it wasn't yet 11 o'clock. We'd then head for the race track. On this one occasion a good friend Cecil and I decided we'd not pay at the gate. We patrolled the perimeter looking for an opportunity to scale the fence. As the two of us identified the ideal spot, we were just about to scramble upwards over the fence when an elderly woman (whom we hadn't noticed), who was sitting on her back door step, with her legs wide apart showing off her pink wrist breaking knickers, shouted *'you'll never make it!'* Undeterred we both leapt up and scaled to the top of the fence before getting caught on the barbed wire! Aware that if we didn't act soon we'd be nabbed! With an almighty jerk of our legs we both ripped our trousers (mine being ripped far worse than his), we then tumbled back down on the wrong side of the fence, to be reminded by the lady 'with the knickers' – *'I told you so'!* Anyhow despite our pride being somewhat hurt, and my trousers both wet from the boat race and now horribly ripped as well, we proceeded along the path with the other punters, till we got to the 'Jockeys' entrance', at which point Cease grabbed me by the arm and said *'follow me'*. As directed I followed Cease. As we approached the Jockey entrance a little old guy with a cloth cap and woodbine cigarette hanging from his mouth, appeared from his little hut, at which point Cease (who most definitely didn't have the build of a Jockey, and had a bushy beard at the time) with an air of authority, said *'Edward Hide'* (a prominent leading Jockey at that time). This was met by *'and who the f..k's he?'* while pointing at me. *'Lester F..king Piggott?!'* (as I stood there in my 'bedraggled' tramp like state), quickly followed by, *'besides Edward Hide's at f..king York, now Bugger off'!* Anyhow as I've said elsewhere in this 'book', I never did get anything for nothing, so of course we ended up paying like all the rest. This would be around mid-day, and we still had another 12 hours of merriment before arriving home, somewhat the worse for wear, and met at the door by my mother with a *'my god'!* exclamation.

Margaret, are these yours?

Reflecting back roundabout this time there was an occurrence that took place that I still find myself occasionally laughing about. It is important that as I relate this laddish tale I point out that at the time I was young, free, and 'single' and hadn't even met my wife to be! I would state quite categorically though that in 37 years of marriage at this time I have never strayed! Anyhow one summer's evening I was out celebrating at a friend's bachelor do, when towards the end of the night I 'got acquainted' with an attractive young lass, and to cut a fairly lengthy story short we ended up in the back of my car in a local layby! This was a barmy mid-summer's night, country smells off the fields and a night that never got dark, beautiful! Anyhow the two of us stayed out most of the night, before heading home around about 5am a little the worse for wear! Funny how an individual piece of music can transport you back many years to certain events. On this occasion in the car I remember playing a piece by Kraftwerk, a German band, called Autobahn, and whenever I hear that music now I can relive that night.

Early the next morning, out to the world, I was roughly woken by my mother; apparently I had promised to take her and my nana shopping to 'Presto's'. I staggered out of bed and headed for my trusty little Mini, while my nana got into the rear. As we sat waiting on my mother, I became aware of my nana shuffling around on the back seat. Just as my mother got into the car, my nana said, *'Are these yours, Margaret?'* At the same time as my mother looked round I also looked into the rear mirror to see my nana holding a pair of knickers up in the air! Well I looked at my mother and she looked at me while grabbing the knickers saying, *'What are my knickers doing in your car?'* Quick as you like and despite my 'sleepy' condition I replied, *'Oh, I use them to clear the windscreen first thing, before work!'* Grabbing them roughly from my nana she proceeded to stuff them into her bag, saying, *'I just think you will, we've a million cloths in the house and you use my knickers!'* I apologised as my nana sat 'tutting' in the back. All over, or so I thought. Anyhow the next night as I lay on the settee watching the television, there's a knock on the door, and as my mother went to the door I heard a familiar voice saying, *'Is Mikey in?'* 'Yes, hinney,' says my mother, *'come on in. Michael,'* she shouts, *'somebody here to see you!'* The girl apologised before asking if I fancied going out. Nothing else to do so I went upstairs to get changed and when I came back down, with my mother in the kitchen, the girl was giggling while pointing at the knickers – unbeknown to me my mother had washed them, before putting them on the clothes horse, clearly still believing the pants were hers! I shook my head and indicated that she follow me out. I explained yesterday's events as we walked along, both of us in stitches laughing!

Just another example of my mother's naivety and innocent take on life! As far as I'm aware she continued to wear those 'second hand' knickers in the belief they were hers!

Swerving at one mile an hour to miss a deer!

Life working in our small forestry gang was often a hoot. Arnott, Colin, Joe and Walter were all entertaining company especially as the work could occasionally be repetitive. There were a million humorous incidents that happened on a regular basis with the vast majority being 'unintentional', like felling trees in gardens which fell straight on top of greenhouses, but not just ordinary greenhouses, oh no, I mean greenhouses with prize plants in them, nurtured and cared for, in prime condition and at their peak ready for the flower shows. On one occasion I was working with the gaffer and when we returned at the end of the day to pick up the others, our digger (a tiny little ineffective 'thing') with a bucket on the front was lying on its side, with the operator at the time (Big Joe) standing looking at it with his hands on his hips, shaking his head casually from side to side. Our boss, Tom, had a false eye, which I always found deceiving, especially if you looked at him from the side. As I looked at Tom I burst out laughing! Not at him I hasten to add, but at the sight of this machine lying on its side, and Tom's baffled facial expression. Anyhow I got a glance from Tom, and if looks could kill, truly I would be dead. We walked over to Joe, nothing being said until Tom looked at the machine, then at Joe and said, *'How the f..k have you done that?'* To which Joe replied without a hint of humour, *'I swerved to miss a deer!'* This useless piece of antiquated metal I swear had a top speed of one mile an hour; even then you'd need a hefty tail wind, and Joe had 'swerved to miss a deer'! At which point, with the two of them looking forlornly at the digger, and Joe having a sly look at Tom out of the corner of his eye, I almost died laughing. This started Joe off as well but not Tom, who mumbled obscenities at the hapless Joe, before threatening to take the damage out of Joe's wage packet. Needless to say the journey home was not pleasant – absolute silence with the exception of me behaving like a 'dick' by lighting up the atmosphere with regular bouts of hysterics, which went down like a lead balloon!

After a year or two with the forestry I began to get itchy feet again and on a whim I packed the job in with the intention of leaving Widdrington for a while. This I accomplished by loading a few clothes into my Mini (which I now had a licence for), told my mother I was off to visit a friend in Northampton and away I went – a prime example of the new 'freedom' I had attained and have referred to previously. I was away for a good six weeks just roaming around the country. I got as far down as Bristol, where I went to see a girl who I had been courting in Malta, Annette Lyons, who was now a nurse. Annette must have got a shock when she saw me. My money had been gradually dwindling; as such I would for the most part sleep cramped up in the back of this tiny little workhorse of a car. The last time Annette had seen me I had had the shortest of haircuts and was tanned with the Maltese sun. Here I was now about four years later, with hair down my back, a few weeks of facial stubble, and badly in need of a shower! Anyhow within a day or two I calculated that with care and 'cruising' at 30mph I might just about be able to make it home!

Back home, and probably as unfit as I'd ever been in my life, I once again visited the labour exchange in Morpeth and once again walked out with a job! This time on a building site employed as a labourer, building as it happens a prison at Acklington, five miles from home. I also began to realise that I needed more at this stage in my life, than beer and the occasional loose woman; as such a change was on the cards!

Reflecting back on my first quarter century

Whilst trying not to lose sight of the title of this book, **60 years an athlete**, I have given a pretty comprehensive account of my early years from birth, through school and right up to and including joining and leaving the Armed Forces. My intention is to invite people into the world that I grew up in, which was so very different from today's world, both in society and sporting issues. Looking back at this stage, it does seem that there was a simplicity in terms of general living then, which was so different from the

Me, Stobswood School

complexities that exist in today's IT-obsessed, hectic lifestyles. I do accept, however, that I have attempted to record my views through the eyes of a child and a young man, rather than through the eyes of an adult, and adults living during the period I refer to back then may well remember those times differently.

Living where I did, there appeared to be a large amount of 'harmony' among the people, and in hindsight I believe the reason behind that assertion is that we were all pretty much the same then; as such there would be little in the way of competition regarding differing standards of living. The vast majority of us lived in identical council houses, the rent was the same for all, and there were very few who actually 'owned' their house; in fact I didn't know anyone who didn't live in rented property. The men got paid pretty much the same wages because most worked at the same places, few families had cars, clothing and footwear was simple and functional, even social lives were pretty much the same. Holidays were spent either entirely around the locality, splodging in the burn at Ulgham, playing at the beach at Druridge Bay, climbing trees at Stobswood, playing sporting games on the 'bottom green', and for the men there was always the oasis of the working man's 'club'. A small proportion of families may have ventured as far afield as Blackpool or maybe even Butlin's Holiday camps, but certainly none of us had holidays abroad.

So where does the title **60 years an athlete** fit in to the overall story so far? Well, Athleticism was (and still is) everywhere in my life although I wouldn't be overly aware of it then, but every single day of my childhood, from infancy, through my youth, and into my adolescence before leaving home to join the military, incorporated forms of physical activity. *Indeed I do believe I have 'always' been an athlete of sorts!* I played specific sports, won some and lost some, but I also climbed trees, ran on the sand dunes, put people's coals in, shovelled snow from paths (for money of course), in the absence of my dad dug the garden, swam in Ulgham Burn, played energetic games, often to exhaustion on the streets and on the 'bottom green', and raced bikes around Widdrington's quiet, almost traffic-free thoroughfares. Perhaps the only thing that separates the athlete from others is that athletes are regularly directed or dictated to by coaches and have carefully planned specific aims and objectives, and keep appropriate training diaries, and until I was fifteen I had none of the latter (and never had a coach), only a zest for continuous physical activity, both sporting and recreational. Certainly, I am sure that the non-specific physical grounding I had for so much of my growing up and into the Marines helped me in more ways than one to develop into the athlete I would later become. It's well known that consistency is an important ingredient essential for sporting improvement, and I had consistency by the bucket-load all through my early years and beyond!

Returning to competitive sport with Morpeth Harriers

Around about this time the novelty of being a 'free agent' civilian began to lose its spark just a little. Back home again I soon returned to training, but with no goals as such apart from the joy of the exercise and generally keeping fit. I always fitted the running in 'immediately' after work, following a hard shift of wheeling bricks, mixing cement or digging foundations etc. I didn't dislike the work and for the most part used the hours there as an opportunity to get physically strong. As daft as it sounds I would turn much of my work into a type of competition, but competing against myself not others, moving around the site at an ever increasing 'rate of knots' while pushing barrows, or loading dumper trucks etc. I'd work hard, and even in mid-winter I'd get a sweat on, often being 'advised' by others on the site to *'slow down for f..k's sake'!* But generally with the additional evening running, and the ever present press-ups, dips and sit-ups I was getting fitter by the week, although there was no real purpose to the training apart from the degree of the contentment I got as always from the exercise and being outside. I was still enjoying a good 'social life', but began to realise that I was going round in circles with no real purpose or direction in my life. Most of my mates were married and had families and I was rapidly becoming the odd one out!

Somewhat strangely I can honestly say that my life changed for good at an engagement party between my cousin Gillian and her fiancé Neil, which took place at the Farriers Arms at a place called Shilbottle. I have been blessed with a wonderful extended family – several have now died – but I had and have both love and respect for all my relations. However once I was past the childhood phase it seemed we had little in common as far as hobbies, interests and general everyday issues were concerned. Having been out of the Marines for two or three years, I was now quietly questioning where the rest of my life was going. I had a recurring feeling, very similar to other times in my life, that once again I was a nobody, with no real identity. As I sat in the Farriers that night I soon became bored with the proceedings. I hasten to add again that it wasn't my family who were the cause of my feelings, but there was becoming an ever increasing restlessness in me whereby I'd ask myself fairly regularly *'is this it?'*. My mother would sidle up to me and whisper, *'Michael, you are going to have to talk to people, son,'* then more sternly, *'they'll think there is something wrong with you – like a halfwit'!* Anyhow from literally nowhere I made my mind up right there and then to return to athletic competition, simply on the basis that I needed something else in my life apart from work and the weekend jovialities!

I had thought about returning immediately to Morpeth Harriers, but became reticent on the basis that I had no idea at all how my current running abilities would fair against 'serious' athletes, so I decided I'd work hard in training for a while then return when I was confident of at least a 'respectable' showing.

My mentor from childhood, Jim Alder, was now in the sports shop retail business, owning a shop in Morpeth called Jim Alder Sports, with another shop in the pipeline, at nearby Ashington. In need of decent training shoes I was soon standing in Jim's shop in Manchester Street. I hadn't seen Jim for around 12 years, the last time being when I was a 15 year old. Jim looked at me inquisitively (there was a spark) until I reminded him who I was. We had a quick chat, and I noted immediately that he hadn't changed one iota – his mannerisms were identical to the last time, talking very quickly as he does, and just as easily distracted! Anyhow I told him I was back in training and hoped to join the club again soon.

The start of another 35 years of consistent training and ambition!

From that point I began training in earnest. Regardless of how I felt after a hard day's work on the building site, as soon as I got in my haversack was thrown in the corner, off would come my work boots and mud soiled clothes, on would go my tracksters and trainers and off I'd jog into the chilly darkness of the Ulgham Road, up around Chisholms farm area, through the Park wood and back home via Stobswood, about six miles in total; a few press-ups and sit-ups would follow before jumping into a cold bath as the fire hadn't been on long enough to either heat the house or the water! I went straight back into training seven days a week; my training diary in the Autumn of 1977 states I was running between 7hrs 30m and 8hrs 50mins a week. I had by now re-joined Morpeth Harriers after a 12 year absence. On the 8th of October I won my first race, a harrier league event at South Shields – described in the Sunday Sun as **'Harris's fine win'.** Although I was running for Morpeth again, I hadn't as yet purchased a Morpeth vest and ran the race in a t shirt! As I passed the finish line, I saw, for the first time in 12 years, Ernie Slaughter (a wonderful Morpeth stalwart) who was one of the official timekeepers on the day. The last time I had seen Ernie had been when he was doing the same timekeeping job in the Sherman Cup event, which I had run in the 'boys' category, a few days before I joined up. Anyhow my face, despite my lack of Morpeth colours, must have 'registered' because as I looked back there was Ernie looking at me over his shoulder. As soon as I could I went back to shake Ernie's hand, at which point he gave me a smile and a *'you're back'!* (As if I'd been on a quick visit to the bog) before scolding me with a *'where's your vest'!* The next few races were recorded in my training diary as an 11th in the Houghton Road Race, a 2 mile road relay which I did in 9m 45s, and the Brampton to Carlisle 10 mile road race on 26th November in 52m 03s. Looking back it seems I had made sound progress in a very short time, but only to be brought crashing back down to earth with a 75th in the Morpeth-Newcastle New Year's Day road race running 1hr 17m 01s, after which I pledged that the next time I would run the Morpeth classic, I wouldn't be out welcoming and celebrating in the new year till 2am! However the next year, due to horrendous weather on the 1st of January, the event was cancelled and postponed for two weeks, till the 14th January 1979 when the snow had cleared a bit. This time I ran the event finishing 15th in 1hr 12m 24s! I'd *improved 60 places* from the previous year; this was pleasing as the event was always full of 'quality' athletes, often with many international runners running alongside the many hundreds of club runners.

Cleveland Marathon, 1981 – 2nd – 2 hours 25 minutes 52 seconds
Winner Ray Smedley
Very windy, gale force

As I write, I must keep reminding myself of the title of this account of my life, **'60 years an athlete'**! Otherwise I will invariably write too much meaningless, trivial drivel not really connected to the story or the title. However, again referring to my diaries around this time and having gained employment at Ashington Leisure Centre, I was now working two different shifts and this allowed me to train twice a day. This period was approximately 24 years after my first ever race, and at the time of these races I was now running around 460 miles a month on a very regular and consistent basis! On the 17th June 1979 I would run my second marathon (you may recall I did one in Hong Kong when I was an 18 year old Royal Marine), at Sandbach, in Cheshire. From a large field of athletes I finished a creditable 15th in 2hrs 28m 35s, my diary reads, and quote *'good for 15 miles but slowly tired by 20 miles, exhausted last 4 miles, legs very tired, hard work just to keep going'*!

It is sometimes forgotten that during the 70s and 80s there was a huge swell in running numbers; as I recall it was referred to regularly as 'the running boom' – all of a sudden everybody it seemed wanted to be athletes.

When you look back at the history of distance running, what you find is that the more competition there is in national teams for places, the greater the individual results attained. It was evident as long ago as the 1920s in Finland – so many world class athletes competing in the blue colours of their country. Likewise in the 1960s and 1970s Britain had so many 'world class marathon men' we were spoilt for choice: Jim Alder, Ron Hill, Jim Hogan, Basil Heatley, Ian Thompson, Tony Simmons, Dave Cannon, Steve Jones, Tim Johnston, Charlie Spedding, Bill Adcocks, Brian Kilby, Don Faircloth, Hugh Jones, to name a few.

North Eastern Counties Marathon –
1st – 2 hours 25 minutes 26 seconds

Likewise in Britain in the 1980s our 800 metre runners ruled the world – Seb Coe, Steve Ovett, Peter Elliot, Steve Cram, Tom McKean, Graham Williamson; there was also 'one of ours' who finished 8th in the Olympic final and I can't even remember his name (Warren?), such was our wealth of talent. Obviously with lesser grandeur than those outlined above, nevertheless in our club, Morpeth Harriers, we had the same in depth competition for places to make the team in local races. Archie Jenkins, Bob Marshall, Mike Bateman, Steve Beatty, Neil Black, Bob Dunn, Don Speight, Paul Bentley, Dave Gray, Ian Brown, Bernie Cordes, Walter Ryder, Alan Catley, Doug Cockburn, Bill Morrison, Peter Carmichael, myself and of course Jim Alder. Additionally there were some exciting talented juniors such as Jake

Harper and Peter Dodds coming through to also challenge for places. There was little between any of us and competition was so keen to be 'just' a 'counter' in the team that it drove us all on to attain notable performances, always having to give our best time and time again just to make the team!

For me, I have always had self-belief; rightly or wrongly I believed that one day I would join those elites of the marathon world, mentioned above. There were people around at the time who were inspirational to athletes like me. Athletes like Ian Thompson who apparently was nothing other than a very good club runner, until he ran a marathon. Having been persuaded to make up a three man team to represent his club in the 'Poly' marathon, he then went on to win the event and run 2hrs 12m in this, his first attempt at the classic distance. In his next marathon he won the Commonwealth gold in 2hrs 9m, in his next the European gold! The stuff dreams are made of.

Summarising my six or seven years competing 'again' with Morpeth isn't at all easy; there was a lot of water, so to speak, under the bridge during that spell. However, I competed in six marathons; all were sub 2hrs 30m. I won the North Eastern Counties Marathon in 2hrs 25m 26s, and was placed 2nd in the Cleveland Marathon to Ray Smedley in 2hrs 25m 52s on a gale force windy day. Appropriately perhaps I won a chair (which I had to carry back on the train) in the Barnsley marathon having finished 9th from a huge field. I was also placed 2nd in the NE Counties 20 mile, and 3rd in the NE Counties 10 mile, won a team winner's medal in the NE cross country, and had other top 3 places in road races. Not a monumental record by any means; however, the strength in depth in the North East during these years was phenomenal. As an example, I once did 1hr 9mins in the 13. 5/8 mile Morpeth to Newcastle on a bitter cold New Year's Day and could only finish 18th. My highest mileage was 139 miles a week and I had many regular weeks of over 100 miles. I ran every day of the week, twice a day; the only interruptions were due to injury, but even then I 'hobbled' through training till the injury healed, rather than 'rest up'. My weight at the time was consistently around 9st 7pounds, *which had my ever worrying mother imploring me to see the doctor as*

I looked so ill! I can even remember Jim Alder saying, quote *'you look hungry, you must be fit'!* On hindsight my training mileage was too much for me. I was born with an innate capacity for endurance as my childhood days reminds me; I could keep going indefinitely but I lacked speed at the 'top end'; as such I would have been better off on 'just' 80 a week or thereabout, and incorporating more quality! What is also worth remembering of those days is that you had to 'hunt' for marathons then, there really weren't that many of them around, and most were never designed to be 'fast'. In the Newcastle marathon, for example, there were three laps, each circuit having a 'lengthy' uphill drag incorporated.

The other thing worth mentioning of that era, certainly amongst 'club' runners, is that many of us **'raced' the 26 miles;** in other words from the off the onus was on attempting to win the event, and certainly there is a huge difference between trying to *win* as opposed to trying only to *finish!*

Oh, nearly forgot, I also got married during this spell, much to the relief of my ever concerned mother. I married Jennifer Elizabeth Brown on my 28th birthday, the 11th August, the same date in 1966 when Jim Alder had won his gold, and I had received my first 'proper' pair of running shoes (not that the latter matters – just thought I'd throw it in!). Weddings were simpler then: we married in Widdrington's ancient medieval little church with all our families and friends present, had a reception at the Waterford Lodge in Morpeth and honeymooned for two days in York, then back to work. After I'd won the Newcastle marathon a couple of years later, we went off to the Isle of Arran for a few days' holiday, and with little else to do my eldest son was conceived on the island – the marathon had been in August and James was born in May – work it out! After being up all night 'spectating' the birth, I nevertheless did my usual training and have recorded in my diary *'ran 10 miles at 7am with a smile on my face'!* I was the proud father of a beautiful, healthy little son, nothing could be better, I couldn't stop smiling.

Blues music and the endurance athlete!

Some time ago when I was playing blues harmonica with the band I was with at the time, called the Rhythm Method, I had a fairly heated discussion with a locally renowned singer guitarist. The discussion revolved around the fact (or novelty) that as an 'athlete' how on earth could I be accepted as a 'blues musician' and play the blues. Although he knew little about me at the time, his insinuation was that athletes are renowned for clean living (the latter is just an assumption by the way, often incorrect), whilst in his opinion, blues musicians were renowned in fact for quite the opposite! His viewpoint was that I was playing the blues by default, in other words there wasn't an 'honesty' or 'sincerity' about my passion for blues music. His assertion was based on his misguided opinion that you had to be physically unfit, probably have a drink problem, smoke 'something' preferably like a chimney, and have a diet that would ensure you'd die early! The latter were, in his opinion, an absolute necessity if you wanted to be accepted as a good and true blues musician.

My all consuming passion for music, particularly Chicago type blues, which I've had since I was 15, is at least on a par with my love of sport, and if I had to choose between the two? No question, I would find it a total misery to live without the music, both listening and playing, but I could exist without putting myself through the treadmill of everyday training for the remainder of my life.

Blues music, as most I think are aware, initially derived around the world due to hardships. The most well-known of these hardships were in the 'deep south' of America, in the cotton fields, where complete families toiled for hour after hour in the intense heat whilst picking copious amounts of cotton, just to ensure they had the most basic of foods to eat while having a roof over their heads. In order to escape the misery and the toil, people would sing with an intensity and feeling that came straight from the heart. Singing the blues somehow helped them escape the pain of their 'oh so difficult lives'!

Whilst I would not wish to compare my 'comfortable' European lifestyle with that of the black people of the Mississippi, nevertheless, there is a comparison. How do I explain, without appearing absurd?

Most serious endurance athletes have a love/hate relationship with their chosen sport, and the hate side probably outweighs the love side for much of the time. For me when I was training 'incredibly' hard (three times a day for most of the year, and working full time, with a family), just waking up in the morning was a heartache! Still stiff and exhausted (like the black people) and probably injured somewhere on my anatomy, from my previous days, weeks, months and years of arduous training, often with little to show for it, I would

Playing with Rhythm Method, 1993

'ease' my fragile body out of bed at 6 o'clock, slide downstairs, grab a bite to eat which would be similar to the cotton pickers, porridge or cereal based. I would then travel in the opposite direction to work and swim an average of 120 lengths in the pool, climb out and have a 'cool' shower, before leaving hastily for work. On the way to work I'd eat two or three apples and a banana, and have a slurp of tap water, while I considered the working day ahead. At lunchtime I'd often run eight or 10 miles before taking a sandwich into the shower, in haste to save time, and then continue back at work. At 16.30 I'd drive home, have five or six jam sandwiches and a cup of tea before heading out for my 3rd session of the day and ride between 25 and 35 miles on my bike, or go and race on the bike before returning home at 21.00. Just another day, with nothing to show for my efforts, and very little, if any, interest either!

Ok some will say (and quite rightly so) that the difference between my 'blues' due to the fatigue and the quite considerable discomfort, and the 'blues' of the black people of Alabama, is that mine is a choice, whilst theirs is a necessity. I accept and totally agree with all of that; however, it doesn't change the concept of the 'blues'. The struggle and the discomfort (for differing reasons) are similar. Athletes or cotton pickers? Well we both regularly have the blues!

At the time of the discussion with my 'friend' whereby it was put to me that I couldn't possibly play blues music 'and mean it' while being a 'pampered' athlete who knew little about the troubles associated with playing that type of music! – trust me, as a working amateur athlete who never took a day off from work due to sickness, or likewise never missed a training session, I knew, and know fully what the blues are. But regardless of all of that I have a passion for music and the blues in particular, that goes much deeper than an occasional hobby. If there is a difference between us (my black brothers and sisters of New Orleans and myself) then it has to be that for me my lifestyle was a choice, whilst theirs was nothing other than an absolute necessity.

For as long as I have lived and participated in sporting competition, I have, and continue to have the 'blues', for there is a certain ever present torment that rides alongside sporting ambition. If honest, and of course I must be in writing an autobiography, I am an addict, similar perhaps to other addicts whatever the differing addiction may be, and the addiction brings with it the 'blues'! Of the latter, I have abundance! I also fully accept that there must have been many times when I was less than easy to live with.

A sporting change and the triathlon years!

As mentioned previously, by now I had another job and had been working at Ashington Leisure Centre for approximately two years. I had originally been interviewed for a Supervisor's post; however, I learned later that the two posts on offer were already spoken for even before the interviews, and right enough the positions were indeed given to two 'in-house' applicants, hence the interviews were nothing other than a paper based exercise. Within hours though I received a phone call informing me that I'd had an excellent interview; however on this occasion I hadn't been successful and the Supervisors' posts had gone. But the lady also added that there was another post available and whilst the wages were less, there was a high turnover of staff within the leisure centres and if I took the post of attendant it would put me in good stead for a supervisor's post as and when one became vacant! I discussed the proposal with Jennifer and we decided it was a good opportunity to begin a career within sport and recreation, and would be preferable to 'labouring' for the remainder of my life! And so began my career in the sports and leisure industry. For the next three or four years I became a pain to management. I found the initial years so frustrating; I was ambitious and wanted to get on, yet my position was not considered to be valid enough to be considered for coaching or supervisory courses. I was desperate to improve my status; as such I pursued any and every course I heard about; I was always knocking on doors. I often got courses that others (supervisors) couldn't be bothered to do – 'I'll do it,' I would shout! I gained coaching qualifications in swimming, table tennis, gymnastics, trampoline, got my bronze medallion, as well as becoming a club coach with Morpeth Harriers in every distance from 800 metres up to and including marathon. I also attended a year's course at Sunderland Poly and came away with a Certificate in Supervisory Studies. I'm sure for the most part the courses I was given were designed just to shut me up! However, I had an earnest ambition to 'get on' and was prepared to work for it.

Some time in 1982, while working in Ashington Leisure centre, I read a brief article in the Daily Mirror newspaper by Brendan Foster (who was I think working for Nike at the time) that would change my sporting life for good. The article (which was accompanied by a photograph showing several 'decathletes' lying exhausted around an athletics track having just completed the last event of a decathlon – the 1500 metres) went on to identify and describe a new craze that was sweeping across the USA – the event was referred to as a **Triathlon!** This incorporates three disciplines: swimming, cycling and running. A view was expressed that whatever happened in America would also happen here in the UK a short while later. The British Triathlon Association had been recently formed and contact names and addresses were given at the end of the article.

For at least the past five years while running with Morpeth Harriers, **I had ran for the most part twice a day throughout the year, mainly seven days a week, accumulating between 80 and 120 miles weekly, occasionally more, but seldom less.** The by-product of the repetitive nature of running, mainly on concrete, was fairly regular injury 'niggles', together with more serious injuries. Strangely though when looking through my training diaries of those years, although I have many injuries noted, I seemed to continue to run through them without being laid up (mind over matter, I suppose). I have many noted comments along the lines of *'Knee very sore this morning, becoming less so toward the end of the run'* or *'right foot still very painful, very worried tonight'* and *'both Achilles tender, especially first thing'*! For the most part it seems I ran through them, because later on the remarks 'petered out' although the training was its ever consistent self!

Right from the beginning I was fascinated by the potential of competing in this new sport of triathlon. On the surface I felt the content was made to measure for me. I was a good swimmer (particularly for a runner), although I had rarely ridden a bike for years I recalled that as a kid few could keep up with me as we raced the streets on our bikes, and my running fitness and ability was well documented! I wrote off to 'Alec Hunter' asking how we could get involved in triathlon competition. Alec replied that if I joined the British Triathlon Association (BTA) there were events coming up around the country and I would be mailed regular newsletters etc. In the first newsletter I received there was one event that caught my eye and stood out immediately – there was to be a National Championship event in Reading on the 5th June! Alec had, in previous correspondence, also mentioned that in my area there was to be a triathlon shortly in Durham. This would comprise a ½ mile swim, 26 mile cycle and a 5 mile run! Pretty soon after reading Brendan Foster's article I had gone into the pool at Ashington and swam a mile front crawl just to see how difficult or easy I would find it! I found it a doddle! I made my mind up there and then that I would go for it, and so I did! I went down to the nearest bike shop in Ashington, Wears Cycles, and bought myself a 'huge' black Motobecane bike for the princely sum of £212.00 (I've still got the receipt), before contemplating how the hell I would 'tell her indoors'! Like most newly married couples at the time, with a newly acquired mortgage etc. we had very little 'spare' cash. I was lucky with Jennifer – although she had little interest in sport, she rarely showed any opposition regarding my participation. Having said that, I hadn't changed just because we'd married, I was an athlete before and have remained one ever since, so no real shocks I suppose.

Whilst I doubt if I would have acknowledged it then (as there is something perverse about the term 'addiction') I was in fact *addicted* to running. At the risk of repeating myself, I never missed training, regardless of work, family, injuries or weather. Although I had now committed myself to the Durham triathlon, I was worried (you see – this *is indeed addiction*) that my running fitness and ambitions would suffer if I reduced my mileage. I was also aware that triathlon may well be a passing craze – then what? So I decided that to safeguard my running progress over the preceding years, and maintain my running ambitions, I would simply maintain my running miles (as near as damn it), while adding on swimming and cycling sessions. **At the time in the winter and spring of 1983 I was running 80 miles a week, swimming six or seven days a week (made easier because my**

workplace had a swimming pool) and also cycling five or six days a week! I was also working 40 hour 'shifts' (the shifts assisting my training) and had a baby son, and a car that wouldn't bloody well start!

I remember at the time (with such a hunger for knowledge) writing to Alec Hunter and asking about such issues as *'do you need two bikes?'*. No! came the somewhat abrupt reply – *'what do you do then if you puncture?'* Fix it or drop out! Said Alec. *'Do you have any advice on open water swimming, what if the water is cold?'* I said. Practise outdoor swimming, he said, and if the water's cold? Well it's cold for everyone, he replied! See, I told you training was non-complex! I was actually swimming in trunks, in the QEII lake in early March, bloody freezing! (Where on one occasion I actually got 'bitten' by 'something' and had the marks to prove it! Just like Jaws!!)

I have always maintained that apart from the 'technical' aspects of certain sports, training is not at all complex, particularly for endurance sports, perhaps with the exception of 'peaking' and being at your absolute best for certain events which does take a degree of expertise. The principles just need to make sense, training should be Consistent, Specific, and to see progress it should also be Progressive. At this time in my life I was a very experienced athlete, I was now 30 years old, with 15 years of 'adult' training and competition behind me (and 10 years as the most active of children), and was a club coach in 800/1500, 5,000/10,000 and the Marathon, and all I did at the time was to use the very same principles involved in running LSD, intervals, fartlek, repetitions, resistance work and transfer them directly over to swimming (I was also a qualified ASA swimming teacher) and cycling!

My training over the following weeks took on a new eagerness, believing as I did that the sport was 'made to measure' for me, and by late spring I was superbly fit, and with the additional muscular strength I'd attained in the pool and on my bike, my weight had gone up to 10st 3lb and there it would remain as my ideal 'fighting' weight for the next 12 years during triathlon competition.

Training week April 1983: run 80 miles, bike 140 miles, swim 12,000 yards.

On the 2nd May 1983 I took part in my first triathlon at Durham and finished an 'unlucky' 6th from the 170 or so starters. I say unlucky because I was sent the wrong way on the run leg, by a boy scout, which clearly cost me some time and probably some places, before I retraced my steps! But I loved it, and definitely I wanted more!

I met a guy that day from Middlesbrough called Dick Hatfield. As we came out of the water almost together we found ourselves changing next to each other; we wished each other good luck before heading out on the bike leg. For the next 12 years I would bump into Dick on a very regular basis and I was always better for seeing him.

Following my baptism into triathlon at the Durham event I had set my sights firmly on the National Championships at Reading in June. Instinct and the previous outing found me very optimistic about my chances 'down south', and my training over the next few weeks really took off!

The month's training leading up to the first National Championships: run 295 miles, bike 600 miles, swim 45,000 yds – averages per week = run 74 miles, bike 150 miles, swim 11,250yds. (Blended into a 40hr working week)

Approaching the Reading event, I contacted my dad (who I hadn't seen for a few years, although we'd kept in touch) who lived in London, with a view to spending the night at his place before travelling on to Reading on race day. My dad hadn't heard of triathlon but regardless agreed to pick me up from Kings Cross and put me up for a night. One of the complexities with multi-sport events is the amount of equipment you needed to cart around with you. Triathlon particularly with the bike and spares as well as the other equipment could be cumbersome. At this time while travelling on the train without a proper cycle carrying bag I simply wheeled the bike everywhere with me, while carrying my other kit in a large bag. Anyhow on Friday the 3rd June I travelled to London and was picked up as agreed by my dad, and on Saturday we travelled to Reading, stayed the night in a hotel before moving on to the race venue at Kirtons Farm early on the race morning. The weather on the day was spot on and the park was buzzing; there were hundreds there, adding to the tension, all sorts of athletes and their followers. After registering I went to my allocated transition area to lay out my kit, where purely by chance right next to me was Dick Hatfield! Dick's speciality was open water swimming and I watched intrigued as he covered his feet in fat! All of a sudden watching Dick I realised the water was probably very cold, particularly in a skimpy pair of trunks. Too late now, I thought, and blocked out any negativity and thought 'what will be will be'. I was still optimistic and figured very few if any would have trained like me. It seemed to me on that day that there were a lot of body builder types there; regardless of the visual spectacle these didn't bother me one iota, I'd been there before in the Marines with the same eye catching types and I always came out on top, and figured today would be no different!

As I've mentioned before and I hope this doesn't sound pompous or arrogant, but I don't know anyone tougher than me, I'm as hard as nails – that's just a fact, and as the saying goes when the going gets tough, the tough get going! I have never failed to deliver in relation to effort –if I'm there, you'll not get an easy race. The harder the conditions the more it suits!

The race on the day started with a blast from a canon, at which point over 200 of us dived into the lake and fought our way around the swim course, especially at the tight turning points where we'd have to slow to get around the buoys and end up bunching. It was a rough swim with lots of unintentional fighting but it got easier as the field began to spread out!

Once out of the water we headed up the bank and onto our bikes. I was now pleased that I hadn't 'greased up' as cycling with lard between your toes could not have been fun! My newly acquired mate Dick was out only two seconds in front of me, which gave me a lift, with Dick being a more than competent open water swimmer. Anyhow my cycling went well, no one came past me, and I continued to pass others, confidence rising and despite the effort I was feeling relatively comfortable. Just the run to do and although the early mile or so was uncomfortable I soon got into my stride. With a mile to go as we finally made our way around the lake to the finish I was in 3rd place and about to move another place up to finish 2nd! The event took me 3hrs 40mins and 45s. It was won by an Army Sergeant called Jim Woods, a British Biathlete, and behind me in 3rd place was Danny Nightingale, an Olympic Pentathlon Gold medallist, so I was indeed in good company.

1983, first ever National Triathlon Championships, Reading
Finished 2nd

In the melee at the end and with the large crowds I couldn't find my dad; some time later when we did meet he asked me genuinely if I'd 'dropped out'! Clearly he'd missed me and assumed the worst, and when I told him I was 2nd, I'm sure he thought I'd made it up! Anyhow in the first National Triathlon Championships I'd finished a creditable runner-up, from 172 finishers. I eventually got £200 and a sizable silver cup. I was hooked and so was my dad.

Twelve years later in my last National Championship event in Guernsey before retiring from the sport, and at 43 years of age, I would finish 8ᵗʰ. In between those years I'd win three British

Championships, finish Runner-Up three times, be 3rd twice, have a couple of 4th places and have a 5th and a 6th placing and 10 National Masters titles.

One of the reasons for my successes in the British Triathlon Championships was that right from the beginning of my entry into the sport I felt that if you were ambitious, then the best place to identify your 'pedigree' was to compete against the best in the country, and the best were likely to be at the British Championships. If you won at these then you had a legitimate right to a claim of being the best in the UK on that day! Hence every year as from January the 1st I'd set my stall out and all my training and competitions leading up to the 'big ones' were designed to 'peak' at these events.

Just to get something off my chest!

Much has been written about early triathlon competitions. A lot of it has been written by people who were barely out of their nappies at the time, almost 35 years ago. They will dig out a photograph of a bike with a 'shopping bag' attached to the handle bars, and add accompanying tongue in cheek text along the lines of *'my, haven't times changed'*! I am one of the very few who can legitimately comment on 'changes' over the past 30 years, having been around in 1983 and competed again in 2015 some 30 plus years after the advent of the sport. I find a lot of the throw away, ill-informed comments total rubbish, whilst at the same time appearing to be totally disrespectful to triathletes of the past, also incredibly annoying. It's my view that apart from an unhealthy infatuation with expensive equipment and the one-upmanship that that fixation brings with it (i.e. trying to improve by obtaining superior equipment), that the sport has barely changed at all in 30 years. The content is clearly the same – triathlon consists as it did in the past of swimming, cycling and running (no change there then) – and you can only physically perform those exercises as you always have. Split times may well have improved (partly with the provision of wetsuits etc.); however, surely that is the same in every sport over the years... compare the 1896 Olympic marathon winner's time in Athens to the marathon time of London 2012's winners! It is worth remembering that back in the 'early' days of triathlon, in an effort to 'prevent unfair advantages' for some, that triathlon was **'self-help only';** as such wetsuits were banned as were tri-bars for a while. You were also, unlike today's 'elite', disqualified if you drafted! I was amazed to hear that in the 2012 Olympics certain triathletes were employed purely to assist the efforts of others, a bit like the Tour de France. This was never intended within the ethical side of the sport, though of course it does seem these days that nothing really matters apart from providing 'winners'. Clearly the latter is pertinent to the elites, where the cycling leg has now become a 40km procession.

Another change, and not for the better, is the selling of 'must have' equipment as advocated and promoted by an array of magazines. Ok this is business and I understand that, it all helps to sell magazines. However, what intrigues me is the following. I recently bought a 'triathlon' magazine, more intrigued by the front cover displaying 'Jenson Button', (a Formula One racing driver), than anything else! I can see no legitimate reason in the world (apart from glamour) why a 'Formula One' racing driver should figure on the front cover of a triathlon magazine denying as it does potential valuable exposure for our struggling triathletes. This says much about the state of sport in general in the UK. Clearly Jenson's fame – through 'Formula One' and not triathlon – and his considerable personal fortune are more important and interesting than any one of the thousands of normal triathletes out there. On top of that of course the photographs are clearly designed to give maximum exposure to all his various sponsors such as Asics, Hubb, Ichiban, Rudy Project, Sci'con, Mobil and even Johnnie Walker! You open the 'triathlon' magazine to find two A4 size posed 'facial' photos - wonderful! Then on the next page is another photo pretty much the same as the preceding three, then you get to the last page of this 'fascinating' article and yes, you've guessed it, another facial photo! Tell you what though, had there been two male editors of this mag' and they had done the same portrayal of em, let's say 'Pamela Anderson', I wonder what the response would have been?

But you know, apart from the immense 'glitz' and hundreds of adverts from cover to cover in the triathlon magazine, the sport is pretty much the same now as it was in 1983. As previously mentioned I was there in '83 and as I write this piece I was there again this year in 2015, finishing 15th at 64 years of age from a field of 262! *In my day* (and all of a sudden I feel a little like Corporal Jones from Dad's Army) you never got 64 year olds getting in the top 20 of sizable fields, so just maybe (no offence intended) the quality of the fields is not as good as in the 80s and 90s! And that's beside all the following modern advances: the sleekest, lightest and most flexible of wetsuits, together with 'leakage' proof goggles guaranteed not to mist up. The lightest and stiffest cycles with components guaranteed to make you go quicker, together with an array of wheels to complement the machine. Then of course 'fast' wheels require 'fast' tyres, then as the 'research indicates' by acquiring the latter, you're sure to save goodness only knows how much time (and effort). Then there's aero helmets tested in wind tunnels to save up to 45 seconds over 40km! Wow, now that's got to be worth £250, surely! Then when you get off the bike, having saved all that energy, you'll really motor along when you step into those super-fast running shoes – and just take a look at the must-have special laces! Wait a minute now because I'm not quite finished! If you are really serious you'll need a computer – I mean how can you possibly cycle fast without one? Oh nearly forgot, we've got power meters as well, and pulse monitors, then if you've any money left (or put yourself into the red, who cares it'll be worth it!) why not spend it on these laboratory tested nutritional products and supplement pills – they're all designed to make you go quicker. Finally, with all that training you've missed due to 'shopping', can you really afford 'not' to have the 'must haves'?

Here's something to think about though!

Performance enhancing 'drugs' are designed for the very same purpose as all that expensive equipment, aren't they? That is, to give you the edge over the competition. The only real difference is that expensive equipment is legal, and expensive drugs are illegal, but the philosophy is pretty much the same – isn't it? That is simply to make you go quicker, however you get there!

A short while ago as I was out having a drink with a very good friend of mine called Ian Miller, Ian reminded me of a conversation we had a few years ago when he mentioned at the time that he fancied getting a new bike, primarily to make his cycling easier and with it to actually go a bit quicker. By all accounts I replied, **'Keep your money in your pocket, Ian, and go on a diet – you'll be healthier, the ride will be easier, you'll naturally go quicker, especially on the hills, and you'll save quite considerable expense!'**

It's worth reminding ourselves of the golden age of British marathon running in the 1960s, 70s and on into the 80s, where we had an *abundance* of 'working', yes 'working' amateur athletes who continually turned out times in marathons that our current batch of marathon runners can only dream about. This, despite the advances in footwear, clothing, support products, nutrition and without 'jobs', and without jobs that complemented their running. In those days a personal best of 2hrs 16 mins would rate you a very respectable runner (of course), BUT also a long way short of a place in a GB team. In the current financial climate whereby many 'ordinary people' (unlike Jenson) have little in the way of spare cash – and call me old fashioned (and you will) – why not take a leaf out of the books of the hard men of the past, and train incredibly hard whilst fuelling the miles with Jam and banana sandwiches while drinking tap water and cups of tea? Say no more! Tell you what though, there was little wrong with the past, marathons/triathlons or otherwise!

Back to 1983 and that first year of British Triathlon competition!

Following the Reading championship event, as I journeyed the long way back up to the North East on the train while wheeling my 24 inch Motobecane in one hand, and bag and 'cup' in the other before getting on the train, I had some quiet time to reflect on the last few months culminating in the success of the event. I had feelings of relief, satisfaction, and quite a considerable amount of optimism regarding the future. The event had been a wonderful success, lots of people from all over the UK, a sizable field and no doubt some good publicity would follow. A lot of work had been done to achieve my runner-up placing, and now with a degree of satisfaction my hunch about my potential as a triathlete had been justified.

For the next couple of months all my energy would be directed towards the British Long Course Championships which were to be to be held in late August 'in my neck of the woods', the North East of England. I believed at the time that the longer the event, the stronger I would be – I could win this one!

My family were indifferent regarding my success, but my wife Jennifer was pleasantly surprised, I think? Her interest heightened when I told her we would get a cheque for £200, a sizable sum then. As close as I'd been previous to that amount of money was when winning £50 for a recent victory in the North Eastern Counties marathon! On the financial side these were difficult years for the Harris household, my wages were poor at the leisure centre, we had a baby boy, Jennifer wasn't working due to motherhood, my car was a wreck (hence the train journey down to London) so £200 was a very welcome 'present'.

I would add at this stage that there is continuous reference to certain words these days, used in the main by our athletes in a bid to receive even more acclaim for any recent sporting successes. One of those words is **'sacrifices'**. Oh how I have begun to detest that bloody word! The vast majority of our successful athletes are and always have been 'professionals' – whether we choose to accept it or not, the truth is that that is one of the reasons why we in this so affluent country of ours have been so successful as a nation over recent years. Their sport is their job, and having made that 'choice' it must be wonderful to receive funding to progress their careers. Oh, to wake up, go training, go home, eat, drink, and rest, before training again and repeating the process, often with quite considerable support put in place by the lottery etc. to help them along. Then when they achieve their goals, we have to listen in apparent awe at how much they have 'given up' to achieve their incredible success with all the 'sacrifices' they have made to win 'medals for Great Britain'!(Very good of them, eh?)

Having given my account in the previous chapters of the state of Triathlon in 2015, and with it my not too complimentary take on where we are currently with all the changes, I am acutely aware that if I keep 'moaning on' then I will be perceived as a 'Victor Meldrew' type miserable old git! Trust me (regardless of what my wife says) I don't come into that latter category. But, I cringe every time I hear certain repetitive words like 'sacrifices', and how they hope to 'inspire' others to follow in their footsteps. I have never referred to any of my sporting efforts as sacrifices and never will – they were a choice, and I made the decisions! No one forced me out 365 days a year; I volunteered! Here is an example of an average day for me in 1983 after the Reading event, and an amateur in every sense of the word!

5th July 1983: **Out of bed at 6am, cycle 17 miles 'to work', followed by weights. Lunchtime – run 9 miles around the 'rec'. After work, swim 2000 yds before cycling two hours home immediately followed by 2 mile steady run!**

The above was run-of-the-mill at the time, and as you'll see that type of consistency prevailed all the way through my 12 years in triathlon. I had no acclaim for my successes and almost no interest – and 'our super stars' who revel in all the acclaim and the quite substantial financial rewards can only reflect on all the 'sacrifices 'they've made, often while sitting comfortably on one of the many chat show programmes!

Weekly training mileage week ending 13th August 1983: swim 10,000 yds, Bike 220 miles, run 95 miles, as usual all incorporated into a 40 hour working week!

On the 28th August I took part in the British 'Long course' Championships and finished runner-up 'again'! My comments in my diary read as follows: 1.5 mile swim in Kielder reservoir, water bitterly cold (no wetsuits then) and choppy, pleased and relieved when I climbed out! Bike leg 65 miles, very hilly, up to 6th into Durham despite my chain repeatedly coming off the ring, had to ride last 10 miles or so on the small chain ring, annoyed! Came through to 2nd on the 14.3 mile run (1 hour 28m) on very hilly course. Legs cramped up later having started run at 5m 30s miles, slowing to 7/7min 30min miles.

2nd National Championships Long Course, Kielder Water, 1983
Exiting the swim 'freezing' before cycling down to Durham and 15 mile run
2nd again!

This event took place on a very chilly late August day. The water as mentioned in the very deep Kielder reservoir was bitter cold. We swam straight out and rounded a small boat on the horizon before returning to shore. This swim was very worrying; by the time I rounded the turnaround boat, I was becoming noticeably 'very' cold, and additionally in the centre of the lake it was very choppy; as such vision was impaired when trying to negotiate the 'route' back. At this stage I was swimming alone, isolated and in a pair of trunks, with no safety cover. The canoes and other craft were hovering around the last swimmers, but this left the rest of us precariously vulnerable. I was only out there 47m 20s but it seemed an eternity.

When I left the water I can still remember the 'boy scouts' offering us hot drinks in plastic cups as we wobbled from side to side up the ramp, totally disoriented. As I took one of the cups I was shivering so much I proceeded to throw the hot liquid high into the cool air, unable to grasp the cup long enough to drink. To this day I remember this kid running alongside me to the bike transition area repeating 'do you want another one' while keeping well out of the way of the falling fluid! Alec Hunter told me some time later how worried he was, not having counted the athletes into the water, and when he saw us athletes towards the head of the field coming out in such dire states he feared for those towards the rear of the field. Even a day or two later he was half expecting a phone call to say a body had been found!

Anyhow at the end of the event, which was won by Stephen Russell from Kent (which required an amazing amount of organisation from Alec and his crew), we were all pretty happy we had 'survived', and although I was disappointed to have been runner-up again, on reflection I was reasonably content on the basis that in both National Championship events to date I had at least been consistent!

A trip to Nice for the World Championships and a member of the 'first ever' two man British Triathlon Team!

About three days after the event, whist at work at the Leisure Centre, I received a tannoy message asking me to come to reception to take a telephone call. It was Alec Hunter saying how hard he had been trying to contact me but didn't have my home phone number before asking, **'How would you like to represent Great Britain in the World Championships in the South of France, all expenses paid?'** I didn't tell Alec (I was too embarrassed) he couldn't contact me because we didn't have a phone at home, we couldn't afford one! Anyhow it took me all of one second to accept, the money was to come from the event sponsors, Weather Seal Double Glazing. There was little time though as the event was happening on the 10th September, less than two weeks after our championships. I secured a few days' leave and before I knew it I was on my way to London again, still pushing my bike along the platforms! I was picked up at Kings Cross by Alec in his big Volvo Automatic. As we pulled away and headed through central London, all of a sudden without any warning Alec said quite nonchalantly, *'In a minute or two I will have to leap out and pick up your GB tracksuits; when I get out, dive into the driver's seat and drive round 'the block' once or twice till I come back and then pick me up!'* Before I could say 'what', he was out and gone! Bearing in mind this is Central London in rush hour, and I'm in an 'automatic' which I've never driven in my life, and told casually to 'drive around the block', well you can imagine my shock and confusion, particularly having immediately stalled the car as I attempted to pull off, horns blaring, lights flashing and one way systems operating, all of course without any regard for a country lad from Northumberland! Somehow, I managed to manoeuvre as 'ordered' before picking up Alec, who had to run into the central lane to get in the car!

Well to cut a long story very short, myself and Steve Russell travelled down to Nice with Alec and his lovely wife-to-be, Viv. We travelled to Paris first of all before staying the night, got a very early morning run in around the streets of Paris, and then put the car on an overnight train to Gap before driving the remainder of the trip down to the beautiful French Riviera. Not the most relaxing of journeys, but nevertheless wonderful to be there.

Down in Nice, the weather was superb and in total contrast to Kielder the water was 'lush'! We soon met up with other Brits who had paid their own fares and made their own way there, Mark Kleanthous, Sarah Springman (a future multi GB and European Champion), and Pete Moysey, to name just three.

On arriving at our 'digs' we were met by Steve's two 'coaches' who had travelled out independently to assist 'him' but not me it seems. One was a cycling coach/mechanic, the other a running coach. Despite there being only the two of us in the GB team they refused point blank to check my bike out or provide any assistance at all; in fact they barely spoke to me. Very strange really; I can only think they felt me a threat to 'their' athlete!

Anyhow the race followed on pretty soon after we arrived and the weather was superb. A 3,000 metre swim, 120km hilly cycle and culminating with a 30km run. At the start there were hundreds of triathletes lined up on the shingle beach all ready to head out into the swim leg, heading directly for the first buoy only 400 metres away, which ensured the opening swim would be pretty rough and very congested at the turn. The Americans ruled the world then – Dave Scott, Mark Allen, Scott Tinley, Scott Molina and many more, all were pros mostly from California. I eventually finished 14th with only the American pros in front of me; Steve did slightly better, finishing just two minutes ahead of me in 13th place.

Later that night we celebrated by walking the streets of Nice and having a huge ice cream before falling into our beds and leaving the next day for the long slog journey home! For my efforts I received £650! A small fortune for us! We bought a new fridge freezer, new television and washing machine, and for a while I had a happy wife!

Arriving home, still wheeling my bike, there was no celebration, no interest and life continued the same as before, and within a day or two I was back to work with once again few enquiries; training resumed three (and more) times a day with my sights firmly on 1984!

ALEC HUNTER!

All our triathletes, past and present, owe a huge debt of gratitude to Alec Hunter. Alec's vision, business mind and amazing energy ensured the British Triathlon Association had been well and truly founded. At the time in 1983, and for several years afterwards, Alec was at the helm of British Triathlon. Despite running several

businesses at the time he somehow continued to put a phenomenal amount of time and effort into ensuring triathlon in the UK went from strength to strength. Regardless of what I say here it won't be enough. But Alec's immense contribution should never be forgotten. Thank you, Alec, on behalf of those who were there then, and on behalf of those who are here now!

The next 10 years, as a working amateur triathlete, family man and not so 'ordinary' lifestyle!

After 1983 and two 2nd placings in the first ever British Triathlon Championships together with a top 14 placing in the Worlds in faraway Nice, I looked forward to the coming years with excitement, intrigue and a massive amount of ambition. Arguably I was already the best triathlete in the country but with two runners-up spots I still hadn't won a triathlon and that bothered me big style! In 1983 I was already 32 years old, with many years (28 in fact since my first race) of sporting competition behind me together with thousands of hours of training, for the most part in absolute solitude. I had without a shadow of a doubt the most incredible cardio-vascular system and an all-round musculature system to die for, and I knew better than most how to 'suffer' both in training and competition. The latter 'pain tolerance' is an essential ingredient when things get abnormally hard. We were informed that, once again, with the successes of last year's championships at Reading and Durham, the 1984 events would take place at the same places, but at different venues!

Strength training with a difference!

Looking again at my 1984 training diary, from the 1st January I was straight back into three times a day training, but also there are regular references to 'sea coal humping'! The vast majority of houses in the North East were heated by fossil fuel in those days – coal! Coal was expensive, yes even up here in Geordie land, with mountains of the stuff all over the place. At this time we lived at number 4, Palmer

Terrace, a two-up, two-down next door to Ralf and Margaret Aspey (I have always been blessed with great neighbours and Ralf and Margaret were no different, super people to live next door to). Ralf had a Land Rover and a sturdy trailer, we had no money, so, with Ralf, I would make regular visits to the sea and shovel sea coal into sacks straight from the freezing water and carry them up the steep, uneven cliffs around Cresswell. Not pleasant work, especially in January, February and March – the bitter cold salt water would 'trickle' down our backs as we toiled up the slopes to fill the trailer. Just like the building sites I had worked on I used these 'essential' journeys as training; comments in my diary often read 'excellent session'! **On the 8th January 1984: I have recorded a.m. – 'sea coal session' in brackets (running up banks with sacks full of dross, jogging back down) a.m. 5 miles run, cold and windy, bit tired, p.m. Bike 1 hour followed by run 3.5 miles straight off bike.**

Week of the 15th-21st January, I did 23 training sessions in the week, but have also recorded sore 'right knee' and sore 'right groin'! Heavy snow fall! At this time as usual I was working a 37 hour week and additionally on an ASA Swimming teachers' course, and an Athletic coaches' course at Gateshead, some 25 miles from home!

8th Feb: a.m. run 15 miles p.m. run 5 miles, late p.m. swim 2000 yrds. 9th Feb: bike 3 hrs, run 6 miles, swim 2,000 yrds. 10th Feb: a.m. run 10 miles, p.m. bike 25 miles flat out!

At this time there are no rest days – And it gets harder!

What I find strange whilst reading these diaries after such a long time is that there's an almost total lack of family type comments. Having said that of course these were designed as 'training diaries' and therein lies the difference I suppose. My son James, whom I loved with every fibre of my body, was two years old at this time, the cutest, most beautiful blond haired little lad who made me so proud; no one could pass him by without smiling. I was a dad and a husband, but have recorded almost nothing about family life.

Jennifer!

As mentioned previously I was married on the 11th August 1979 on my 28th birthday, following a three-year courtship. Jennifer was a very attractive, dark, petite, and quiet young lady, who came from a very respectable family that I grew to both like and respect, and worked as a secretary for the Northumberland Health Authority. We met at a party in Widdrington, I walked her home and our relationship progressed steadily thereafter. I can well remember when we got to her door that first time, and I asked her out and she said quote, *'I'll think about it'!* Confused, I had no answer to that. I can remember walking away thinking *'what the hell does that mean?' (or words to that effect!).* A week or so later we met again at the 'club' and went through the same process. Looking back she wasn't easy to get to know! A lot of the attraction for me (apart from physical) was that she appeared quiet, a little naïve and innocent, and the latter was in contrast to some I had 'known'!

What is perhaps strange in our relationship is that we have nothing at all in common. I most certainly don't mean this to sound in any way derogatory, but Jennifer has little interest in anything apart from family, reading romantic novels, and holidays; she doesn't get overly enthusiastic or worked up about anything, let alone sport or music, my own passions. The latter is actually an enviable trait, on the basis that it makes life for her pretty much stress free – little upsets her, apart from me occasionally, and she goes with the flow. Me, well I am totally different, and apart from sporting issues, I am obsessed with music – absolutely obsessed – and our house is saturated with it! I play guitar and blues harmonica whilst listening to music at every available moment. I love history and natural history, I have a huge allotment and a million books – although I don't class myself as an avid reader, I find reading too slow and I'm easily distracted.

Like many couples I guess, over the years we have had our disagreements, from my perspective often because of her oh so casual response to many things, although of course she may well see it differently. As mentioned we rarely talk sport, she has little interest, she'd travel to events with me and the lads, not to spectate and shout me on, but more because she can sit and read her novels and gets a 'fried breakfast'! One of Jennifer's irritating traits is her ability to detach herself from 'the moment'! Here is an example (which some may find amusing?). Using your imagination, here we are, standing beside a huge lake where several hundred triathletes are about to dive into the water and contest an arduous triathlon event. I turn to Jennifer and ask her to 'zip my wetsuit up' (it zips from the rear), at which point she audibly struggles with the zip, uttering effort based groans, not dissimilar to giving birth, 'by *it's tight mind, Mick, are you sure it fits?'* before triumphantly stating *'there, I think that's it about done, 'almost' to the top, but you better ask someone else to check it, just to make sure'!* The latter is quite likely to be followed by *'ee mind, Mick, remind me on, we have that Council Tax bill to pay on Tuesday'!!* My seven months of incredible gut wrenching preparation has come down to this! A zip that 'may be' done up properly, but then again 'maybe not', and a flaming bill, as I stand there brimming over with copious amounts of pre-event adrenalin! I have said elsewhere that I was always proud to be a working amateur athlete; however, the latter example just exemplifies just how amateurish I was. Regardless, I somehow went on to win almost 50 triathlons. Bet the Brownlees never had pre-event preparation like this though! I am now smiling, wondering what her response to that will be, but I'm not making any of it up, and maybe I'd prefer her the way she is, rather than being high as a kite in anticipation of my performances etc. We've been together 40 years, I've never strayed, ever, and I'm certain she hasn't either. She's always looked after our money (or lack of it), been a good mother, is a great cook, and of course adores our little grandson; she's also through much practice become a very accomplished snorer! Regardless though she gets a Valentine's Day card every year (I'll catch the ba....d at some point, you watch!) and of course I do love her nevertheless – sometimes! Can I just add though, please don't interpret my comments too negatively, like two good mates, we don't take ourselves too seriously, as such we find it very easy to take the pee out of each other without falling out, but our continuing longevity as a couple presumably says much about our relationship.

Photo for newspaper, with James, 1984

Winning British Grand Prix Title, 1987,
Milton Keynes

British Grand Prix final, 1987, Milton Keynes
1st with Rick Kiddle and Jon Ashby

Feb Sport Cross Country Champion, Singapore

Triathlon years – 1984, 1985, 1986, 1987 and British Champion!

I had an uneasy start to 1984; this was due to having been so close to two British Championship wins in '83 but coming up just a little short on both occasions. There is a very thin dividing line between 1st and 2nd, but in reality the gap is huge – few ever remember the runner-up and in reality only winning matters, if you are serious about your sport. I couldn't help but wonder whether I had missed my best chance of becoming a National Champion! However, driven on by obsession and belief in my abilities, I trained incredibly hard, without let-up! I am amazed, looking at all my diaries, as to how hard I trained, day in day out, week after week, month after month, and year after year. Also, just like my school reports identify all those years ago, I was never absent from work, 100% attendance always! Additional notes on the 19th February read – *trouble with car, it won't start, had to buy a new battery.* As I recall at the time we also had niggles like the lawn mower wouldn't work, or the television went on the blink. I mention the latter simply just to identify that despite all the training and work related issues I had fairly consistent everyday problems that would niggle away at me, mainly related to a lack of money, although I'd hasten to add we were never in debt. On top of this, I was soon to learn that Jennifer was 'expecting' again; this wasn't a surprise and certainly planned, but with both of the pregnancies I was amazed just how quick the conception happened, having decided to 'go for it'!

At the Leisure centre, I worked two different shifts – one from 7.30am till 3pm, and the other 3.00pm till 10.30pm – both gave ample opportunity to cram in the miles. Also during my break periods at work I'd train again! The main asset for me at the centre was the swimming pool, which saved me a lot of money and a lot of additional travelling time.

At this time in the North East the Miners were on strike for many weeks. Our swimming pool was coal-fired and before too long the coal ran out. Being a 'swimmer' you could view this in one of two ways: either a massive inconvenience, or a bonus, the latter based on an ideal opportunity to get some 'cold water' conditioning swimming in. As you'd probably guess I took the latter view. I got the swimming pool to myself, and just carried on as before but now swimming daily in the freezing water! Must have been a strange sight though, with me walking around the centre shaking like a leaf an hour after the swim, trying to warm-up in the middle of summer!

June 1984, Ashington baths
Triathlon training, pool temp 58° due to miners' strike
Usual distances 2000-2500 yards, 80-100 lengths, followed by cold shower!

I can well remember one day Arthur Scargill attended a rally in our leisure centre which was attended by hundreds of miners; the atmosphere on this occasion was up-beat as opposed to angry or worried. In the North East, as you can imagine at the time, there was major support for the plight of the miners. As I remember, Scargill's speech on the day was truly amazing; although I wasn't a miner (my family's history on my mother's side was drenched in the coal industry) I stood with all the guys and listened; he even stirred me up! The passion and the camaraderie amongst the miners really was awe inspiring. Arthur Scargill was highly regarded, by the vast majority of miners, and there seemed an honesty about him that was endearing – he very much appeared that he was one of them, as opposed to just doing a job. There is no doubt, I'm sure, that he did his utmost to safeguard the future of mining in both the North East and nationally, although the mining industry despite his efforts and the support he clearly had was soon to plummet. He did say as I recall that if the government got their way, there would be no pits left, and as history shows he was right!

An example of training when doing an average early shift reads: 28/3/84, 17 miles Bike to work, followed by Swim 2,500 yds, plus a few weights, lunchtime run 1 hour, p.m. Bike 2 hrs home.

An example of a late shift reads: 5/3/84, a.m. Sea coal humping (good session) a.m. Bike 3hrs (good effort) p.m. run 10 miles in 62mins 5s.

Approaching the National Championships in Reading, things, judging by my diary, seemed to be going well; most weeks were the same with a few adjustments. **Weekly hours' training through May reveal: 24hr 10mins, 23hrs 45mins, 23hrs, and 23hrs, so very consistent!**

Eight days prior to Reading on **Saturday 9th June: a.m. Bike 2 hrs 35 mins (excellent hard effort on hilly course) followed by 5 miles run in 30m 32s, pm Swim 1500 yds, p.m. Run 45 mins (felt quite good).**

Pretty much the same as the previous year I travelled down to London on the train, got picked up by my dad at Kings Cross before spending the night at his place at Waltham Abbey. But before leaving I swam 1000yds, cycled for 30mins, and when I got to Waltham Cross I ran for 25 minutes. The next day, i.e. the day before the race, I ran for 25 minutes, biked for 15 minutes to check the bike was ok after the previous day's journey and then had a 15 minutes swim.

British Champion!

Race day 17th June 1984 dawned fine, very warm and calm, and ideal conditions. I have written in my diary that there were 350 competitors;

however, the result sheet shows only 279 actually finished!

I can clearly recall getting a very 'serious' swimming brief as we all lined up in front of the lake, by I think a guy called Roger Parsons. There were a lot of headmaster type 'warnings' about anyone caught doing this, that, or the other would be disqualified. By luck and a strange coincidence I happened to be standing next to Jim Woods, last year's event winner; Jim still in the Army and myself a former Royal Marine, we were quaking in our boots about the sternness of the briefing – NOT! Anyhow the customary rough swim was somewhat 'pleasant', the water being quite warm; the cycle was quite congested till it sorted itself out and I came through well with a terrific run leg to win in a heavy 'downpour' by over a minute. I have written in the diary 'very pleased with the win, as everybody who was anybody was there'! Jim Woods (last year's winner), Marin Dyer (a future National Champion), Stephen Russell (the current long course champion), Glen Cooke (a future multi National, European and 2nd in the World Championships), Bernie Shrosbree (national team for years and winner of survival of the fittest), Howard Jones(National team), Pete Mosey (who would win the following year's event at Milton Keynes beating me by three seconds in the process), Rick Kiddle (a future National champion) and my friend Sarah Springman, and so on, Sarah finishing a creditable 93rd on the day before herself becoming a multi-National championship winner and European champion.

The event was again superbly organised – thanks again to Alec, Dick Poole and others!

My recollections after the event were mainly feelings of relief, on the basis I think that whatever was to happen in the future, I would always be a former *British Triathlon Champion!* **I believed then and I haven't changed my mind, that due to the content of the sport, whoever wins that event (providing the best in the country are in attendance) has a legitimate claim to be the called the fittest man or woman in the country 'on that day'.**

Another memory of that day was that once the heavy thundery showers had ceased, the sun came back out and the whole day became very pleasant with people going back into the warm water for a relaxing swim. As a reward I can clearly remember standing in a queue for believe it or not a celebratory 'hot dog', and listening to two guys in front of me, commenting on *'whoever won it, had to be 'something else'!* At which point, without saying anything, as you can imagine I had a smug smile on my face!

Within the next week or two I would be brought back down to earth, and realising that success is and always would be for me at least, very fleeting! There was no interest at all at home (no change there then), and in a full page article in a major running magazine at the time, despite winning the event I got one line, which went – *'last year's runner-up Mike Harris held on well to take the title in 2hrs 49min 21s'!*

The remainder of 1984 saw me finish a disappointing 3rd in the National long course, a 3rd place in an event called 'wings, wheels and water' which was a televised event at Milton Keynes. And a 16th in the Worlds held for the second year in Nice, where I was 1st Brit to finish from many hundreds of competitors, this despite having punctured at the top of the climbs and all the descents to do with a new tubular tyre and no 'glue' on to hold the tyre firmly in place, hairy stuff! In the latter despite dropping only two places from last year's event, I also dropped a couple of hundred quid in prize money, but the £400 plus was still 'very' welcome.

Pebbles for the Lads!

One of the highlights for me at Nice this time around was a meeting that took place in a hotel foyer! As I waited to book in I heard a conversation taking place in English between four guys. After a few minutes, intrigued and a bit nosey, I approached the lads and asked if they were here for the triathlon. All looking round together, they replied in unison 'yes mate, you?'. Yes I replied and we gave some introductions and handshakes, followed by a quick chat. Unfortunately I can only remember two of the names, Bernie Shrosbree and Mick McCarthy.

Turned out they were Royal Marines, and as soon as they found out I was a former marine, well we were like family! Bernie said that he and one of the others had done the Reading event and I casually said, yeah me as well. *'How'd you get on then, mate?'* said Mick. *'Oh I won it!'* I replied. *'F..k..g hell, you joking? What's your name again?'* Mike Harris! All of a sudden I was 'almost' a super star, more because I was one of them, rather than because I was a decent athlete – once a marine always a marine. Anyhow the meeting was just perfect, the humour was what it always had been and we got on like a house on fire. What I remember to this day was standing on the beach with Mick and hundreds of others all with our official red swim caps on, and viewing the course with all the buoys a few minutes before the off. Excited and ready to go I turned round to Mick and said, *'What sort of time you looking for then, Mick, for the 3,000 metre swim'?* To which he replied, *'TIME? You taking the piss?'* Followed by, *'I've only ever swam half a mile, and that was in a f..k..g swimming pool and with a life guard!',* then just as quickly, *'I don't think I can swim that far'!* He wasn't joking! God I laughed, and so did he, but all of a sudden whatever nerves I had disappeared. Anyhow he got around and they all finished the event, much impressed with my 16th. Following the event we had a few drinks the following day, and with typical marine humour, I remember Bernie going round with a carrier bag and removing pebbles from underneath the breasts of topless women as they were sunning themselves, before placing them in the bag while saying gratefully *'merci, for the lads back home'!* The lads were all SBS. Bernie was the only one who could I think call himself a 'serious athlete'. The other three were just hard bastards with a sense of both humour and adventure!

My Dad!

My dad actually paid for me to travel to Nice in 1984 – without his money I would never have got there, and unlike the previous year, I actually flew out on that occasion. Over the next 12 years or so dad would turn up at many of the 150 triathlons I did, both at home and abroad (occasionally travelling together) when I represented GB.

Before 1983 I saw little of him. As you may recall if you read the early chapters, my mother and father parted and divorced when I was about eight or nine years old, he left home by mutual consent I think, and went back 'down south' where he was originally from. Over the following years we rarely met (although we did keep in touch by occasional letters) except for occasional holidays, when Linda and I would be placed on a train at Newcastle and met by Dad at Kings Cross, before having a holiday at my Granny and Grandad Harris's tiny little cottage in a place called Smallfield in Surrey. My Granny and Grandad were a wonderful loving couple, and always made us incredibly welcome. I only ever saw the sun shine in Smallfield; it never rained and was never cold down there, unlike the North East. Whenever we went there we had the unusual sight (for us) of apples all over the roads in Smallfield (honestly though where we lived, apple trees were rarer than a current Newcastle goal!). While down there we would occasionally get a train from Horley down to Brighton for a day out, and despite the horrible shingle beach had a great time.

My dad has always had an avid interest in sport but more as a spectator, although he did play cricket often when he was younger. We also have a photograph of him receiving a cup from Lord Louis Mountbatten during his Navy days.

I often wonder what would have happened to our relationship had triathlon not come along. Anyhow following Reading '83 we saw a lot more of each other; my dad became as obsessed with the sport as I was, and he'd spend hours analysing result sheets and working out 'split times' etc. My transitions from swim to bike, and even bike to run, were for a lack of urgency, at best ordinary and at worst bloody awful! As such there is no doubt I lost wins by being too lax in pulling shoes on and off etc. At 63 and 64 years of age after another 'dabble' in the sport following a 20 year absence, my transitions are no better, this year despite finishing 15th from sizable fields of 250/300 plus. If I'd been quicker in transitions, and had comparable times to others, I'd have been close to top 10 placings! Some of the time I was faster in all three disciplines than those who finished in front of me, but struggled bloody well changing! I'm once again getting angry even thinking about it now! I still need to grow up!

Following his retirement my dad once again moved back up here for more peace and quiet.

After 12 years of the most intense involvement within triathlon, as you can imagine I could write volumes. In order to somehow summarise this period though, I'll give sparser details.

Oh what a 'cock-up'!

In the 1985 National Championships I finished 2nd in the National short course at Milton Keynes, getting beaten by three seconds in a 'sprint finish' from Pete Moysey. No disrespect to Pete intended but this was a terrible tactical error on my part – I had caught Pete on the run and was going like a train, and for some inextricable reason instead of going right on past him, I slowed and ran with him. We were both well clear, and I thought I had the event well and truly sewn up, only to come round the final bend to see there were only 40 or 50 metres left – we sprinted and I lost out! I was incredibly fit then, my recovery was instantaneous, and once over the finishing line I rather casually walked away leaving Peter rolling around on the floor in apparent agony with cameras flashing! I hold no malice now, I messed up, and certainly Peter deserved his win as he was a true stalwart of British triathlon for many years. Later in the year I finished 3rd in the National Long course at Nottingham. An event that due to the weather (bitter cold and windy) became nothing other than a survival event. The swim was two miles, still in trunks those days, with almost half the field being pulled out with hypothermia. It was won by a new guy nobody had heard of called Mark Knagg, a real nice fellow and a very good swimmer and cyclist and steady runner. Mark seemed to have come and gone in a flash, never to be seen again after a year or two! I also finished 8th in the Europeans in Denmark, with the GB team getting the bronze medals.

In 1986 I decided to concentrate on an Ironman event. I told the BTA my intentions early on and was given the nod and an early selection for the GB team in Sater, Sweden, on the 6th July. My training from early on in the New Year reflected the aim.

As a means of covering lengthy distances on the bike, I got my brother-in-law Duncan to drive me places and drop me off, and I'd ride back without stopping, then go straight into a run.

Testosterone, by the bucket!

30th May 1986: dropped off in Edinburgh by my brother-in-law Duncan at 6.30am, cycled 114 miles non-stop home (5hrs 25mins) with two bananas and two water bottles via Berwick, followed immediately (without going into the house) by a 1 hour steady run.

Had a shower followed by something to eat, at which point Jennifer says, *'Do me a favour, Mick, take the lads out for a bit, I'm shattered.'* So up I get and with one in the pushchair, the other walking (for a while), we set off for the field at Stobswood, one mile away. We kick the ball around for a while before heading the one mile back; by this time I'm pushing James and carrying two year old David 'piggy back' style. Jennifer says, *'You back already?'* Followed by *'mind if you're back to work tomorrow that grass needs cutting otherwise our cutter won't do it if it gets any longer'!* So I cut the grass, and then give the car a quick wash!

Sitting in the house and about to drop off, woken by Jennifer, *'mind, Mick, it's 4.30 if you are going swimming'!* So up I get, grab my trunks and goggles and head for the pool and a two mile swim (140 lengths front crawl!).

When I train hard I often sleep badly, but also rather worrying, I was so randy all the time. I read somewhere many years ago that as you get fitter your body produces more testosterone, and I must have had it then by the bucket load.

So funny now looking back, but in bed I would attempt to give subtle notice of my em, come on, you know, my em 'excitement' before Jennifer (tired out looking after the lads all day) would jump up while saying *'for god's sake, Michael, I'm tired, leave me alone please'!* After which I'd drop off into a deep sleep before being roughly shaken at 6.30 to go swimming before work, and the start of just another day. Honestly she wanted me to go to the doctors to 'get something' to 'calm me down' ha! I mean what would I have said? *'Hi Doctor, can I* have *some 'anti testosterone' pills please?'* He may well have replied, 'Try doing some exercise, it'll help wear you out – you'll sleep better!'

Throughout the year and training for the ironman event, I was also doing Olympic sized events without the success I had begun to expect – not disastrous by any means though, I'd won at Durham, won a silver medal with Glen Cooke, Howard Jones and Sarah Coope in the European Relay Championships. I had a funny looking photo of the four of us posing before this event –, I say funny because Glen, Sarah and Howard had spent the winter training in California, while I wintered in the North East; they were like bronzed gods and I resembled Steptoe (Wilfred Bramble)! I was 5th in the Wirral Grand Prix, 3rd in the Sunderland Grand Prix, 5th in the National Long course, 2nd in the Tynedale Grand Prix and 5th in the Ripon Grand Prix. These were all national events in those days, attracting competitors from all over the UK.

Along with Jennifer I got an all expenses invite to take part in the 'All Ireland Triathlon' at Sligo on the 24th August, and I finished 2nd. I wasn't worried about the lack of wins; I knew my performances were hindered by the very high mileage I had been doing, all of which reduced my speed or quality sessions and therefore my performances in shorter events.

In the Ironman in Sweden, after travelling with the team manager Dick Poole by train, car and boat to Sweden over 24 hours to Sater, I finished a creditable 17th but also inside the top 10 as there were several of the top Americans there as 'guests'. My time on a difficult undulating course, and still without a wetsuit,

was a new UK record of 9hrs 43mins 22secs for the 2.4 mile run, 112 mile cycle and Marathon event.

Summarising 1986 in the back of my diary, quote:

Did a tremendous amount of work this year and yet had a disappointing year – must be a question mark over TOO MUCH MILEAGE!

The old man of triathlon – not quite – yet!

At some time around about 1986/7 someone wrote an article about me they entitled **'The old man of triathlon'**! In 1987 I would be 36 and after August I'd be 37, so some merit in it I suppose, particularly when considering I was still competing at the top level and most if not all of my opposition were at least 10 or 15 years my junior. Age I think for most of us does creep up ever so slowly so we don't actually notice it and certainly if you are super fit at 36 then the likelihood is that you will also be super fit at 37, providing of course that your lifestyle remains unchanged. I cringe when I regularly hear commentators stating things like *'well of course he is now in his 30s'*! Suggesting as it does that he is fine at 29 but 30? It's bollocks!

Well, despite my age, '1987' was to be my best year yet although of course I didn't know it then!

A very good triathlete friend of mine called John Willis had competed in the Otley Triathlon in 1986 which I missed for some reason. Anyhow John commented that the Otley event was exceedingly difficult and mountainous – followed by *'but it'll suit you, Mike'* followed by *'oh and it's the National Championships next year'*!

Having listened intently to John's description of the Otley course, I decided there and then that the event would be my main aim in 1987. There was by all accounts a speedy swim 'downstream' in the river, followed by a mountainous cycle leg which had previously been used as the National Hill Climb championships. The Otley event would go up this climb (and others equally as hard) not just once but being a two lap race twice, then to finish the 10 km run started by running up a lengthy hill for the first two miles, before becoming undulating as opposed to flat. My hill climbing in these years was exceptional so the course appeared tailor made for me, and so it proved.

By this time I had been promoted at work to Assistant Manager and in the process moved from Ashington to Newbiggin Sports Centre and my training diary for the first day of 1987 reads: Working, too much drink last night, pm 8 mile run, ok once I got going! But after the 1st January my diary is totally congested with details of training three and four times a day, this despite my new work responsibilities. I have been looking through my training diary of January, February and March trying to find something else interesting apart from training issues, but there is nothing apart from continuous graft, no let-up regardless of the often dire weather. Often training days consisted of riding over to Rothbury (a 'lumpy' area of Northumberland) while taking the most difficult hilly route possible, a warm-up of 20 miles; once there I would put my gears on to the 52 big chain ring and do repetitions up the steepest hills before freewheeling back down and repeating the efforts over and over again. Once exhausted I'd ride home while still looking out for the most challenging climbs. These sessions were well over three hours, then there was still the compulsory run and swim to incorporate into my working day!

However, I had been approached earlier in the year with a request for me to complete a triathlon for charity on the 7th March, which I agreed to. Apart from the 'good cause', the event was *to finish in St James' Park just before the kick off of a Newcastle United home game*, ensuring as it did excellent publicity for the charity. Well, I used the event as a quality training session and blasted it from start to finish. Right enough, at about 2.30pm I entered one of the most famous football grounds in the country before running around the periphery of the pitch to generous applause, and crossing the line, very nice. I was presented with something from Newcastle Manager Willie McFaul, but for the life of me I can't recall what it was!

On the 17th April I won the Durham triathlon in warm and hazy sunshine.

This may be sounding a wee bit boring now, as there is little of interest to tell at this time. But my training right from the 1st January has been phenomenal in terms of the amount I was doing, the consistency of it all, having trained three times a day every day since the turn of the year. When I say this may well appear boring it pays to remember that most training is boring simply because you are by and large just repeating the very similar process day in day out; it's a bind, it's lonely, and the early months are cold and dark. Often the races seem like light years away and the temptation to miss training is ever present. *I used to regularly say to myself* 'no one's training as hard as me, no one' *and I meant it! When races came along later I honestly used to look at others with a degree of contempt, and remind myself that I deserved to win these, almost as if it was my absolute right. I know how pompous this might sound but if miles had been money I would have been the wealthiest athlete in Europe!*

On May 10th the Royal Exchange were at Newbiggin Sports Centre for their regular annual performances of Shakespeare plays, while doing a National tour. These really put our sports centre on the national map, they were so prestigious. Bearing in mind that I was often the most senior member of staff in the building while these were here and performing to sell-out crowds, stress levels could be pretty high. *On the 17th May I have recorded that I didn't get to bed till 4am yet that same day I ran 8 miles in the morning, swam 3,000 yrds at lunchtime and cycled for 1hr 51m 53s!*

On the 31st May I won the Cleveland triathlon by six minutes!

On 7th June despite going off course on the bike, I finished 3rd in the Wirral GP Triathlon!

An example of my form 10 days prior to the British Triathlon Championships on the 5th July was as follows:

24th June: am Swim 3,000 yds fartlek, dinnertime run 10 miles in 55m 23s, 7 pm raced the 25 mile Barnesbury Time Trial in 57m 15s and was 2nd fastest on the night!

It seemed to me with the above indicators I was as fit as I'd ever been, and if my two boys would break their habit of waking up most nights, and I kept away from any colds or last minute injuries, well – who would beat me?

Despite all the training, racing, work and family life, on the 30th June I had an interview for another job, as Duty Officer at the Wentworth Leisure Centre in Hexham, which I got! Another bonus of working at Hexham was seeing on a regular basis Duncan Robb, a genuinely nice guy, who did a good deal of work for triathlon both locally and nationally. Duncan was always excellent company and it was always a pleasure to have him around!

British Champion – again!

The big day arrived for me 'again' on the 5th July, when all the considerable efforts over the previous seven months and 30 plus years of training would once again pay dividends. I competed in the Otley triathlon and at 37 years of age and an amateur athlete in the true sense of the word, with a full time demanding job of 40 hours every week together with a family I was once again National champion!

My training diary for the next day, the 6th July reads: 'walking in the fields at 3.45am – couldn't sleep, a beautiful serene morning'!

An extended run of form!

A week later I was down in Yorkshire again winning the prestigious Wakefield Grand Prix event from a huge quality field! At this time I had limited sponsorship from Puma, and after the event I was approached by a lady called Dorothy Mouson who was second in command to Derek Ibbotson (the former one mile world record holder) at Puma UK. With the Puma HQ being relatively close she had come along with an assistant to watch the event. She was very impressed with my win and the amount of triathletes taking part, but unaware of my link to Puma. She was also clearly pleased that I was walking around in a Puma tracksuit and enquired about the product. Not knowing she was a Puma rep', I commented that the clothing was fine but the running shoes were pretty 'crap'! I then let slip that I had limited sponsorship from her company. Oh wow she said, we must see you again and see if we can't upgrade our current contract. Before she left I also mentioned that I'd won the British Championships the week before, leaving her on a high – she said she'd be in touch!

I can clearly remember returning from Wakefield with a huge cup, and finding my mother at our house., Jennifer commenting *'you've won again then'!* The lads took the cup and rolled it around the sitting room floor before my mother called me into the kitchen where she was washing dishes and quietly said, *'Well done, son, I'm proud of you of course, but remember while you're 'gallivanting' around, swimming and riding your bike, that you have a wife and two beautiful boys back here!'* What could I do but nod! I smile when I think of her, I loved her so much, and although she died a little over a year ago, I think of her several times every single day, and presumably will for the remainder of my life. Only family ever mattered to her, right from my school days and even when I was representing Great Britain she never ever understood sport! But I couldn't have got a better mother that's for sure.

My very successful season continued for a couple of months yet. All these events were biggies; a 2nd place in the Tynedale GP was followed by my only real disappointment of 1987 which was a 4th place in the National Long Course at Kings Lynn in Norfolk (my car wouldn't start when I was about to drive down, as such I had to hurriedly hire a vehicle and it took me six hours to get there). On the 30th August I won the Yorkshire Dales GP event, won the Ripon GP event six days later, and a further week later at Milton Keynes having finished 3rd in the GP final I was crowned **British Grand Prix Champion for 1987**. A week later I won the Aireborough elite triathlon. A week further on I was part of the Tyne triathlon club who won the Cleveland relays.

The domestic season over, my intention was to crown a wonderful year for me and go to Nice once more for the worlds; however a lack of funds totally ruled that out. To replace it I had recently received a letter from John Rawnsey, the organiser of the Yorkshire Dales triathlon and also the organiser of the 3 Peaks Cycle Cross – John offered me a free entry together with free board and B & B if I'd consider doing his event. Nothing to lose, I agreed. I didn't have a 'cross bike' but Steel's Cycles came to my rescue. Much to my dismay I was tipped in Cycling Weekly as one of the favourites, laughable, never having ridden cycle cross, and this event was massive in terms of difficulty riding up and down three of the highest climbs including Pen-y-Ghent; however, I finished respectably but a long way off the front. On the 2nd November as Guest of Honour I had an all expenses trip to Blackpool to give out awards, being put up in the Pembroke Hotel. I remember the local press had a headline *'triathlon ace in town'!*

Finally on the 20th December I finished a wonderful year off with a win in the Tynedale Christmas Duathlon in Corbridge.

On Christmas Eve we added to our family with a beautiful Springer Spaniel pup who we named Ben, and he would become my faithful little running companion for the next 12 years! Many was the time that the two of us would get up before work, often as early as 5.30am during the summer months, and go to the beach for a run on the most beautiful expanse of sand which is Druridge Bay; on a sunny morning this place was heaven, the two of us in exile, and the only living bodies on the planet. On Sundays we'd run from Cresswell to Amble and back, stopping on the way there and again on the way back for a quick swim in the lake at the country park to cool down before recommencing our two hour run.

Christmas Day 1987

My training diary for Christmas Day reads: 5.45am swim 1,500yds Ashington, 10.00am run 36 mins 47secs Chisholms circuit, pm Bike 1hr brisk before night fall!

I can remember sitting in the staff room at Ashington Leisure Centre on Christmas Eve, when someone made a comment along the lines of 'you'll not be swimming tomorrow then, Mike'! At which point John Davison the janitor-cum-handyman said somewhat tongue in cheek, 'well I've got to be here to check chlorine levels etc. at 5.30 so if you want in there's no skin off my nose'! and of course I couldn't resist John's very kind offer and shortly after 5.30 on Christmas morning there I was swimming up and down the pool... before racing home in time to see the lads get out of bed to open all their presents!

Triathlon years – 1988, 1989, 1990, 1991, 1992, 1993, 1994!

Following my best year yet in 1987, my confidence for the forthcoming years ahead was very high. 1987 had been a bit special for other reasons apart from my racing results. I am sure that due to a not-so-good 1986 where I only managed a 6th and 5th in the Nationals because of concentrating so much on Ironman, and with an influx of very promising young triathletes coming through, many had written me off, but that only gave me even more determination to prove them wrong. Although now 37 years of age I felt I had several years left at the top of triathlon in the UK, providing of course I that didn't rest on my laurels so to speak, and there was little chance of that! At the end of 1987 I had three British Championship wins, three runners-up placings and twice 3rd, all in British Championships, top 10 placings in Europe and two prominent placings in Nice – not bad for an amateur athlete from the North East with a full time job, and a young family. In previous years as far as publicity or exposure was concerned I had never received what I believe/d I could have expected, based on my constant outstanding record over the preceding years. For example over the 12 years I was involved in triathlon I was never featured on the front cover of a triathlon magazine, and when I think about some of those who had graced that iconic page, I felt at the time 'slightly peeved'. Because of my age, and my location in the North East, I was probably viewed by the powers to be at that time as unfashionable and probably on 'borrowed time' regarding the future of triathlon! And here I was now in 1988 at 37 years old, when everyone had predicted age had caught up with me in'86, hailed in one of the write-ups as 'Britain's domestic triathlon monarch'! I had just completed my best year yet in sporting competition, having won the British Short Course Championships (now referred to as the 'Olympic distance') and won the season-long British Grand Prix Championships; on the way there I had won some of the biggest triathlons in the country. My only disappointing event was the National Long Course, having finished 4th; however, there were reasons for the latter performance as mentioned above, too much mileage!

To put the record straight and to pay him a very respectful tribute, my friend *Glen Cook* was without a doubt the best triathlete in the country probably from 1986 onwards, and arguably the best in Europe as well. Certainly on nine out of 10 triathlon courses Glen would have beaten me, providing he was fit at the time; the one exception 'may' have been at Otley or perhaps Yorkshire Dales simply because of the nature of the courses, such as the fast shorter swims and the massive hills the events incorporated both on the bike legs and on the difficult run sections, which suited my lighter frame. I first came across Glen in 1984 and I can well remember passing him on the run stage at Reading. I then spent time with him as part of the National Squad in Wales around about 1985. It was clear Glen posed a major threat. His swimming was second to none, his biking had excelled and I felt then that only his running was a potential weakness. I can clearly remember analysing Glen, particularly his running (unbeknown to him). In '84, '85 he had what I would call an 'awkward' running gait, not fluent; his feet turned outwards and I can well remember thinking at the time that he may well incur running related injuries when he upped his mileage, due to his foot plant. However, I think I was proved wrong – he turned into a 'very' capable runner and with it a superb all round athlete. Glen and a few others, including his wife to be *Sarah Coope* (herself soon to become a National and European champion), had taken a professional decision and wintered in California enabling full time training in what I can only imagine must have been superb environments with outdoor 50 metre swimming pools and a wonderful climate well suited to triathlon, certainly far removed from wintering in the North East with the snow, rain, and howling winds.

Along with Glen, *Robin Brew* arrived on the scene round about this time, another nice guy and another superb athlete. I believe I'm right in saying that prior to turning to triathlon Robin had set an Olympic record in swimming in Moscow. I hope I am not being unkind but I wonder looking back as to whether Robin fulfilled his potential; he had for sure some wonderful wins (and brilliant sporting career) and Glen having known him for a few years rated him extremely highly, but as far as I can recall I don't think he won a national or European title, and when you have his talent that's a bit of a shame, but of course he may view it differently, and certainly if he was there at any event around the worlds he was a major threat. I well remember training with Robin in the hills of Portugal when we were both there in 1992 but for different events – a very capable cyclist but his swimming was the best in Europe at that time I think.

Back to 1988!

After such a successful year in 1987, 1988 was to be a strange one, for various reasons. I was put off the National short course for the first time because of the venue, it was either Deal in Kent or Canterbury (not sure which) and living where I do I might just as well have gone to Hawaii! The other reason was that on the 28th March I had a job change and became Sports Development Officer for Northumbria Police. On the actual day I got the job, Jennifer rang me at the Sports Centre at Hexham and told me we had just received a cash buyer offer for our house. We had been trying to sell the house for upwards of a year with a view to moving closer to my then current job as Duty Officer at Hexham Sports Centre. I had a lengthy, almost 100 mile return, commute to work every day, made worse at night as I often had to lock up and set the building alarms at midnight before heading home. At that time depending on which shift I was working, **I had to leave home in the morning at around 5am for a 40 mile drive to get a swim in before work, did my usual run of 8 miles or so at lunchtime, and by the time I returned home at 6 o'clock had to then motivate myself to go out on the bike for up to two hours... long days!**

In 1988 I did 22 triathlons, had 13 wins, and in the remaining events, which included a few GPs (where I won Otley again), I was inside the top 5 except at Swindon where I was 8th. But think about this for a moment because this is how this 'amateur' athlete functioned. **When travelling to events such as Swindon my day would go like this: Away to work at 7.30am, work till 3.30pm, drive the 17 miles home, pack the car with bikes and spares, wetsuits and all sorts of support items. I would then wait for my two lads to arrive home from school (in '88 James would have been six and David four) before the four of us cramped tightly together in an 'old banger' headed off on a seven hour car journey down to Swindon on a busy Friday night (I have also commented 'don't feel well, muggy head, sore throat'). James was a particularly poor traveller; he was an** 'are we nearly there' **type after five miles. Arriving late at night we'd then either look for our prearranged digs or find a B and B! I did all the driving as Jennifer 'wasn't keen' on motorway driving. The following day I'd start thinking about the event only to finish a disappointing 8th from 380, before loading us all back in the 'old banger' for the return journey home. Back to work the next day, but only after an early morning swim at 6.30am!**

Perhaps you can now see why I have issues with our current 'pros' who talk about all the **'sacrifices'** *they make – they don't know they're born! And then of course there's multi millionaire 'Jenson' on the front cover, but hey I'm cool, ha!*

Despite the various wins Otley GP was the pick of the bunch I think for me in 1988. The event was different from the usual – it started at 6.30 on a barmy Saturday night and we swam through the town before heading out on our bikes, which according to my diary was 4 x7 mile circuits coming into the town centre each lap, and being cheered on by, quote 'thousands' who turned out from the pubs etc. to shout us on. Having won the Nationals there the previous year I was becoming a crowd favourite – it felt good though to be appreciated. There were bands playing and a carnival type atmosphere prevailed, and I was interviewed on a band stand afterwards. Later they even sent me a newspaper where I was photographed and on the front page with a headline – **Morpeth's Mike Harris wins Otley again!**

My training through the year was the same as normal, three times a day, mainly seven days a week. There is no doubt at all that on many occasions I 'over trained' and my tapers before events weren't tapers at all! Two days before Otley for example my day went like this: am Swim 2,500 yds, Lunchtime run 34m 11 s 'flat out' in shorts and vest course PB, pm bike 2 hours steady but plenty of hills (feeling good, on a beautiful night).

Been going through my diary for 1988 trying to find something interesting, something perhaps out of the ordinary but it's all pretty much run of the mill I'm afraid, with little it seems except the norm. One big change that year though was obviously my occupational move, and starting with Northumbria Police – a wonderful job (almost) for the next 24 years which I aim to devote a special chapter to following the triathlon years; I need a full chapter as there were so many differing elements to this unique occupational position!

In 1989, I appeared on the front cover of *Today's Runner magazine* (wearing Puma running apparel, which went down well with Derek Ibbotson at Puma)which I think was the biggest selling running magazine in the country at that time. I had a four page spread inside, and the crux was 'how can runners successfully make the transition into triathlon?'. This is clearly what I had done, arriving in the sport from running. Following on from this article I was also given the role of answering readers' letters and queries in relation to triathlon; I think I got £5.00 a letter, but hey, not to be smirked at, that was probably two rolls of tub tape in '89! So happy days were here again and our finances had gone from terrible to awful!

I can very clearly remember at the time when the running magazine came out with me on the cover, and travelling down to London on the train for a photo shoot and to pick up some cycling apparel from Freewheel, a big cycling mail order company at the time who had been sponsoring me for two or three years. Anyhow I was really getting quite a kick out of seeing my face in all the WH Smiths shops, and at one point as used to happen then the train pulled up in a station – York? – and there was a guy standing with a newspaper barrow opposite my compartment window, and there I was looking at myself through the train window. However, I was very quickly brought back down to earth when I got home and walking into the local cricket club one night to be greeted by the usual: *'Hi Mick, yi still fit? Fancy a game of futbarl on Sunda? Too owld like the rest us noo, eh?'*

I swear I could have won an Olympic gold medal and no one around here would have known, or if they had they wouldn't have let on! I know it sounds trivial, but one of my biggest regrets in my life is that despite my sporting record over so many years, locally no one gives a monkeys, and I include my family in that. It's never been something you could bring up yourself, you need a prompt from somewhere, and a prompt locally has never been on the agenda! Maybe my grandson will one day ask – **'Granda, were you an athlete once?'**

Who's nicked my shoes?

Anyhow at 39 years of age I still finished 4th in the National Long Course in 1989 at Rother Valley and had another seven wins. On the 23rd April while representing the Northern Area in the Inter Regional Championships someone 'pinched' or 'borrowed' – no, definitely 'pinched', I never got them back – my running shoes from my transition point, and I was lent a pair of size 9s (I am a 7) for the 10km run, yet still had the 2nd fastest run split of the day. Actually as reminded in my diary this was a *'freezing' cold day, quote - with snow, rain, ice, bitter, bitter cold can't ever remember being this cold, finished the run with a very bad calf* – well there's a surprise!, size 9s and soaking wet!

Following the last competition of 1989, which was the Cleveland relays in October, inexplicably for me there is little training recorded in my diary. I was on holiday 'somewhere' in October after which I have nothing logged; however, I have trained almost every day of my life and I am certain that this period would have been no different, especially with having a gym and sports hall within 10 metres of my office. Because of an ever increasing involvement in Police self-defence I was going to Judo sessions fairly regularly at the time in Ashington for additional expertise. These sessions were hard work, and although clearly I was very fit, the physiology was so different from triathlon. Judo for the most part is an anaerobic activity, with pulse rates elevating very quickly, before fluctuating but still remaining high for short periods, as opposed to the lengthy aerobic exercise of triathlon.

However, relating back to my training diary of **1990,** at the introductory stage I have written *'from October to December have done little swimming, some biking, ran often, done judo and weight training, have sore ribs from self-defence course'.*

Despite being out celebrating the New Year in on the 1st till 5am, I ran for 40 minutes later in the day, with a sore Achilles and a 'bad head'. Thereafter I was back to twice and occasional three times a day training. At the end of the week ending January 20th I have recorded *'obviously very fit and happy with my present condition, Achilles a bit better'!* On the 11th February I did the Weardale biathlon which I can't remember at all and finished 3rd, despite 'struggling on hills and stitch on the run'. Later in the day I swam for 50 minutes. On the 15th I went down to Batley in Yorkshire to renew my contract with Puma and Derek Ibbotson. Picked up my allocation and returned home. **A word about Derek Ibbotson.** Over the preceding few years I was to meet with Derek once a year down in Batley. Derek had been a very high profile world renowned athlete, and as mentioned previously a former World Record holder for the one mile. Derek was a very energetic guy who walked as if he was in a massive hurry; he was also a gentleman as far as I was concerned and treated me with real respect. I would accompany him down to the 'factory' and literally help myself (although we had a written agreement regarding kit); I also got a healthy amount of kids' clothing for my two lads – tracksuits etc. A short while later for reasons I still don't know too much about, Derek lost his job at Puma, and his number two replaced him. At that time I was to lose my sponsorship with Puma as well. But Derek wrote me a nice letter explaining that the latter was not his choice and he felt that I had served Puma very well and personally thanked me. The reason for my contract not being renewed, I learned later, was because at the time Puma was sponsoring several very high profile sprinters and because they wanted more, the 'small fish' had to go! But I had massive respect for Derek, not just for the way he dealt with me but also because 'back in the day' and in another wonderful innocent era he had been a truly gritty athlete who always gave his best. If you are reading this and you are unaware of Derek – google him and you'll see what I mean about the effort he put into his racing!

1990 appears to have been pretty ordinary from the athletic side. It seems I only had five wins, three seconds and a couple of 3rd places. I had a 13th place from 326 finishers but had the 4th quickest run in the National short course, my worst position by far – I punctured twice in the National Long course and without any more spares had to pull out. **The latter, despite thousands of events, was the only event in my life that I have failed to finish!**

Before putting 1990 to bed, a word about the **Aireborough Elite Triathlon** which I won twice and was a close 2nd the last time. The reason I single out this event is because of the level of difficulty that went with it. The format was different from the standard triathlons. The event started out with a 1,000 metre swim (14.26) in a crowded swimming pool; you then had to scramble to the start of the run (which wasn't adjacent to the pool) quickly, as any additional time over your official run start time was simply added on; you then ran 9 .5 miles flat out (51.11) on a very undulating course, then changed your shoes and briskly made your way to the cycle start, 22.5miles (1.5.36) the ride, after a 10 mile run, was incredibly hard. There was a lot of uncertainty with this event because it went on all day, with hundreds of competitors, as such it was much later in the day that you'd actually get your time and position, so you had no idea really as to whether you were first or last. A great event and superbly organised (when you consider the complexity of it) by Mike Shutt and his very professional team!

1991 started quietly; training was twice a day on average, but as most athletes know the winter months are generally a hefty slog, the weather is totally unpredictable and all too often in the North East particularly harsh, and of course the hours of daylight are severely limited too. Also, competitions can seem an eternity away! However, if you are ambitious you recognise the importance of consistent training regardless of the time of year, certainly, and you need a lot of discipline and determination to see these months through. There is an old saying in athletics which goes *'summer races are won in winter'* such is the importance of consistency, if you are serious!

The Rhythm Method

Joining a band

In January I had a fortuitous meeting with a guy who became a friend for life. While working at Newbiggin Sports Centre in 1987 I had met a local squash player called Tom Maley. Tom was a very competent squash player, and as such was in and out of the centre on a regular basis and of course we'd always pass pleasantries when our paths crossed. It's strange really how often you can see a person and yet know almost nothing about them. Ships in the night! Tom, as mentioned, was a very good squash player, but apart from that I knew nothing at all about him. Tom became a renowned Sculptor with incredible high profile pieces of work such as the statue of Sir Bobby Robson outside St James' Park, as well as several other notable and eye catching Sculptures prominently placed around the North East reflecting Miners at work. A wonderful talent! However, looking through my 1991 diary I note that on a Friday night I was out socialising in Morpeth with a good friend of mine called Ray Tweddle. As we walked past a pub called the Black Bull, we were enticed inside by the sound of 'live music'! On investigation, we ascended some stairs, paid a pound on the door and went inside where there was band playing lively Bluesy type music.

With the lights down low the band members were simply figures in the darkened room, but the music was spot on. Most budding musicians like myself tend to pay particular attention to the band's playing credentials and as I cast my eyes around they eventually came to rest on the drummer and the drummer in this band was none other than my squash playing acquaintance Tom Maley! Pleasantly surprised to say the least, once the band had a break I approached Tom, we shook hands and had a quick chat, and of course Tom knew me only as an athlete and Assistant Manager at the sports centre – he had no idea that I had an incredible passion for music, particularly R and B. Anyhow Tom offered us a lift home in his van at the end of the night's entertainment. While chatting I mentioned that I played blues harmonica and then thought no more about it, until that is on Sunday the 13th January, when there was a knock on my door, and there was Tom standing saying, *'We are having a band practice, do you fancy coming along with a couple of harmonicas for an informal jam?'* Well I couldn't wait, and quickly picked up three or four harmonicas with a range of keys and off we went to North Shields. Once there I was introduced to the other lads, Foxy, Charla, Ken, and Jim. As I recall I was given a mike, and invited to join in. Well I must have impressed a little bit, and was invited to another practice at Tom's house a few days later, following which Jim said they had a gig on the Friday night, the 25th January, at the same venue as when I'd first seen them three weeks or so previously, and I was welcome to come along and 'join in'!

On the 25th I went along travelling with Tom and have recorded in my training diary: *'played my first gig with the Rhythm Method at the Black Bull - great, went really well'!* I couldn't believe my luck if I'm honest, here I was still an ambitious athlete but with an opportunity to play blues music with a very capable band. My association with the band would last several years with lots of regular gigs in the North East, while at the same time trying to maintain my standing within triathlon circles, do my bit as a dad and a husband and of course going to work every day. Jennifer was more bemused I think than anything, she couldn't give a toss really about music or even triathlon, but true to form she just let me get on with it. Jennifer and I have often had an uneasy association, but we've been together up to now for 40 years and despite 'occasional disagreements' we are the same now as we've always been. I do realise of course that there are many women out there who would never have put up with my lifestyle. Once we were married I well recall my mother saying, *'mind, Michael, when you're married, Jennifer gets the pay, son, so she can pay the bills and things',* and that's the way it's been right since 1979. I get a few quid pocket money, depending on the prevailing household finance at the time. It's funny really but my mother's philosophy came from a time when in the North East the man would come in from work on a Friday and before he even sat down for dinner, the week's wages were put down on the table! Like a lot of people I would imagine, as a kid I can still remember little piles of money on the dresser, dinner money, coal money, insurance, and rent money, all neatly laid out ready for collection. Those were days when benefits were almost non-existent and debt was frowned upon, even seen as a disgrace I guess.

By April I was pretty fit and things appeared to be going according to plan, my pulse was 35 bpm, and blood pressure was 115/72. On the 12th May I finished 2nd in the Blyth triathlon. We then set off for a holiday at Butlin's in Skegness but on the way down we stopped at Peterlee where I won the East Durham triathlon by seven minutes, followed by a 3rd place at the Prince Bishops triathlon on our way back. A week later I was 9th at the Bridlington GP where I crashed my bike on a roundabout during a very heavy downpour while well in the lead, which resulted in quite severe mechanical problems with wheels rubbing on brake pads etc as well as severely grazed legs. I was 2nd in the South Tyneside triathlon on 30th June but once again finished with a very sore right Achilles tendon and on 21st July won the National vets long course title but noted in my diary 'annoyed I couldn't give my best due to continued Achilles problem'!

In no way attributable to playing with the band etc. 1991 was my worst year in triathlon to date, and by August the 11th, my birthday (my 40th), I had a boat load of injuries. On the 11th I won the National vets title, however have scribed in my diary – *ran very well despite very severe Achilles tendon pain, during and after, swollen and discoloured, in a lot of pain!* The following day at work I had written – no training limping very badly!

So ends 1991!

1992 started pretty quietly, but from half way through the first week I was back into two training sessions daily but only averaging about 90 minutes a day, with more at the weekends. A comment in my diary reads 'feeling quite fit and confident, ankle certainly getting better but stiff in the mornings'. Of course work would always interfere with training, as it does for most, and for me, because of the active physical nature of it, one of those interferences would be...

Self Defence Training!

I was referred to by three different job titles with Northumbria Police; these were Sports Development Officer, Force Physical Training Instructor and the Force Senior Self Defence Trainer. That's value for money – even if I say so myself, and I never once rang in sick! One of my roles in my job with Northumbria Police was training cops and some support staff in what was referred to in those early days as self-defence training (later to be renamed 'Personal Safety' training). In my early days with Northumbria Police, all the Self Defence training was carried out in Judo Suits which perhaps gives an indication of the very active content! Having qualified as a Self Defence trainer in 1989 following a three week highly active and demanding initial course at Harrogate, in order to hang on to the certificate I had to return to the same venue once a year for a week's refresher. In 1992 I went down on the 24th February; the fact that I have recorded 'no training' that week up to the Friday the 28th (when I did 65minutes on the bike) gives an indication of how physically demanding these courses were – they were truly physically extreme!!!

When at Harrogate for either initial training or refreshers, I would join trainers (generally about 12 others) from all over the UK. Most were cops, but a handful including me were civilian support staff trainers. Regardless, we all did the same training. The nature of the subject ensured most trainers had a back ground in martial arts, and most were several kilos heavier than I was. You weren't 'paired off' with someone of similar weight as you would be in competitions, you worked with all; you can imagine therefore being continually partnered with guys who were several stones heavier than yourself – bloody hard work, whether either pulling, pushing, striking, throwing or wrestling no quarter was given or expected! My only background in martial art type activities when starting with the police, came from some 'unarmed combat' whilst serving in the Marines. It is fair to say that these courses at Harrogate were brutal in both their content and the ferocity of the effort given; an easy way to describe the activities is to see them as 'ferocious fights'! And with fights you have winners and losers – unofficially of course! The form of self-defence we did was also recognised as an official martial art, referred to as Taiho Jutsu, therefore there was a grading system, white for novice up through the various coloured belts to Black as the acknowledged expert. Apart from the essential Trainers certificate you left with, at the end of each week there would be a 'grading' and having put in a very painful week we all wanted to leave with a different coloured belt to the one we had started the week with!

By now you will be aware of how incredibly fit I was; however, these weeks down in Harrogate were something totally different from the swimming, cycling and running I was conditioned to. We would start the week off on a Monday morning at 9am and I swear by 10.30am we were already physical wrecks! An hour and a half after we first stepped onto the mats we had a coffee break, sitting down in the lounge soaked wet through, in pain and with so many bruises they more resembled a rash than a bruise! Standing up again after 15 or 20 minutes you were even worse, until the warm-up, then you'd quickly become accustomed to it all again. Honestly (and we were all pretty much the same) you'd quietly wonder at lunchtime how the hell you were going to get through the rest of the week, or weeks, depending on the course duration.

It wasn't unusual to lose one, two or more students over the duration of the course. But that was never going to happen to me unless I had a broken bone or something of that severity. I completed them all with a smile on my face, despite the agony I was in most of the time. Break Falls were the key – we were thrown literally hundreds of times each day but once break falls were perfected, you learned to cope!

I did several three week courses down there as well as the one or two week refreshers, from 1989 till I left the force in 2011. I never missed my allocated course, and through the years progressed to black belt and became a qualified 'Trainer of Trainers', the latter enabling me to train and authorise police officers to become 'In-Force Personal Safety trainers', through a two week course I'd facilitate. The pressure I felt was based on the 'possibility' of returning back to Northumbria without a certificate, due to either not completing the course in its entirety due to injury or failing the course for some reason, such as being judged as incompetent. A lot of pressure!

A little more on personal safety soon!

My sons!

Back to 1992, and on the 15th March I took my eldest son, James (and his friend Simon) to his first race at Jarrow. I have commented in my diary 'he ran great came in 12th from about 150'.

As I have mentioned previously, it's my view that sporting competition gives us all the opportunity to carve out an identity, not necessarily through attainment in the form of winning, but rather through the effort given, which is much more important than winning. With so many people present for this outing I can clearly remember saying to James, *'You must get up the front at the start, son, otherwise you'll get bogged down and never get through!*. Our James totally ignored my advice and in an attempt to become inconspicuous, stood several rows back, but once the race had started he did amazingly well to come through the field in so little time to finish 12th. Left me wondering how well he would have done had he took my initial starting advice... I am proud of both my sons and love them more than anything; as such, whatever they do, as long as they're healthy and happy, try hard, are honest and have morals, I really don't care about their physical prowess. With James it became very clear that he had little interest in 'standing out in a crowd', either through sport or work, and as mentioned he's a great kid, a wonderful husband and with his equally wonderful wife Julie, has given me and Jennifer the most amazing little grandson, Dan. Dan is indeed lucky to have parents so devoted. James appears to be very content, and that's a great place to be. Contentment is elusive to many (including me unfortunately), but oh what a virtue it is, rather than to keep searching and looking for something else instead of what you've already got.

Just like me and my sister Linda, my two sons are very different. Apart from being a talented footballer, David initially showed greater promise as an athlete – I hasten to add not because that's what I wanted or expected, but like myself as a child, running around came natural to him. I well remember when he was playing football for Alnwick, after covering every blade of grass during the game, we'd return home whereby he'd quietly disappear, only to go straight to bed still wearing his muddy strip including shin pads and stockings, black as a 'miner's gaze', totally exhausted! I can also remember going down to Swindon on the 30th May 1992 for a triathlon and as my diary indicates arriving the day before the event, we went to the venue to check out the swim and the run course (2 x 3mile laps). Anyhow arriving at the park, I said to Jennifer that I would be gone for 20 minutes or so with the intention of familiarising myself with a run around course. As I started to jog our David was quickly by my side (he'd be about seven or eight years old in 1992). I stopped and told him to stay with his mam as the distance was too far for him, but seeing his obvious bitter disappointment, I rescinded and off we jogged together. Apparently he found much of the three mile trek pretty easy; certainly he ran the whole distance before sprinting to the 'swings' on conclusion of the run, apparently none the worse for wear. At school he developed with the help of Morpeth Harriers into a classy young runner, won Northumberland County titles in cross country as well as 1,500 metres and 800 metres, and he also finished 4th in the North Eastern counties cross country and in the Northern Cross Country champs from 17 counties he was 4th again and only 12 seconds down on the winner. David was a natural talent, he was born with an innate amount of stamina, and had a real turn of speed, greater than mine, and many times I've analysed why he suddenly lost interest, and have never found a reason – certainly he could have gone on to greater things. But it wasn't to be, and like with James, providing he's happy I have few regrets other than perhaps he didn't make the most of his god given talent. Like his dad though he's never been unemployed, he never misses a day's work, and always pays his way.

There is another subtle difference between my sons though, which is quite interesting, and perhaps best summed up this way.

Many years ago when perhaps my training was at its peak in terms of hours spent training, I would normally do my long workouts at weekends. I well remember on one of these occasions, as was the norm, heading out for a five or six hour solo bike ride, on a bitter cold winter's morning, windy, temperature hovering around freezing, threatening rain, hail, and later snow. I toiled away, travelling initially up the coast to Seahouses, on through Bamburgh, and almost up to Berwick before turning in-land and heading for Wooler. At Wooler the clouds gathered big style; it was now about 2.30pm and I still had at least two hours left, which meant I'd cycle the last few miles in the dark. I was freezing by this time and becoming more tired by the minute. Anyhow, in line with this simple tale, when I eventually arrived home, I had a bite to eat, before unusually for me went to bed to warm through and drowse before going swimming. Within minutes of crawling between the cold sheets and taking up the foetal position, much to my surprise, in walks James (he'd be about two or three) in his tiny underpants and vest and gets in beside me. As the two of us lay there, him facing away from me, I instinctively reached out and put my arm around him. Within seconds James took hold of my protective parental arm and without further ado roughly removed it as he edged further away! I well remember at the time having a smile to myself in relation to James's instinctive actions. James by nature was never a cuddly laddie; he didn't seem to need the physical affection that some others relish! Now then, in total contrast and at the risk of embarrassing him, our David is different. When we would have wrestling type 'fights' in the sitting room and be rolling around the floor, they would start off in a 'laddish' fashion, but every now and again David would linger for a few calculated seconds, for a dad to son cuddle, before recommencing the fight. The two of them are as different as chalk and cheese, and that's people from the same parents – intriguing though!

In 1992, now aged 41 I had a 3rd in a duathlon in April, and on the 5th May finished 9th from many hundreds during the Newbiggin 6 mile running event with a 30m 58s – this race was the third training session of the day for me having swam in the morning and cycled in the afternoon. On the 10th May I was 4th in the Blyth triathlon and on the 30th May following a seven hour drive down to Swindon won the National vets title, with the 10th fastest run on the day from 750 finishers. On the 14th June I won the National vets Sprint triathlon at Hull finishing 8th overall.

Combining being a triathlete whilst playing with my band in the pubs and clubs of the North East! Have a look at this!

On the 18th June I travelled out to Vilamoura in Portugal to represent GB in the European Masters Triathlon Championships. To cut a lengthy story short, I finished 2nd in the event just failing to catch the winner by only 12 seconds, and ran a 32min 10km. Once I crossed the finish line, I was immediately 'shadowed' by an official as I had been selected for a random drugs test and had to give a urine sample. So desperately dehydrated, for several hours I was unable to give enough quantity of urine (despite desperately swigging copious amounts of water) to allow the test to prevail. Eventually I succeeded! This testing station worried me at the time as it was chaotic, no one it seemed could speak English and I think there were three samples taken and placed in three separate tubes, but it all looked so complicated and messy as such it all appeared to me to be so subject to error. I had been drug tested at events before but none appeared as dysfunctional as this one.

Having taken so long to give my sample, I had missed one or two flights home. Eventually around about 3 or 4pm, having been up since 5am, I boarded a flight home. At the airport I was picked up by Tom Maley, we sped home, whereupon I said a quick hello, before quickly putting my bags, bike etc. into the garage, ran upstairs and had a quick shower, put my Bassman amplifier into Tom's van before racing through to Bubbles Wine Bar to play with the Rhythm Method till 11.00pm. I got home at 12.30 in the morning, had a few hours' kip before leaving for work at 7.30am, still managing a swim on the way! Some day though!!

I was soon back to normal though, training three times a day, and on the 17th July after work we loaded the car with my gear, on this occasion with Jennifer, David and my nephew Michael and we drove seven and a half hours down to Ironbridge for the National Long course championships, arriving at 10.00pm. We then had a Chinese meal (chicken and mushroom with boiled rice) before grabbing a few hours' sleep. The 'next day' we were up with the larks to compete in a 2,500 metre river swim, 56 miles hilly cycle, and 20km run. I have the results sheet in front of me; I was then 42 years old and from the 432 finishers I finished 14th and had the

3ʳᵈ fastest run split of the day covering the 20km run in 1hr 11mins 46s! We waited around for several hours before I got my medal. I then drove for another six and a half hours back up to the North East! *As an amateur athlete, just another day, and they go on about their bloody sacrifices!*

On the 26th July I was a tired 5th in the North Tyneside triathlon.

I was even more fatigued and had another Achilles tendon injury when I finished 10th overall in the Weardale triathlon 'on a bitterly cold, windy day'. I didn't want to do this event but felt obliged to as Tyne Tees television had previously asked if they could follow me throughout the event, and having agreed several weeks earlier I felt an obligation to honour our agreement. But oh the turmoil of once again running a 10k hilly course with a chronic Achilles injury!

The day after the above I have stated bluntly in my diary, limping badly, season finished!

1993 and my final year in triathlon – 1994!

Looking back now at my racing results over the preceding couple of years, although there were some fine performances and I was head and shoulders the best over 40 triathlete in the country if not Europe, there was a definitive decline. I'm not sure if I realised it at the time though. January 1993 was nowhere near the same as preceding years; I still trained every day and attended Harrogate again from the 17th of January, but the amount I was doing in training was far less. I was still playing regularly with the band and in February I have recorded, 'seem to be quite fit, despite a lengthy 'rest' period', and rests in previous years were unheard of!

In addition to the above comments on February 13ᵗʰ I have written: Training going well at twice a day, and in the space of one week I have gigged with the band twice, been an 'extra' in Jimmy Nail's Spender television series for some desperately needed extra cash,

and done a charity 'modelling' job for Linda Norris at the Holiday Inn!

Modelling clothing – honestly!

The modelling job is worthy of a mention! A journalist called Linda Norris had done an article on me in the Sunday Sun newspaper, and a while later she rang me at work and asked if I would do her a favour as a sporting 'celebrity' (the only time ever I have been referred to as a celebrity – thank god!) and model some sports clothing at a charity event to raise funds for North East born Arsenal footballer Ray Kennedy who had been diagnosed with Parkinson's disease. How could I say no? Anyhow Linda said it would be simple and all I'd have to do was wear some sports clothing and stand around next to a couple of clothes rails. Nothing could be simpler, or so I thought! Also I was told there would be other 'sporting stars' present.

On the night, after work, I went along to the Holiday Inn at Seaton Burn and was amazed at how many people were there; in fact I could barely get parked, such was the interest.

Entering the reception area I was met by Linda who took me along to a large room where several professional models, mainly female, were rushing around. I was introduced to several (they were gorgeous – and that's not sexist by the way – just complimentary) and we made small talk until all of a sudden someone entered the room and shouted 'ok folks, you've got 10 minutes, get ready please'! Try imagining this now! – All of a sudden, and with a turn of speed that would have graced any triathlon transition area, all the girls were 'stark naked' before putting on swimwear and other sporting apparel! It struck me at the time that it was obviously a wind up – 'Beadle's About' or 'Candid Camera' – as I looked around for hidden cameras. OK, I'll play your silly game, I thought and shouted to the girls, 'Hey, where do I get changed?' – 'You get changed here, Mike, where we can see you!' came the reply! The organiser reappeared and demandingly shouted over to *'pip pip, Mike, you're going to have to be quick, you've got 5 minutes'*! It then struck me that this wasn't indeed a game and somewhat stunned I stripped alongside the rest and began to change into my delegated swimwear, only to discover that all the 'gear' was a size or two too big for me! And I'm talking 'swimwear'! Bloody hell! Anyhow all this was happening so quickly and before I knew it I was being ushered up some steps on to a stage behind some curtains. The next step was then explained which went along these lines: when the music starts and the curtains open I was to walk forward to the centre of the stage, look left at the model on my left, smile at her and nod, then do the same from the right hand side and as they both approached me in the centre the three of us would walk in unison down this lengthy catwalk, get to the end, turn around and retrace our steps! The hall, although darkened, was absolutely packed! Can you see me? Swimming gear two sizes too big (not flattering me at all), a beach type cap on me noggin, and carrying a pair of shades! It must have resembled a 'Benny Hill' type script!

This went on for about an hour as I recall; after each appearance we hurried down stairs back into the changing room, where we all stripped naked 'again' before re-emerging in different beach attire and carrying a towel, beach ball or something appropriate to resemble a day at the 'seaside'!

The girls were wonderful, very professional and didn't even seem to notice my *bare credentials*; I noticed theirs though, oh yes, wonderful, and perks of the job!

A short while later I got a smashing letter from Linda saying how successful the event had been while thanking me so much and saying how much money had been raised!

Just another day for this celebrity athlete, musician, part time actor and model – Ha!

Like father like son!

On the 20th February we had a few days' holiday in Malta, my place of birth, and where I'd been based for a while when in the Marines, and as was the norm I trained twice and thrice a day, but for shorter durations. While in Malta I took my family up to St George's Barracks where I was stationed in the Marines, and whilst driving up the road leading to the old main gate, James (who often suffered with travel sickness) let it be known that he was about to 'throw-up'. Stopping the hire car just in time, James rolled out on to the pavement before being sick. I watched him while smiling affectionately, remembering happy memories, as in the exact same place 20 years previously while coming back from a night out, me and my buddies would also be spewing copious amounts of Maltese beer. I couldn't grab the camera quick enough, whilst getting a good telling off from Jennifer 'for my inappropriate behaviour' – no sense of humour! Anyhow we still have the photo, happy days! I suppose for any normal people looking at my diary even in 1993 they'd probably describe it as extraordinary; for me while comparing it to previous years it was anything but, it wasn't even ordinary. Through March and April I was training every day, some days twice and at other times thrice. I was still playing with the band regularly and 18th April I was running a two week Self Defence Instructor course.

Like father like son! James being sick, Malta, February 92

Running the Instructor courses was exhausting. At this time I ran them all by myself (with usually between 12 and 18 students on each course) and a normal day would be as follows: *7am swimming, drive to work and on the mats by 9am for three hours, as the students went off to the canteen – well fatigued (I extended their lunchtime till 13.15 for recovery) – I went up to the top field and did 45 minutes of interval running, Rush back (take a sandwich into the shower) and was back teaching at 13.15 for another three hours. The class would limp away home and I'd do a bit of general admin before driving home and going out almost immediately on the bike for between 1 hour and 1 hr 15 minutes!*

I did the Blyth triathlon on 9th May, finishing 4th overall. On the 23rd May I won the National Short Course vets title in Swindon before travelling the 300 miles home.

On the 12th June I travelled with Jennifer to Gretna Green for my good friend Dave Aylwin's wedding before travelling straight from there down to Aylesbury for the National Sprint triathlon where I won the vets again. On the 17th July I travelled once again down to Ironbridge in Shropshire for the National Long Course champs finishing once again (same as last year) 14th from 500, with the 5th fastest run time, winning the vets very easily in the process! I returned to work the next day to supervise another two week Self Defence Instructors course! On the following Sunday I organised the Police Triathlon Championships and on the 30th played with the band at Bedlington. I have a very clear memory of that gig, because a guy stripped absolutely naked in front of me and danced as I played harmonica. The manager of the Station approached and I thought he was going to escort the guy out, but instead he whispered in my ear, 'See the effect you have on him?' before advising me to 'ignore him, he's harmless'!

Throughout all the above I still managed to train at least twice a day and more often three times – amazing really even if I say so myself!

My season finished disappointingly in the World Championships on the 22nd of August where despite being one of the favourites I could only manage 6th. Although I have noted my performance as 'felt OK', I have also written very disappointed, 'did my best and therefore no excuses'! And so ended the 1993 triathlon racing year.

Triathlon years almost over!

I truly can't remember the definitive time when I decided to call an end to my triathlon years, but I do remember (helped I think by my fading results) having a longing to be 'normal', put a bit of weight on, get up a bit later on a Sunday morning, read the papers, take the dog out walking instead of running, play with the band without having to worry about tomorrow's triathlon while loading my amp into the car etc. etc. and how nice it would be to sit down after work instead of stuffing jam sandwiches into my mouth before heading out on the bike 'again'! I would soon be 43 years old and by this time I had almost **'40 years as an athlete'**! Little did I know that despite my impending 'retirement' I would still have another 20 years to go before I would get to **'60 years an athlete'**!

Final Triathlon year – 1994!

I'm feeling like this is getting a bit repetitive so I'll not linger too much on '94. Suffice to say my training was as consistent as ever but noticeably less in terms of miles covered; my lifestyle, though, changed little. On the 1st May I was 2nd in the Cleveland triathlon and first vet by miles. This was 'Dick Hatfield's event – you may recall Dick's name from my first ever event almost 12 years ago. A week later I was at Market Bosworth finishing a very disappointing 3rd in the National vets, my worst position ever in vets' competition. I finished 4th in the South Tyneside event at the end of July. On the 21st of August I won my 9th National Vets title in the Short Course Championships at Wakefield!

And finally on the 4th September 1994, I flew to Guernsey (my dad meeting the cost, and still with me at many events 12 years after

Reading) for my final event, the National Long Course Championships. I had a great race, finishing 8th overall at 43 years of age, and winning my 10th National vets title by a huge margin of 20 minutes.

I well remember after the event, while flying back up to Newcastle, thinking what a great way to finish my triathlon career. Remembering that 12 years ago, I had travelled down to Reading and finishing 2nd in the first National Championships and here I was 12 years later at 43 and still in the top 10, bettered only by seven youthful athletes!

The day after the Nationals in Guernsey, I wrote in my diary *'travelled home – walk through the woods with Ben'* (my Springer). A good start, I think, in my bid to become a 'normal' bloke!

In summarising my 12 years in the triathlon world, I had won 13 gold medals in National Championships, 3 silvers, and 3 bronze medals. I had 47 open wins, 85 top 3 places, won 10 Northern Championships, was a former British Ironman record holder, had top 10 placings in Europeans with 3 medals, and a couple of top 15 placings in the Worlds, a great record in anyone's books. Despite it all though I remained a little known amateur athlete from a distant cold corner in the North East of England. But all those medals were simply proof of what can be achieved initially by dreaming, then turning the dreams into reality by nothing other than consistent effort! A good time to bow out? No chance!

Newcastle United, and who the ---- let the cat out of the bag?

Around about this time, I was sitting in my office at work one day when the phone rang. I picked up the handset to hear a guy with a broad scouse accent say, *'Can I speak to Mike Harris?'* 'Speaking,' says I. *'It's Terry McDermott here, Mike, from Newcastle United. I've been given your name and I'm after a favour!'* A wind up was my first thought, so 'P--s off' says I, laughing, followed by 'who's this?'. Laughter on the other end was followed by *'No honestly, Mike, let me explain'!* If it wasn't Terry McDermott they were making a bloody good job of the impersonation! Anyhow he went on to explain that the current very successful 'toon' team under Kevin Keegan's guidance were trying to find somewhere quiet to train, away from the media and public, hence Police HQ had somehow come into the frame, and *could I arrange it?*. For obvious reasons I was sworn to secrecy, no one was to know! By now I was convinced it must be Terry and we agreed to meet at HQ so he could have a look over the facilities, in particular the football fields. Anyhow Terry duly arrived at HQ a couple of days later; I met him at the main gate and proceeded to show him the changing facilities and the field, after which he said, *'Perfect – can I leave it with you?'* After he left, I went up to the Superintendent's office; closing the door behind me I quietly explained the situation and asked for his approval, while making a point that the whole thing would be a waste of time if 'word got out'! 'No problem,' he said, 'go for it, Mike, but keep me informed.'

I swear I told no one, the Super swore afterwards that he told no one, yet when the team arrived in their luxury coach at the main gate and I jumped on board as their escort, the short journey to the changing rooms became like a trip down the Wembley Way! Worse again when we went onto the 'top field' which ran adjacent to the A696 – there were more spectators than at a toon home game! There were lines of cars bumper to bumper on the A696 main road and everyone from Berwick to Newcastle seemed to be having a day out! Shaking my head vigorously I awkwardly apologised to Kevin and Terry, both of whom just laughed, and didn't seem at all surprised, taking it all in their stride. Their training went on for a couple of hours, job done. As we walked back to the gym, Kevin said to Terry, *'Have you got Mike's present?'* at which point they both shook my hand, thanking me generously for my help and saying how much they appreciated it. I was given a plastic bag and inside there was a recently signed football top and a signed football. **Here's a little secret though!** Ever wondered what the pros eat in changing rooms? Well on this occasion at least, 'Jaffa Cakes' were the trend with the Mags! In our changing rooms, which were fortuitously right next to my office, they left boxes full of them – kept me and my hungry family going for weeks. When I looked into the reason for their 'biscuit' preference, these delicacies, I think

I am right in saying, are pretty high in energy but low in calories, a beneficial quick fix! Interesting eh? You heard it here first!!

I had previously heard all about Kevin's leadership skills (which I think were obvious) and his down to earth attitude, which clearly endeared him to the fans. As we parted I remember thinking 'who wouldn't want to give their best for this guy?'. Polite, warm, sincere, jovial, funny, knowledgeable, all of which are sound humanistic qualities in any environment, sport or work. When I next saw the Super' and before I had a chance to say anything at all he looked at me and said, 'It wasn't me mind, Mike'! **'Nor me, Boss,'** I quickly replied! With both of us shaking our heads we went our separate ways, me thinking, *'it must have been him'* and no doubt him thinking *'it must have been him'*. Which begs the question if it wasn't either of us *'who the .... let the cat out of the bag and told the whole world of the toon's secret day out?'*. Alas a mystery never to be solved – my money has to be on him though!!!!

And another!

Playing with Smoke Stack Lightnin

One day, not long after I'd decided to call it a day as far as triathlon was concerned, there was a knock on my door. As I opened it, there was a guy called Kevin Stansbury standing there with a note. The note was from an icon of music within the north east band scene called Bob Davison. Bob has been playing with bands for many years, a superb singer/guitarist and a genuinely nice guy. I had occasionally jammed with one of Bob's previous bands as they played locally in pubs and clubs, called the King Snakes, great fun! Apparently he had been trying to find me for quite a while, to see if I fancied joining his new band. He knew I lived somewhere in Widdrington, hence the note delivered by hand and by Kevin, a local Widdrington lad himself. I rang Bob who wanted me to double up and play guitar as well as blues harp with his new band, and we arranged to meet at the Diamond pub in Ashington. On arriving I was introduced to the owner of the pub called Dave Langdown. Apparently, Dave was a drummer who owned not just the Diamond but also the nearby Bubbles Wine Bar. Dave was also going to be part of the band, and we struck up an immediate friendship. I really can't speak highly enough of Dave, one of the most obliging people I ever met, and I am lucky to be able to call him a mate, we are sound friends. Owning the two pubs was very fortuitous for us for two reasons: it gave us somewhere to play as bands were a regular occurrence at Bubbles, but additionally it also gave us a great venue for band practices. Bob also had a bass player lined up, Alec Alloa from Morpeth, another nice guy. Anyhow Bob had a cassette tape ready with suggested numbers. I took it away, listened to it and within a few days we had our first band practice. The band wasn't yet complete though and Bob's long term band associate Graham Kelly, an excellent guitarist with very good vocals, also joined us. We were to be called Smoke Stack Lightnin. Anyone who plays in bands will be quick to tell you that there are often major clashes of personalities, often confounded by musical differences. The latter didn't happen with us – we all got on like a house on fire. The R and B music we played was loud (with four guitars, a harmonica and drums) and fairly raucous, great fun and I loved it. We played all over the North East and as far away as Aberdeen and Wetherby, always travelling together in Dave's work horse of a van.

It seems in my life that as soon as one door closes another immediately opens, and this was just another of those fortuitous occasions that came along literally from nowhere and at the right time.

Despite the perceived disparity between band music (and the obvious socialising that goes with it) and sport, I never stopped training during this spell, still seven days a week, and my love of physical activity never waned, as I now competed in ultra-fit competitions.

Anyhow we must have played together for about three years or so, before, like most things in life, it ran its course and we amicably parted. More or less as soon as we went our separate ways, along came John Hall, who pestered the life out of me to start racing again, on a bike! How could I resist?

24 Years with Northumbria Police (and as it turned out 'another 24 years of sporting competition'!)

As mentioned previously, while working as Duty Officer at the Wentworth Sports Centre in Hexham, although I was happy there, I applied for another job, had an interview in February 1988 and on the 28th March I became Sports Development Officer with the 6th largest police force in the country, Northumbria Police. It was at this time that I met a Police Sergeant called John Lowes, and for many years John and I would meet at work during coffee breaks and have a good laugh while discussing affairs of the day. John is just a bit special! He was a Police PTI at Training School before I met him, but sadly he went on to develop Osteoporosis whilst in his prime. No reason for it, he was to all intents and purposes very fit and strong, healthy and with a lust for life, and with a loving family. I read a quote many years ago which I've never forgotten – *'handicaps are given to ordinary people to make them extraordinary'*. John certainly falls into this category, a firm friend who despite his physical limitations would never dream of asking for special attention. He puts many of us to shame, and revels in helping others, a rare quality! I was very fortunate to have met John and to have spent so much time in his company, and certainly my life would have been poorer had our paths not crossed in March 1988 and continued to this day.

Having found my ideal job, I would spend the remaining years of my working life totally immersed in training and advising both police officers and support staff in a variety of subjects, and always with the same amount of enthusiasm I had for all my sporting endeavours. I was incredibly fortunate to get the job. It's my view that interviews are often a lottery and apart from the obvious credentials you require, you also need a bit of luck, your face needs to fit with the interview panel as well, and there is a very fine dividing line between being 1st and 2nd – it happens in employment just as it happens in sport! Although I have no doubt that at the time I had all the suitable credentials, being a multi discipline athletics coach, gymnastics coach, trampoline coach, table tennis coach, swimming teacher, diploma in sports psychology, a supervisory studies certificate, first aider etc. As well as being a former member of the uniformed services, I was also a 'self-coached' British sporting Champion at the time as well. On the day of the interview I also wore a Great Britain Blazer. The latter (the blazer) I accept as 'bullshit', nevertheless I'd earned the right to wear it when appropriate and on hindsight bearing in mind the association between the job and my sporting pedigree it was perhaps a congruous move.

I had bought the product of a healthy lifestyle myself, and having willingly bought the product it becomes pretty easy to sell on to others; in other words there was no deceit, unlike perhaps some other salesmen. I do accept though, due to my sporting ambitions, that personally I regularly went over the top regarding exercise and that's not necessarily healthy. Without hesitation though, I can honestly say the role I had with the police was much more to me than just a job. In fact I actually took a pay cut to be with Northumbria Police; however, as I proceeded through the years my organisation regraded me three times, ensuring as it did that there was monetary rewards for my efforts.

In my life I have given a huge amount of loyalty to the differing bodies I have belonged to, whether that be my schools, the Royal Marines, representing Great Britain in sport, and that pride and loyalty extends to being an Englishman, a Brit and a Geordie, and even with the bands I played with I always wanted to be part of the best, and I don't care how soft the latter sounds, I am saying it because I mean it! My high profile position with Northumbria Police was to be no different. I was absolutely passionate and loyal about both my role and my employer. *I say all this now as later on in this chapter you'll see how wanting the best for my organisation would result in me being bitten, for want of another expression! If nothing else it is interesting how things can change so quickly and how you can fall out of favour, for telling the truth, however unpalatable that may be!*

My individual role with the police was unique, I was the only one in roughly 5,000 employees doing this very specific role, and my duties were wide and varied. The Job title (Sports Development Officer) at the time was a bit misleading, although I was Secretary of the Athletic Association, in all honesty there was little to do in relation to 'sports development' – each sporting section in the force, and there were many, had their own elected committees and I was seen as the go-between, but the committees were already full of enthusiastic and very able personnel.

For 24 years I supervised literally thousands of physical tests, both at the recruitment stage and throughout training and probationary periods. Additionally there were differing tests for specialist bodies such as Firearms, ARVs, ASGs, Dog Handlers, Surveillance, Air Support, Public Order, Mounted section, Marine division, Special Constables and in the later years several uniformed Civilian Support Staff roles. I also supervised, as you can imagine, thousands of physical training sessions, a lot of the time I didn't just direct, but I think I gained some credibility by working out or running alongside the classes, in so doing leading by example, a good way to enhance respect. Health awareness subjects were also part of my remit. Later on my role would change to a degree with greater emphasis being put on self-defence training; with the latter I was to gain yet another job title 'Senior Self Defence Trainer', at which point I was also given a team of six dedicated trainers, initially to train up and certificate before supervising and directing in order to facilitate force wide training.

Other roles I had were delivering Conflict Management and Health Awareness talks in classroom type settings to various groups. In the early days of my employment the latter sessions of health awareness could be (not by choice) hilarious! When I first started at HQ I was guided by a police PTI called Dave Aylwin. Dave and I became good friends and remain that way even today many years later. As I was learning the ropes so to speak, and getting my head around how different groups operated, Dave would offer advice. It is fair to say that policing has changed massively over the years and certainly the police force of 1988 would be unrecognisable in relation to the force that operates in 2015, for various reasons. One of those reasons is the 'type' of officers that were working in 1988 and coming to the end of their 30 year career. Political Correctness was almost unheard of in 1988 and certainly 30 years previous to that, i.e. in 1958 when some of these officers would have been joining the force, the term would have resulted in merriment and invariably subjected the user to a degree of ridicule! I mention this simply as a means of identifying the type of officers I had to advise from time to time and on a fairly regular basis. One of the courses I helped with was referred to as a Sergeants and Constables Development Course. Lasting a week or two, it was designed to bring the older and therefore more streetwise officer up to date regarding changing procedures and the ever increasing use of computers etc. The course organisers clearly thought that an input on health followed by a 'bit of a run around' in the gym would be beneficial; hence my own involvement was called upon.

When I was initially requested to do an hour's input on health, I sought guidance from Dave Aylwin. Dave was blunt with his advice which went along the lines of *'talk to them on health and fitness – but watch this lot, queer buggers these, Mike'*!

Anyhow not having enough time to compile an interesting talk before the first one was due, I had the idea of just encouraging class participation by inviting a question and answer type session – they ask a health/fitness related question and I in my wisdom would provide them with an answer. Sounded pretty good to me: gets the class involved and the answer is both pertinent to the individual yet well within the remit and scope of the overall session.

Anyhow casting my mind back to the day I have in mind, it is fair to say this group of very experienced officers were 'not very responsive' to the subject of health, to say the least. Questions were awkward and often irrelevant, e.g. laddish comments such as *'does size matter?'*

followed by a juvenile smirk, or childish giggle! One person in particular seemed to be hell-bent on giving me a hard time. However, one of the questions he asked was very pertinent and went along the lines of:

'We work irregular shifts, therefore we eat irregular meals – what would you suggest?'

Well, say I, **'look at 'what' you're eating rather than 'when' you're eating it'!**

'Aye, well, howay then, give us a clue,' he replies!

So I say: **'Instead of having a chocolate bar with your coffee at midnight, have an apple'!**

Now I'd be the first person to concede that an apple doesn't really go with a coffee (I mean you can't *dunk it,* can you). But what I meant was to cut out the negative calories in the chocolate and replace it with a healthy choice such as an apple, maybe five minutes after the coffee.

The guy replies – *'I cannit keep an apple doon, me, chuck it straight back up again'!*

'Ok,' says I with an attempted look of empathy, **'how are you with a pear?'**

He then shakes his head from side to side before declaring – *'Na, cannit keep one of them doon either'!*

It may help to try and visualise the scene. At this time the remainder of the class are absolutely non-committal, body language, positive or negative is non-existent and verbal contributions are restricted to grunts or muffled yawns. Clearly during this period, it was unfashionable to be both a hardened cop and be health conscious at the same time!

Back to the scenario, in desperation I say **'well, what about a banana'?**

'Howay lad,' comes the reply – *'have you seen the price of bananas?'*

I well remember at this point looking him in the eye and with a smile, and telling him head on, 'I get no pleasure in this but the likelihood is you are going to die early. As far as nutrition goes, you know what's **good and what's not so good, but you refuse to adjust and make changes for the better, so be it**!' To which he replies, *'well thanks for that, like'!*

A short while later we all went down to the gym for a bit of PT, and the same guy goes into the changing room to get changed and comes out with a Rab Nesbitt style string vest on and a pair of pyjama bottoms kept up with a draw cord, together with a pair of slippers. When I challenged him (in good humour) about his choice of 'sports clothing' he replied, *'Well it's as close as I've got to a tracksuit and trainers, do you want me to stay or...?'* I said, *'Hey, if you're happy so am I'* and he completed the 'run around' in his best 'recreational/sports' clothing!

A well-known statistic at the time in 1988, in relation to longevity, was that the role of a police officer did not enhance the potential of a long and healthy life, especially following retirement. Unfortunately a fairly high proportion died within a handful of years following their initial retirement from the force. I do believe at the time the average male person in the country lived till around about 75 and females till 78; however a lot of cops were tragically gone before they reached 68! The reasons for this were partly due to the way they lived their lives with the negatives of shift work, poor diet, stress, and lack of 'appropriate' exercise routines all contributing to their fate.

I relate the above little story simply to show the diversity of the groups I dealt with in my early years with the police, but also to acknowledge that ignorance and laziness resulting in poor health are so often self-inflicted. I mean who wouldn't want to be fit and healthy? Surely the latter is attractive if only to ensure you are able to spend the pension you have earned and worked so hard for. Good health requires a degree of self-help, and cutting your nose off to spite your face is lunacy.

Watching the Tits – help!

Another somewhat similar incident has just come to mind, but this time with a different group. The group in question on this occasion were probationers and as the group were about to finish their probationary period and therefore become verified cops, it was thought pertinent to remind them that a fit and healthy lifestyle was advantageous. Once again I was deployed to give a fairly relaxed input on Health Awareness. By this point I had devised a written questionnaire, which would result in the class having to attempt to write alongside the question an appropriate answer. Typical questions were: 'what is the difference between complex carbohydrates and simple carbohydrates?' 'What is the difference between aerobic activity and anaerobic activity?' 'What are water soluble vitamins and why are they important in your diet?' Etc. Once the students had completed the knowledge check, we would come back together as a group and systematically analyse each question.

On this occasion as the group were answering as best they could the questions, I was totally distracted by some wildlife activity outside, which I was viewing through a window at the rear of the room and the back of the class. HQ at Ponteland was a hive of activity in relation to wildlife (one of my passions in life). My buddy Alan Pearson and I used to hang nuts out, put seeds in containers etc; as such we were visited regularly by foxes, red squirrels, even the occasional otter, and a host of birdlife including tree creepers, nut hatches, woodpeckers, and numerous different birds from the tit family.

Anyhow as I was sitting observing the tits on the nuts, I suddenly became aware of a police woman sitting perhaps six or eight feet away from me, looking at me and appearing slightly embarrassed. Realising that she must have thought I was staring at her, I quickly tried to allay her fears, and without any thought looked her in the face and said, *'It's ok, don't mind me, I'm only looking at the tits!'* Well she went a bright shade of purple and glanced down at her chest, as did the rest of the class, suspecting I guess that she had a blouse button undone or something. Quickly realising what I'd said, I blurted out, 'Great Tits!' (for the uninformed Great Tits are a type of 'feathered' tit) shock horror! Now the whole class were looking at her chest. Quickly gesturing by pointing to the window I blurted out, 'I'm watching all the tits, look behind you, on the nuts, look!' It was akin to a script from Fawlty Towers, total silence, with me nodding frantically in the direction of the tit activity. Time stood quietly still for a moment or two. All of a sudden, thank god, there were a couple of giggles followed by fairly raucous laughter. I said to the young lady, *'Hey I'm so sorry, please forgive me if I've embarrassed you, it wasn't intended!'* And with a sheepish smile she nodded and left with her colleagues. I wonder if she, or the class, ever recount that incident, which perhaps these days would see me locked up, despite the innocence of it all!

What I found through the years while working with Northumbria was that you didn't have to be physically fit to be an effective cop, but it was definitely advantageous. Without a doubt there were, and are, excellent officers who did outstanding jobs but who could be classed as lacking in elements of physical fitness such as an ability to run, perhaps in aid of a colleague in dire need of assistance, or for public order duties, bearing in mind that a team is only as good as its weakest member. Without a doubt though, good health and physical fitness are virtues in any walk of life, and it was part of my role to educate, motivate and develop awareness in things appertaining to general health and physical fitness to enable operational effectiveness and additionally assist in improving lifespans in retirement!

Fitness tests!

When I began my career with the police, the fitness tests were pretty straightforward, and easy to train and prepare for because you didn't need specialist equipment. I didn't compile them, I just took over running from where my predecessor Simon had left them, and most forces did pretty much the same tests. When civilian applicants arrived at force HQ, amongst other assessments, they were also expected to run 1.5 miles in under 12 minutes for men and under 13m 30s for women, followed by at least 20 press-ups (female applicants performed them from the knees to compensate for natural strength limitations associated with their gender), 20 sit-ups, 20 burpees and a flexibility exercise (sit and reach).In order to encourage effort applicants were graded, so the faster you went or the more you did the higher your mark. So you'd be assessed by one of four scores – excellent, good, acceptable or poor – with the 'poor' you had failed the test and were either rejected or given 're-runs' till you passed.

A while later as a means of improving fitness standards, particularly of new recruits, other additional tests were incorporated to run alongside the long established tests. So there was now a 1.5 mile run, press-ups, sit-ups, burpees, flexibility, and if the applicant was acceptable on these they would return a while later (after a week or two rather than a day or two) and then complete a 20 metre shuttle run test, which was maximal and progressive thereby once again allowing each applicant to impress by doing their best, plus an upper body strength test, grip strength and standing jump, and body fat measurements were taken from four parts of the body using skin fold callipers, the readings accumulated and referred to a chart resulting in a reading of percentage of body fat. On another day applicants had to do a water safety test, which included a slow 1.2 mile jog down to the village swimming pool at 7.30am followed by a couple of lengths' swimming, and a couple of minutes treading water. Finally if applicants had passed all the latter they would be 'kitted out' with public order equipment before undergoing a shield run/walk, facilitated by our public order training department and designed to replicate a public order street type scenario.

The vast majority of people passed these tests; however, as with other things in life some had to work a little harder to be successful, but the end product was a secure job for the next 30 years!

I mentioned earlier that there was a huge difference between the police service when I started in 1988 and the police service I left behind in 2011. For 22 of my 24 years with Northumbria Police I had a wonderful job, it was tailormade for me, I was so lucky but never took it for granted, and was as proud as punch being there – how many people could honestly say that about their job? There were countless people I genuinely looked forward to seeing every day, I didn't have enemies, partly because I would do almost anything for anybody, I didn't know how to say no, or sorry I haven't got time. I had some wonderful colleagues, support staff as well as cops, and many of my colleagues I class as very close friends and that will never change. I was treated with the greatest of respect for 99.9% of my 24years there. However, I have purposefully left the 0.1% out for a reason, which I'll come to soon.

A continuation of '60 years an athlete'!

To remain within the references of my book, I have again referred back to my training diaries of this time. Having finished with triathlon, it wasn't long before I was enticed back into another physical challenge; the new challenge was made easier because although I was no longer competing, I still 'worked-out' every day and remained exceedingly fit, even if I was now 50 years old. The new challenge I refer to was labelled **'ultra-fit' competitions,** which were gymnasium based. In brief, the individual disciplines incorporated into the event were normally treadmill running, rowing, stepping, cycling, bench pressing, shoulder press, rope climbing (we had ropes at work and when in the marines I excelled with rope work), press-ups, sit-ups and finishing off with shuttle runs whilst carrying a medicine ball. As far these events were concerned, from the off, where there would be 10 or 12 athletes in a row (there would be 'waves' throughout the day), you simply completed one exercise as quickly as possible before briskly moving on to the next. Each competitor was designated an official who would both ensure you were performing each discipline correctly whilst also counting your reps. On conclusion your time was recorded and once the last wave had finished, you were given times and positions.

On Sunday the 11th March 2001, I have recorded 'tried the ultra-fit circuit 1hr 20 mins, did it 3 times, very hard work'. Then on the 15th I have the first mention of 'ultra-fit' training, after which my diary is very consistently involved with gym work for a competition on 19th May at RAF Gosford, Wolverhampton, **called the X Zone!**

Old habits die hard, and my training was incredibly intense over the following weeks, on average training in the gyms (at work and Red Row) for around 1hr 45m a session, with gym work consisting of aerobic/anaerobic stuff and loads of weights and core work. Also I note my weight has increased from my triathlon years of 10st 3lb to 10st 11lb. This type of training does make you feel good because it is so complete, upper body, legs and cardio, and as far as all round fitness goes this is the 'bee's knees', but at the extent I was doing it I don't suppose there is any longevity with it. Mentally and physically you are sure to 'burn out', unless you reduce the intensity and the duration of sessions.

On the 19th May I travelled down to Wolverhampton at 6am; it took me 4hrs 30mins to cover the 263 miles and I was off at 13.30! The event comprised 2km recumbent cycle, 50 press-ups, 2.5km run, 60x20km seated shoulder press, 1,500 rowing, 50 sit-ups, 2x rope climbs, stepper 9.30mins, cycle 4km, and medicine ball shuttle runs!

Quote, *'totally knackered at the end, very disappointed, tired almost from the beginning, pushed myself to the very limit'!* Baffled by a lack of form on the day, I have noted that I was dehydrated before the off with urine being 'cloudy' –how could a seasoned athlete have allowed the latter to happen? – unforgivable! The latter makes sense though in relation to my lacklustre performance – if I was dehydrated (possibly by not drinking enough even on the journey down) at the start of the event there is no doubt, in the confines of a sweat drenched hot gym, performance would suffer big style, and so it did! A friend (David Riddell) who actually worked at Gosford as an RAF serviceman, who watched the event, told me a week or two later that I had won my age group; that being the case I had another national title, but I left straight after my wave for the lengthy journey back rather than wait around another few hours, and as far as I can remember I didn't receive a result sheet or trophy so, who knows?

Another entry in my diary on the 27th May, different from the run-of-the mill entries, reads – *Border Canary sitting on 4 eggs!* I used to breed and show canaries for a few years and there was an art to getting all the eggs to hatch at the same time, ensuring as it would that all the chicks had an equal chance of survival! Just thought I'd mention it! Whilst it will happen all over the UK, there was a 'northern thing' in relation to guys having a shed or pigeon ducket where spare time would be idled away. As a kid there were loads of pigeon duckets all over our region and every day if you looked skyward your gaze was met with regular flocks of circulating pigeons, in training for races of several hundreds of miles.

Still with the Police and the beginning of a prolonged period of racing bikes!

During this period, I worked with a police officer, a guy who I had known for several years who was to become one of my most trusted and loyal friends, **John Hall!** I had taken John as a young cop through his probationary period, and a handful of years later he had enrolled on the first Self Defence Instructor course, which I supervised along with another colleague. John, along with one or two others, had to be the most enthusiastic instructor I have ever met, he was a delight to train, incredibly enthusiastic, disciplined, had a hard work ethic and sought every opportunity to improve his knowledge and better himself.

After a few years John was seconded to work with Public Order Training, at force HQ, and while there he took every available opportunity to come down to my gym and 'busy himself' within the realms of self defence issues. At this time, having lost my training partner to pastures new, I suggested that another staff member become a Trainer of Trainers, and John was selected to attend Harrogate for the three week initial course and to qualify as a Trainer of Trainers. Once qualified, John was my shadow, eagerly following me all over, often in his own spare time, in a bid to gather as much additional information as possible. Later we worked together and developed a sound double act. As an experienced operational cop, he had much to offer the constant courses I ran and our relationship, professional and personal, couldn't have been better!

John had been an enthusiastic racing cyclist in his youth and had begun to race once again in Cycle Time Trials. Following each race he would give me a running commentary on his performances. This began to be followed by very predictable enquiries which went along the following lines: '**You must still have a bike or two, Mike? Why not come down to the Barnsbury 10 nights, you'll get a good work out?**'! If only I'd known where these throw away invites would lead!

After a while John's constant daily badgering got me thinking; my thoughts were along the lines of *'well I don't suppose I've anything to lose, I've got a bike, even if I've barely seen it over the preceding two or three years'*! My main concern even at this early stage was that I would once again become 'obsessed' with competition. At this time despite the fact that I trained as always every day of my life, I considered myself to be 'almost normal' and had quite serious reservations about once again getting engulfed into competitions. I was after all a recovering sporting addict! I was also now in my fifties!

Never the less with the X-zone finished and out of the way, on the 20th June 2001 I turned up at Seaton Burn for my first cycle race since 1994, the Barnesbury mid-week 10 mile time trial! I remember telling Jennifer that I would be late in and would attend the race straight from work, to which she was heard to murmur 'oh god'!

I had only recently taken my road bike out of the shed, to discover there was a 'bleb' in the tyre, and with no spares I took it anyhow. A few of the lads gathered around had a look at my 753 road bike before taking the piss in relation to both my tyre and my antiquated racing kit!. Anyhow on a windy but sunny evening I rode a 25m 40s '10'! Finishing well down the field, before returning home and Jennifer asking *'well, did you win?'* and she was serious! My pride already seriously hurt she further rubbed salt into the wound by affirming *'well what do you expect, you're 50 for goodness sake'*! Three days later I had been entered for the police nationals, and agreed to the entry only because the events were held up here in our region – *'so you might as well, what have you got to lose, Mike?'*. So, on the Friday night on a difficult, twisty, lumpy course down in Cleveland I did a 26m 29s '10' and the next day I returned and did a 1hr 4m 11s for the '25' although by all accounts the course was considerably long, and still riding with the ever growing bleb on my front tyre didn't help!

Driving home after the event I had mixed feelings but the overriding one was that I should never have started after such a lengthy time off the bike and I had nothing to gain by being involved again, but now I had taken the plunge so to speak I couldn't possibly leave it like this. Regardless of my now 50 years, I had been a quality athlete with a reputation and I would now have to attempt to get back a degree of respectability before calling it a day, again!

On the following Wednesday, the 27th, I rode another of the Barnesbury 10s, riding a similar time of 25m 23s with John Hall, my tormenter, riding a 25m 02s and John Bent, another friend and cop, beating me by a massive 1m 15s. I have commented in my diary *'found it hard work, sure I'm not going at all well'*!

If you cast your eyes right back to an early chapter titled 'The start line 1955' there are similarities between my first cycle race after the lengthy layoff, and my first race as a four year old in 1955 – honestly my feelings after the preceding few days and regardless of my age were very similar to how I felt all those years ago having been last of three in my first race! Embarrassment, frustration, anger, even shame! I know how ridiculous this must sound, nevertheless it is the way I am (show me the boy and I'll show you the man!), I'm not proud of it, and if I could alter it, then for sure I would if only because those feelings aren't easy to live with or in any way positive or complimentary.

Are you the Bent brothers?

Having mentioned John Bent, I am reminded of an amusing incident which would occur a year or two later. John Hall and I were at a race and standing there in our skin-tight lycra hugging shiny racing kit when a cop called Mark Ambury, who had recently transferred from another force to Northumbria, walked up to John and I and looking us both in the eye said, **'Are you two the Bent Brothers?'** Well, we both looked at each other laughing before I said, **'No, mate, it's just the way we're standing!'** Mark didn't see the joke of course, and had been looking for either John Bent or his brother Peter, both good friends of mine, in order that he could register his interest in joining our cycle club. *'Are you the Bent brothers?'* Ha!

Interesting now looking at how the content of my training diaries began to change as a result of my return to cycle racing and those notable early hammerings. Clearly I was once again getting the bug, but I think it was more to redeem myself before hopefully once again retiring to a more leisurely life befitting a 50 year old 'has been'. However, on the 6th July I even went out and bought a pair of second hand Zipp 404 racing wheels. *Little did I know that for the next '12 years' I would be chasing cycling 'wins'!* My progress during this initial 'back on the bike' phase was encouraging: two weeks after my first race I knocked almost a minute off my previous PB, and a month after the first outing I had both John Hall and John Bent well behind me. A week later I was 5th fastest on the night and another minute quicker, the next week I was 4th in 23m 25s, and two days before my 51st birthday I knocked another minute off doing a 22m13s '10'! In my last race of my very short season I rode a 57m 22s 25 mile time trial! All encouraging stuff!

Digressing a bit!

Other entries in my diary are in total contrast to sporting ambitions. Border canary sitting on four eggs, 7pm Conflict Management training at Newcastle (I did these as and when requested as an outside interest). Psychology GCSE exam, Biology GCSE exam (courses I financed myself). Attended Lou Warmington's retirement do; went to Sorrento for mini holiday and visited Pompeii – wonderful. So life was rarely boring I suppose.

On the 2nd September 2001, I travelled down to Harrogate for another three week self-defence Trainer of Trainers course. Every now and again in the police force someone would take up a new position, and immediately, almost as a means of justifying their newly acquired role, a new and different system would be hurriedly formulated and put into place. This new course was one of these 'replacement' products, and as a result we all had to be trained up in the 'new stuff' before heading back to Force HQ and re-training up an entire police force – nightmare stuff, and so often the new material was clearly no better than the tried and tested old routines! You can imagine having 4,000 cops all up to date but now requiring training in newly acquired different systems of self-defence, new physical techniques, with new terminology, guidance models and new recording systems to formulate and put into place.

Almost two weeks into this course an event happened which would change the world as we knew it. During a break on the course we walked into the coffee lounge to be confronted by some of the most horrendous footage ever seen on television; it would become known as the **9/11 terrorist attacks in New York**! In the 15 minutes or so we were in the lounge it was almost impossible to take in what we were seeing, words can't describe the muddled disbelief of what we had briefly witnessed before returning back to the self-defence mats as if nothing had happened! In denial I suppose, I somehow believed that once we got to the lunchtime break the scenario we'd witnessed would somehow have disappeared.

On Sunday the 16th September I have written in my diary, 'went to church this morning'!

Religion and me!

I pray every day of my life (just like cleaning my teeth) and why not? I don't shout about it and rarely if ever even mention it, it just doesn't crop up. I pray for my family because I love them, and at the risk of appearing slightly mad, I pray for animals and mammals and all sorts of other life. I abhor animal cruelty, it torments me; I put animal cruelty in the same box as child abuse. I occasionally wake in the night thinking about recent news items, maybe about child cruelty or child sexual abuse, or the aforementioned animal cruelty, and praying helps me deal with things, a little like talking something important over with a friend, yet conversely I'm not overly religious. I don't read the bible and I rarely go to church. I'm not sure about it all, how can you be? Logically it doesn't make a lot of sense, yet what a wonderful thought to think there is an afterlife where you are reunited with good people, family and friends who have gone before us. There is a line in an 'Albert King' song which says *everyone wants to go to heaven, but no one wants to die*' and the latter includes the clergy – it seems there are few with an arm in the air shouting 'take me next please' or willingly queuing for a definitive place in the next life! So maybe a lot of the Clerics are like me, we simply live in hope. Maybe praying is not so dissimilar to 'singing the blues' which has apparently helped people for hundreds of years ease the pain of their troubled lives. I'm in no way obsessed with it all, but I tell you what – there's worse ways to spend a little time, and for me if nothing else, it makes me feel good!

I like churches; some of my fondness is because I love history. For almost 1,000 years people have attended Widdrington's sturdy little church, and when you go to this small medieval building it has a serenity about it, with an aged smell that is hard to define, it's quiet and peaceful, the people who go there are good people (if it's good enough for Peter Carmichael, it's good enough for me), they attend for good reasons so on the odd occasion I go I know I'm in good company. Even on my wedding day as the church began to fill up and as I sat there with my best man Ian Wright, waiting for Jennifer, I remember being lost in the architecture of the place as Ian (covered in nervous sweat) rambled on about his speech and goodness knows what else. But you don't have to go to church to pray, you can pray anywhere. On the 16th of September though, I was kind of drawn there, I just went quietly upstairs, got changed and without telling anyone went to church, to offer something for those innocents who had died in such horrendous conditions in the World Trade Centre and the surrounding areas. Perhaps the one thing that differentiates most Human Beings from animals is empathy; we can, with a little imagination, transport ourselves off to anywhere, good or bad and being 'united' in grief for others is a valuable human trait.

I knew a guy once who used to attend the Self-Defence Trainer refresher courses I was running at Force HQ. A super guy who never attempted to hide his faith. Once the courses were over he would always politely thank me before adding 'I'll pray for you Mike'! As soon as he was out of sight I'd quietly find a mirror and check that I wasn't looking as 'peaky' as his remark somehow insinuated. A super gesture, nevertheless.

On the subject of churches!

Several years ago I was on a lengthy solo cycle ride, and having arrived at Elsdon I stepped off the bike for a quick slurp of water. Finding myself next to Elsdon's wonderful historic church, and unable to resist, I lay my bike down and went inside. As I stood there in my cycling kit looking around the little church, my attention was drawn to a noise on one of the splendid ornate window frames. On further inspection there was a colourful little butterfly frantically trying to exit the church through the closed window. Without a further thought I took off my cycling shoes and struggled up onto the windowsill and cupped the butterfly in my hands and was just about to climb down and release my winged friend into the sunshine when the door creaked open. Feeling a wee bit daft, I looked around to find the local vicar entering, as yet totally unaware of my presence. Wondering what to do next and not wanting to startle the vicar I cleared my throat to identify my presence, and the vicar almost .... himself! There I was perched precariously on the sill several feet off the ground in my lycra, as our eyes met! The vicar was clearly taken aback and confused, before I blurted out words to the effect of *'oh hello there, I've just caught a butterfly'* while nodding in the direction of my cupped hands. After a few seconds with me smiling pleasantly trying to allay any fears he may have had, I clumsily struggled down nearly 'setting my neck', whereupon the vicar smiled before saying 'bless you, how nice'. Both of us relieved, we walked to the door together before I released our mutual little friend into the welcome fresh air. I occasionally wonder though what his thoughts were – was I viewed as a 'miracle' who just happened to be passing by to fortuitously rescue the butterfly? Or, more likely perhaps, as a nutter who would be responsible for the vicar always locking the church door in future?

12 YEARS RACING ON BIKES!

Me, Time Trialing

How do you condense 12 years into a concise readable account? It's this easy – '**I won 80 bike races, and had literally hundreds of top 3**

placings on the bike, the vast majority of which were when I was between 50 and 60 years of age'! There, all done! But it's not the winning that is interesting because the competitions are over so very quickly; but the journey taken to win these races can be compelling, and is for the most part a very uncomfortable struggle! If you look hard enough around my home you'll see a few trophies, but the awards say nothing – most aren't even pretty ornaments. **My diaries say everything.** *For 40 plus years ever since I began keeping training diaries, I have sat down at the end of most days and recorded the detail, 365 days a year.* **I can lay a very real claim to being one of the best 'trainers' ever** – not because I was the best athlete ever, far from it, but very, very few trained as I did and still do, although approaching 65 my body needs more rest now between efforts. This may sound a bit pompous but how I would have loved to have coached someone like myself. Totally committed, disciplined, honest, and ambitious and in simple terms a 'real trier'. Most coaches could ask for no more than the athlete who does their absolute best every time they turn out, regardless of the pending results!

I have already outlined above my re-entry into cycle racing. In the first few months of 2001, having started racing on the bike there was little time for improvement because the racing year was almost gone. Besides I knew I would need a winter or two of consistent training before I'd see real improvement in racing performances, so turning to my diary of 2002 I have noted that in the first week of January, only the main roads were 'rideable' due to snow and ice; regardless, I rode them anyhow. The weather in the second week was better, *'much milder – but not warm'*, hence 13hrs 30mins hours on the bike, even with a day off having decided to visit the Battle of Flodden mid-week and back to college for an evening 'Counselling Skills' course I'd enrolled on. All my additional courses took place outside of normal working hours and were designed to enhance my job related skills, and I paid for them all myself! On Saturday 19th January I went with Jennifer to my good friend George Story's 50th birthday at Blaydon rugby club. I have always been into practical jokes, and George was my main man in this regard, daft as a brush; both of us needed little encouragement to cause merriment at the cost of some unsuspecting victim.

Through February I often trained twice a day and noted in my diary on the 9th March –'training really well, no wasted sessions – had 70 bike sessions since January, 14 over 2hrs 30mins', not too sure if this sounds that much but these were all effort based, seldom 'twiddling' gears for the sake of it.

On the 17th April the Barnesbury '10s' began again. The format for these events was that you simply turned up on the night, paid a pound, raced, received your time at the end and went home. On the 17th I paid the princely sum of £2.00, and raced twice flat out and one after the other and finished in the top 5 for both; clearly my strength was encouraging. On 12th March I did three training sessions in the day, all quality intervals; 30th March I did 3hrs in the morning and 1hr 26m pm. Sunday the 20th April I rode 2hrs 35m in the morning and 2hrs hard effort pm. These are just a sample taken at random from my diary.

Quickly leafing through 2002 I raced 44 times, it seems I have several top 3 placings, was riding regular 56 minutes for 25 miles on different courses and **had my first win on 21st August and at 51 years of age! The latter being the first of 75 wins over the next few years. But it had taken me about 18 months of consistent graft to win an event. I said in the chapter labelled 'The start line 1955' (when I was four years old) that** 'the win didn't come easy and they never would'! Well, you can certainly say that again!

At the time of my first cycle win I was 47 years into **'60 years an athlete'!** Still with another 14 years to go to get to where I am as I write this.

On the 10th May 2003 I had my first open win in the Zeus '10' which opened the flood gates for many other victories that year – seemed like I had arrived. Effort rewarded!

In 2004 at 53 years of age, I had 25 top 3 placings with 14 wins almost exactly 50 years after my first race!

On the 10th July after a falling out at home (which I truly can't recall about what!) I travelled locally for a 10 mile time trial. I was off at number 5 but number 4, 3, and 2 failed to start. Already annoyed from the previous argument, I also would now have no one to chase, so a truly solo effort would result, and just before I'd thought it couldn't get any worse, it also began to rain as I approached the start line making the roundabouts slippery – still annoyed with my previous 'falling out' it looked to all intents and purposes that this wasn't going to be my day! However fuelled up with additional adrenalin **I rode a 20m 20s '10' mile time trial** (that's as near as damn it 30mph for 10 miles on public roads), on an old steel framed bike finishing almost a full minute in front of the runner-up. At 8am the next morning I **won another 25 mile time trial in 55m 42s,** a week later **I won the Wansbeck 10 in 20m 48s,** on the 28th **I won again in 20m 55s,** on the 4th August **another '10' win in 20m 41s,** and a week later **yet another win** in an identical time as the last one **20m 41s** – and so it carried on until the last event of the year when **I won the Christmas '10'** beating

Harry Walker by just two seconds. Harry, who I have massive respect for, is a real hard man, and a former National 30 mile record holder; we have the same birthday, however I am 18 years his senior and that means I was serving in the jungles of Malaya when he was born, and here I was at 53 years of age having a wonderful season. But the beauty of sport is that all those wins (and there would be many more to come over the next few years) were earned through sheer consistent hard work. **As an athlete you truly reap what you sow!**

Get obsessed!

Regarding the latter I well remember having a fleeting conversation with John Hall when I'd mentioned that I was off to Paris for two or three days with Jennifer one weekend, when John quipped, *'What, away? You'll miss your training!'* 'Not at all,' said I, 'the flight's early at 7am but I'll get up at 4.30 and do an interval session in our utility room before leaving for the airport, then find a gym for the next day, return home late the day after and do another session in the utility when we get back, no problem!' *'You're obsessed, Harris,'* said John. To which I replied, *'H*ave you ever won a bike race, John?' *'No,'* came the reply. 'Well would you like to?' say I. *'Oh yes,'* said John, *'just one would be nice!'* 'Well,' says I, **'get obsessed, mate!'** Although it was all clearly 'tongue in cheek' there was a serious message there and I'm sure I don't need to elaborate!

Back to the police one last time (remembering I was there 24 years).

During these years I was still working hard with Northumbria police, I loved my job and as a bonus, what could be better than an athlete having the privilege of going to work in a tracksuit? I have also mentioned earlier that I felt valued by my employer and particularly within the rank and file of the organisation. Despite the fact that we were only separated by about 100 metres, our Command block personnel had very little to do with me; in all my years working within the gymnasium block I can only ever remember one Chief Constable coming into my office and chatting about work related issues, yet it would be fair to say that I had some sort of influence on almost every aspect of operational police work. Some Chief Constables I never met at all. Mike Craik was the only Chief Constable who occasionally attended self-defence training sessions, mainly if he was about to go on the streets carrying his Personal Protective Equipment – as such he realised he needed his official CS, Baton and Limb Restraint authorisation, so he attended training. During Mr Craik's years Northumbria had a most tragic incident whereby a much respected constable called Joe Carroll was involved in the arrest of an offender in rural Northumberland. Once arrested, the detainee, who was noticeably under the influence of alcohol, was handcuffed and placed in the rear of a police car for transportation to Etal Lane police station some miles away from the incident. As the police car travelled along the A69 the detainee reached through between the front seats of the vehicle and in an agitated state pulled on the hand brake, resulting in the vehicle crashing and with it Joe's tragic death. As a result of this tragedy steps were taken by the Chief to put into place preventative measures to ensure as far as was reasonably possible such an incident would never occur again; it is worth mentioning that we always complied with National guidelines in Northumbria – the new measures were additional. Many discussions took place between myself and other appropriate personnel before I was given a directive to advise all operational cops and staff on our newly formed policies and procedures. In order to once again train the entire force (a huge undertaking), with my staff and the assistance of Technical Design we formulated training videos for viewing of best practice, before training in the physical techniques and actions and finally we designed a written test to affirm understanding of the subject.

As from 2006 a full time self-defence team had been recruited, and over several months I trained and equipped the team to cover all aspects of personal safety, within my role as Senior Self-Defence Trainer. During the next six years or so we self-produced many DVDs as training aids, some of which lasted 30 minutes and longer, with me and my team acting out all the character roles. On completion, these videos would be viewed by thousands of cops and staff. I was very much proud of all this footage, simply because I'd start with just an idea and a blank sheet of paper, and with no outside help (apart from Technical Design who were always helpful) I'd write all the script before directing all the varied actions. These had to be 'spot on', primarily because everything on the footage could be used as evidence in both internal and external enquiries regarding the training officers had received. These were all self-generated projects, we didn't have to do them, we could have simply trained by referring to the National Manual of Guidance, but we did the additional material simply to further enhance the quality of the training we delivered in Northumbria Police. Another self-made initiative I undertook was to author two books on behalf of the Sports and Social Club, and the Training Unit, *A Guide to Health and Fitness and a Guide to Personal Safety Training*. Many hours were spent in my own time writing these at home, with Robbie Burns providing humorous caricatures to accompany the text. Thousands were printed and presumably many will still be in circulation around the force, all designed to help and assist my colleagues.

In line with the above, I was continually required to work with Professional Standards Department (PSD) and assist in inquiries relating to the actions of police officers and staff during operational duties. The format would run along the lines of: A complaint would be registered with PSD, who would then analyse the actions and the nature of the complaint, and because I was responsible for the training I would be quizzed in order to identify whether the individual/s had complied with training they had received, and if not then assess their behaviour from other angles. The law of the land is not prescriptive as such, but it is advantageous if officers had been seen to act reasonably and their actions were deemed to be in line with training they had received. I did find some of these investigations, from a personal perspective, very difficult. Coroner's Court investigations being one of the most difficult of inquests. Despite the obvious tragedy of a death in police custody, the nature of these investigations were particularly stressful for all concerned. I knew many of the officers involved in the various investigations, yet from the professional side clearly I had to divorce myself from any inclination to act on their behalf and as such be seen to be totally impartial. The worst cases for me were when officers' actual jobs may well have been in jeopardy, and my own evidence, written and verbal, may have been one of the deciding factors in the final outcome. I hope this doesn't sound patronising but police officers are first and foremost human beings and the uniform changes little in that regard. A lot of actions are instinctive, and with instinctive behaviour we don't actually engage the brain particularly in situations deemed to be imminently dangerous, more so when their person is under threat. Police officers and other uniformed staff often get 'frightened' during certain incidents (although many may deny it) and all the training in the world will have little effect when severe threatening behaviour occurs, survival may become the instinctive issue. Being frightened and acknowledging it, is a sound defensive issue that courts and investigating officers should take into consideration. Clearly this is not a 'training manual' so I'll leave it there except to say that physiological changes that result from fear are many, and rationale also disappears very quickly. Changes which occur may well be instantaneous and will limit or inhibit responses. So, questions relating to 'so why didn't you do that, or this, or the other?' are often elusive to the officer at that time; certainly give someone something better at that time than what they've got, then common sense dictates they would take it – wouldn't they? So why didn't they then? I'll leave it there but in this very concise paragraph you can see my job had many variables and complexities!

I have always taken it as a tribute that there had been an almost total lack of interference from Senior Officers or Line Managers within the realms of my occupational roles. I took that as a compliment as to how well my duties and the training of officers and staff had been conducted. Clearly there were few concerns; otherwise they'd never have been away.

I had also received Judges' written compliments for the evidence I had given at court, finding my evidence **'deeply impressive'**! Before I left my job I also was presented with a certificate from the Head of Professional Standards, a Detective Chief Superintendent, for my **'professionalism and assistance over many years in the**

investigation of crime and misconduct'. Nice to be appreciated!

In my last three or four years with Northumbria Police there were many changes within the organisation and many of us struggled to see the rationale behind much of the change. Because of a lack of finance, I struggled to get the most basic of training equipment, while at the same time new occupational roles were being created seemingly left, right, and centre, often with the attachment of quite hefty wage packets. New job titles were invented without real explanations as to their intended functions. I well remember a brief chat with one 'fortunate' employee whose wage along with the new title had just gone up four grades, and when I asked how the person was coping with the complexities of the new role, I was told that the most difficult part of the day was wondering what to wear having got out of bed in the morning before heading off to work! I seemed to be attending several additional meetings on a regular basis for no apparent reason and the vast majority of the attendees would walk away muttering 'what the hell was that all about?'. Of course with the new positions came a need to justify the new roles, so even more meetings were forthcoming; one meeting seemed to result in another meeting, the crux of all these being that additional work would then materialise for us team leaders before being handed down to the rest of our already struggling teams. In hindsight I was very fortunate with my training team – I had a big say in who we recruited as I was on the interview panel. I was responsible for their initial and ongoing training and day to day welfare, and I still see Kim, Damian, and Dave socially, we remain firm friends, often laughing about certain 'things' which happened during my watch, so to speak! Other notable friends, and I have many, were and are Bill Manderville, Ian Miller, Taff Bailey, Robbo, Dave Little, Kevin Bray, Alan Pearson, Helen Gregory, Jane Stabler, Az, Sati, Monica, Darryl White, Steve Blackwell, Geoff Nainby, Ann Bell, Linda Pringle, Pauline Graham and George Storey. We laughed as much as we talked, which says it all really!

The 'blip'!

I have mentioned previously that 99.9% of my job and indeed career with Northumbria had been great, but the 0.1% (which occurred after 21 years of service) I refer to had left a very sour taste in my mouth and even now almost seven years later still rankles somewhat.

For reasons which beggared belief, *the fitness testing procedures* for new recruits and those in their probationary periods had been gradually reduced to a pitiful nonsensical gesture, with no credence whatsoever apart from the end product which enabled the all-important tick in a box. Comparing the content of the fitness tests we'd had for many years with the complete drivel we ended up with in my last three or four years was nothing short of shameful! What was even more shameful was the ever growing numbers of applicants and recruits entering the force who had quite serious difficulties passing them. It bothered me big style that people were coming into the force and judging by their obvious lack of physical fitness, would be unable to perform certain active policing duties at the 'start' of a 30 year career let alone mid-way through. As the person supervising the tests I felt a professional obligation to inform the powers-that-be of the current levels of physical fitness, rather than have them at a later date perhaps state that they were unaware of the falling standards primarily because no one had told them; additionally, the latter was officially written into my job specification, i.e. *to keep management informed of trends and developing situations!*

The tests I refer to required the individual (in clothing and footwear of their choice, and indoors) to jog at a 'very' gradually increasing pace, beginning at walking pace, between two lines 15 metres apart for a period not exceeding 3 minutes and 25 seconds. Then to identify a degree of upper body strength perhaps required to apprehend a non-compliant offender, or to carry a shield, they would then push a bar one way before pulling it back the other way, all done, before a 'congratulations you've passed', and as mentioned this is at the 'start' of a 30 year career.

Despite my protestations about the inadequacies of the test I found there was absolutely no interest whatsoever. Yet there was massive interest in 'reducing absenteeism', work that out! I wrote several reports, but didn't receive replies. I knocked on doors and verbally expressed my concerns, all to no avail. As mentioned previously I was immensely proud to belong to Northumbria, I only ever wanted it to be the best police force in the country, and when I felt strongly about something I expressed my views, but only with the intentions of improving or maintaining the standards the force had had for many years. Increasingly following meetings I was told quite vociferously that *'my comments were unhelpful'*, accompanied by *'it's a good job that ---- wasn't there'*. Nevertheless, I always felt comfortable speaking out primarily because I was only telling the truth regardless of how unpalatable that was. Certainly I got absolutely no pleasure from extolling the negatives.

With the above background I attended yet another meeting on 22nd May 2009, in the Bailey Hall, Police HQ. To cut a long story very short, we were given an update in relation to our performance and were continually told how well the organisation was doing and how we were meeting all our targets etc. At the end of the ACC's input he said words to the effect of *'I have gone over slightly but we still have some time left for you to voice your own opinions, or ask any questions'*! There were no takers and a somewhat uncomfortable silence reigned. *'What, nobody got anything to say?'* prompted the Chair.

This is pertinent so I'll mention it. I would estimate that the vast majority of the people in the hall on this occasion were female employees; I was myself the only male on a table with at least another seven or eight very pleasant female colleagues, some I knew personally and others were strangers so to speak. I mention this purely as an attempt to paint a picture, whilst trying to seek a logical reason for the hostility that would soon be thrown my way, apart perhaps from the fact that I was a male with the audacity to criticize female physical performances – having spoken out several times about the futility of the testing procedures and how the operational effectiveness of the force would be in jeopardy should we continue to recruit along the current pathways.

When outlining the considerable improvements the force had made over the preceding weeks, the ACC was particularly vocal in celebrating recruitment of so many more female officers. I have mentioned before how absurd the physical fitness tests were, and how many were struggling to attain even the bare minimum – well the vast majority of those 'recruits' who were so obviously labouring badly to achieve even the most minimal of standards were female applicants. Many were woeful – fact! For the most part, males performed satisfactorily – fact! Result sheets were the proof if needed. Many of the girls found running slowly for a little over three minutes extremely taxing. Their recovery rates were often shocking. And perhaps above all it was obvious that few had taken any time to prepare themselves for the tests.

As I sat there quietly listening to all the accolades being given and being so apparently well received by the floor, I couldn't help but silently reflect on how atrocious the standards were, whilst wondering whether the Chair and other members of the Senior Management Team had any idea about the probable repercussions of employing people whose physical fitness standards were so dire at such an early stage in their career. None of the people 'up front' had ever viewed the testing procedures, most had never even entered the gymnasium, yet clearly the assumption must have been that we were doing exceedingly well simply because we were meeting the guidelines in terms of gender numbers arriving to take up the position of police constable.

Prompted once again by the chair to encourage something in terms of verbal feedback from the floor, and with no other takers, instinctively I found myself standing up and giving a personal introduction as to who I was and my position within the force, deemed necessary I thought as there were so many new employees present whom I'd never met. Once done, I referred to the recent statistic that had been displayed during the presentation and the verbal explanation which accompanied it, notably that 'we had succeeded in recruiting so many more female officers'. Although as far as I was aware females had always had the same opportunities to enrol as male applicants. I hadn't prepared anything for my very brief impromptu input simply because I had no intention of speaking; frankly I'd never even thought about it. No turning back, I proceeded to inform all those present how totally inappropriate *from the physical perspective* many of those newly recruited female officers were, and how if we continued to recruit such a high proportion of the same physical quality that we had been doing then the force would struggle to perform some types of operational police work, such as public order issues requiring officers to run around in boots (not lightweight trainers as per the test), often for long periods while carrying PPE including shields while wearing helmets etc and in all climatic conditions. The latter scenarios of course were just about to happen in several of our major cities as mobs went on the rampage, looting and pillaging, while setting fire to buildings etc. And officers being relied upon to run around for extended periods attempting to control and arrest offenders. Well I'll tell you now there were large numbers of officers (yes I'm sorry but mainly female) we were recruiting at this time that were incapable 'at the start of their new careers' who would be unable to perform these tasks, so then what?

Of course no one in the hall wanted to hear what I had just said (as daft as it must sound, I didn't even want to hear it), especially as the element I was referring to was so much the opposite of what we had just been told, nevertheless it was the truth. I got solace from telling the truth to the police force and that couldn't be wrong – could it?

I could have stood up and said the opposite and congratulated all the Senior Management Team (SMT) on their recent successes particularly that the recruitment of so many physically fit female officers was so welcome. BUT I would have been lying! And this is the police force which should thrive on honesty, even if the issues raised were somewhat unpalatable!

You must remember that I had tried other methods of highlighting my concerns such as several reports with pertinent statistics attached, and verbal warnings but to no avail, so this was an unplanned final attempt to at least have some say – *'hey if he feels this strongly, perhaps we had better have a look at it, after all he's been here for 22 years and this is the first time he's done this – maybe, just maybe he may have a point, I mean what do we know, none of us have even watched a fitness test, let alone analysed one, mmm!'*

The opposite happened, I became almost a verbal punch bag as abuse was hurled my way, and I was immediately labelled a 'sexist', because I had the gall to mention females rather perhaps include males in my criticism. **To put the record straight, I had only been referring to recent female 'recruits', not the female gender as a whole, because the latter would have been sexist and I most certainly could never be referred to as a sexist!** I was shouted at from one or two women across the hall, one of whom I had been friends with for years. The woman sitting next to me who I had had a pleasant conversation a short while ago just prior to the meeting, looked up at me and said, quote: 'I have a friend who's just joined, she will be well enamoured at what you've just said'. I looked at her and said, 'Is she fit?' Somewhat surprised she replied, 'Presumably so, she's in,' to which I replied, 'Well I'm not referring to her then'! What I meant was that there were obviously some coming through who were fit and physically able to do all aspects of their operational roles. I'll say it again; I was only highlighting the ever growing number who had pretty shocking levels of fitness.

All the SMT at the front looked at each other in disbelief, while rolling their eyes skyward. The scene was reminiscent of a Charles Dickens storyline where Oliver Twist dares to ask for more – 'more'!!! Can you believe what he's just said? My good god, he criticised female recruits, he must be a sexist! Although I'm guessing, the chair no doubt said before too long who the hell is he? Followed by I want him spoken to, and harshly, we can't tolerate such outlandish criticism!

Well, once the meeting was finished I got up and left with all the others. I immediately received some very welcome support from both males and females, and was ignored by others, but there is little doubt that over lunch in the admin blocks there would be some interesting if not harsh banter. I was told a short while later a couple of 'complaints' had been received – but not 'written' by all accounts. The complaints were presumably fortuitous for the SMT as they would now have to be followed up.

With it now being lunchtime I did what I always did and had a work-out. Afterwards, returning to the gym office I was confronted by two of my staff, who, whilst grinning asked what the hell I had been up to, as there had been a couple of urgent phone calls for me to contact the Chief Inspector as a matter of urgency. I opened my emails and there were another similar couple of messages.

I walked down to the admin block, knocked on the door of the Chief Inspector's office which was open, and was greeted with a smile and a whispered 'what came over you' before being ushered inside and closing the door behind me. I sat down and replied along the lines of I didn't understand what all the fuss was about, I simply told the truth about a certain group of people who would cause the force problems if we didn't recognise the issue and do something to rectify it! 'Mike, you came across as a right sexist!' 'What, for telling the truth?' I said. Silence ensued, as we looked at each other!!! Before she then said, 'There are a lot of unhappy people out there (in admin!), not to mention the SMT and god forbid if Mrs – had been there? An apology, Mike, would go some way to putting it right!' 'Not a chance,' said I, 'apologise for what exactly?' 'Well, if you are adamant, then this is unlikely to go away!' said the Chief Inspector. Clearly at a stalemate, with her agreement, I got up and left, awaiting the next step!

A short while later, I got a call from my Inspector asking me to come and see him!

I walked down to admin once again. 'Come on in, mate,' said the Inspector, followed by 'we've got a problem, Mike, we've had a couple of complaints about what you've said.' As mentioned previously the complaints apparently were from Administration staff, employees who had never seen a fitness test, and never seen results either past or present, so the complaints could only ever be about my use of the term 'female' recruits. There was no malice from the Inspector as, difficult as it was for him, he appeared at least sympathetic. He had recently attended the gym at my request and viewed the fitness tests and the resulting end product of what we were about to accept, which had now become the norm in terms of not just the overall results but possibly even worse the lack of effort given.

Clearly the Inspector was doing what he was told – 'have a word with him, get him to see the error of his ways, issue an apology and maybe we can cautiously move on' etc.

I wouldn't apologise, I'd done nothing wrong, and there were no untruths! I left 45 minutes later, feeling slightly sorry for the Inspector; stuck in the middle, this wasn't easy for him.

Returning to the gym I was met by one of my long term 'friends' who had shouted the abuse across the room, before getting the briefest of hugs and although now smiling commented, 'Mike, if there is an issue with the tests, what you should have said was that 'all' the recruits – 'males' and females had problems with the tests, not just the females!' 'No,' said I, 'currently the males are ok, the females are not, I'm not prepared to lie in order to make people who know nothing about the issue feel good!'

Two staff members who were in the office at the time and had seen the tests on many occasions, turned around and said to my friend, 'You really should see what he's on about.'

Before I left for the long bank holiday weekend break, I had yet another email telling me now that the Head of Training wanted to see me at 4pm on the Tuesday when we returned.

Over the Bank Holiday weekend I rode 200 plus miles on my bike, driven by sheer frustration!

As directed, on the 31st at 4 pm, as a 58 year old, feeling like a five year old, and even if I say so myself, the most loyal of staff members without a blemish on my record, and with 20 plus years of service and not a single day off sick, I stood outside the door of the Head of Training (who turned up 20 minutes late) waiting patiently, as other staff members went by, smiling genuinely while uttering positive comments.

I had a brief chat with the Boss, who in the nicest way told me to be careful in the future with ill-advised comments, job done we amicably shook hands, I left and went home.

All of that because I had the nerve to tell my force some home truths, that many female recruits (by no means all) currently entering the force had woeful levels of fitness – how dare I?

It is worth mentioning that, nationally, there were countless uniformed personnel who fully agreed with my sentiments regarding the fitness tests; I was in no way alone. Every now and again an article would appear in the National press whereby a journalist would write an article on the subject, then volunteer to participate in a formal test before passing with flying colours and without any preparation – enough said!

Would I do it again? Nope, I achieved absolutely nothing, no one listened apart from those who could hear nothing other than imagined sexist derogatory comments; worse again, no one cared, and for the first time in my working life I got a boat load of grief, and I'm still occasionally mad about it all! Everything seemed to revolve around the couple of verbal complaints; no one was apparently interested one iota in the issues that I'd raised. No one came to see me about the very real problem that I'd identified, no one had a look at the results, and no one came to observe the tests, there were no discussions, absolutely nothing! The whole saga seemed to revolve around nothing except the two complaints from, well – who knows? In hindsight, the whole thing was like a Monty Python script!

Mid December, headline news on both leading television channels, had the woman who was Chief Medical Officer describing that 'female obesity was a bigger threat to the country than ISIL'! I can't help but wonder what would have happened to me, had 'I' (as a male) dared to utter such a comment while working for the police!

But a short while later at the Northumbria Police Annual Awards at the Civic Centre in Newcastle, I got **'The Outstanding Contribution Award'** and a standing ovation – funny old world eh?

Putting it to bed!

This is my life story, to date at least, and if I don't tell the truth as I see it, or if I somehow self-censor myself and only talk pleasantries regardless of what I believe, there can be little point to it at all. I mention this because I got absolutely no pleasure from the last chapter; in fact several times I've even thought about deleting it, it's left a sour taste in my mouth. I mean why tarnish 24 years with this one unfortunate incident? I would love to be able to go back to the 22nd May 2009 and be a fly on the wall and observe it all again but impartially as a bystander. Maybe it was me? And maybe I could have said my bit in another way? Maybe if I'd said it was the 'males' who had a fitness problem it would have been so much more acceptable to the females present. As it was, telling the truth resulted in me being the target of so much unnecessary ridiculous aggression and most of it from people who because of their non-involvement in the subject hadn't got a clue about what I was referring to!

The last couple of years for me with the police were, em? Uncomfortable. For the first time I wasn't really enjoying my job, but perhaps I was never meant to really enjoy my work? Maybe I just got lucky for over twenty years, in which case I have a lot to be grateful for. Amongst all the many wonderful people I knew and worked with, good friends then and now, and colleagues who were a delight to work alongside, there was a much smaller group of people often with 'authority' who I felt were weak, with few leadership skills and were hiding behind an invisible cloak or curtain which, due to their occupational status, protected them from analysis, and I didn't trust them. I figured several were there purely as a career move, and as soon as there was more money elsewhere they'd leave at the drop of a hat. I felt they had little regard for staff, and staff were there simply to do as they were told, as such not permitted an opinion, and if they didn't conform, well so be it, there were always others who could replace them. I would reiterate, many training staff at HQ had real pride in their work, they wanted the best for the organisation, and as such clearly had quite legitimate views. With some figures of authority their jobs, I felt, were too much for them, and perhaps made that way by others another step or two up the leadership ladder, therefore so much pressure to achieve the aims and objectives as dictated to them. I have consciously left the word 'bullying' out because it is open to so much interpretation. Many people where I was working seemed to spend their lives whispering scathingly in the shadows; either unwilling or too frightened to express an opinion in case they were labelled as 'trouble'! Uniformed staff in particular could and had been in the past moved at the drop of a hat, having fallen out of favour for various reasons, and to be fair it was safer and certainly easier to smile pleasantly while nodding approval regardless of personal thoughts, and say nothing, but then continue nevertheless to whisper their discontent in safer confines!

The learning curve for me, although it came very late in the day, was that popularity is very fickle; people will change like the wind if it serves them better. But at the end of the day, the person who nails their colours to the mast so to speak and openly supports you because they earnestly believe it's the right thing to do, are worth ten of the others! I honestly thought at one point that I was about to be suspended pending perhaps an allegation of sexism 'which wouldn't be tolerated!'. I even suggested this to Jennifer, who bless her said 'well so be it' with a 'trust you' thrown in for good measure as she finished her coffee! All this though has led me to a much greater respect for the so called 'whistle blowers' who are persecuted, silenced and even booted out for daring to tell what amounts to the truth.

Retirement from work!

Sometime in early 2011, there were moves afoot in Northumbria police to promote Voluntary Redundancies in an attempt to save x amounts of money. It wasn't Northumbria Police's fault, and they were simply adjusting to the financial restrictions being placed on the organisation by the government. Prior to this I had never given early retirement a thought; it's the sort of thing that always seemed to happen to others. As mentioned previously I had never been unemployed and had taken it for granted that I would work till 65 and who knows maybe even beyond. However I was quietly told by 'a source' that the 'grade' I was on was likely to be phased out and discontinued; as such perhaps my longevity in post was also limited, and maybe I would be well advised to at least look into the proposed 'Voluntary Redundancy Scheme' and leave my options open. I made a phone call, received the info, then set about assessing the financial implications with Jennifer. Having had 24 years with the force plus another 10 years in local government the payoff was better than I thought it might be. As well as the 'lump sum' I would receive, I would also be entitled to a monthly pension straight away. It was also pointed out that the 'offer' may not linger too long. As I understood it, the following year offers may well be reduced, and who knows with the future as uncertain as it appeared to be, I, along with my grade may well be forced out anyhow without the current enhancement! I also began to realise that despite my loyal service, and almost unique expertise due to time in post, I was simply 'another' expendable commodity. We decided to go for it, and on the 28th February my completed forms went in. I requested that I would prefer to leave on my 60th birthday in about four or five months' time. That timescale also suited the force and would allow them sufficient time to make adjustments in my absence. After almost a quarter of a century with the force, I think it fair to say I had almost become part of the furnishings. Indeed I had been with some officers right through from their probation and early years and up through their promotions, progressing to Chief Superintendents, and as expressed by one in an email, I had always been one of the 'constants' in his career. Certainly one of the beauties of being a civilian was that I had always been on first name terms with all my uniformed colleagues regardless of rank, except Command Block who out of respect I always referred to as Sir or Ma'am.

Many of my friends and colleagues were genuinely shocked when I said I was on my way out, some even saying 'I bet you don't go' and they meant it! Presumably there were others who truly couldn't have cared less. But as the record shows I did go, and on hindsight and despite some reoccurring reservations at the time, I have had no regrets. I miss the daily social side of work, the 'good mornings, how's it going'? I miss the 'crack', the occasional but ever diminishing humour. I miss the work, how many could say that and mean it? (Such a lot of it was my hobby and a personal interest anyhow.) But I have to say, I don't miss one little bit the political sensitivity that became so ever prevalent, and the repeated references that I seemed to make every day, such as my continual 'no offence' comments following the expression of a view in case I had unintentionally 'upset' someone!! I don't miss the growing army of politically correct professor types (no offence to professors – see what I mean?) waiting around every corner ready to snipe at every opportunity in response to some unintentional upsetting remark!

I was allowed to put out a force-wide email to say a personal heartfelt goodbye, and at the same time to express my sincere gratitude to the thousands who had made my job so perfect for 20 plus years; it wasn't slaver, I genuinely meant it. I had formed great friendships and been privileged to work alongside so many highly professional people, cops and staff, who had been a joy to work with. Enough said. In my last week or so I had received so many emails, I barely had time to read them all let alone answer them.

I have never in my life had a personal birthday party, engagement party, or personal leaving 'do'. However on the 9th August that changed and at the police club in Newcastle I had a super farewell evening. I had asked Andy Nevison if his band would play for me; I got an immediate 'yes of course' and they refused to accept a fee. In the lead up I remember how concerned I had been just wondering whether anybody would turn up; however, there were loads and I was afforded an excellent send off!

Two days later, I was a former employee of Northumbria Police!

I am looking through my 2011 diary as I write the above and my training is as relentless as ever; additionally I had started swimming again before work. The examples below are taken at random:

29ᵗʰ March am 45 minutes front crawl, dinner time intervals on the bike, pm 30mins run on grass.

4ᵗʰ April; 7.00am swim at Ponteland 100 lengths front crawl, dinner time 30 minutes Motion Bike session, pm Bike1hr 44m 25s hard effort.

15ᵗʰ May am swim 140 lengths front crawl, pm bike flat out 1hr 38m 19s PB on this course.

And so it goes on 'as usual'!

It seems in 2011 I continued to race on the bike throughout the year but not as consistently as in previous years, I had several top 5 placings but noticeably I can't find a win. Maybe now in my **60th year and with 56 years as an athlete** I am beginning to encounter some physical limitations, surely not!! – more likely though, I just needed to train harder! A highlight of the year, however, was travelling down to Hull with Keith Davison (a good friend and quality cyclist for many years) and **at 61 years of age I rode 10 miles in 20mins 25sec, and a short while later a 25mile Time Trial in 54m 35s.**

Racing the bus again (58 years since the last one!)

Around about 2013, quite mysteriously, an amusing tale about me kept materialising from fairly unlikely sources. For example, while sitting in Helen Batson's house (the sister of my good friend Ossie) Helen said words to the effect of *'eeh, we laughed when we heard about you racing the bus'!* How the details of this scenario Helen was referring to had got around I really don't know (a short while later I was also approached about the same incident at the cricket club, and even my sister-in-law Sybil had commented on it); however, the likelihood is that the detail of this very brief calamitous affair came from someone actually on the bus and watching the incident unfold at the time.

When I reached my 60th birthday in 2011 I was entitled to receive my 'old person's bus pass' (a proud moment, and the first thing I ever got for nowt). Although I don't use it a great deal, one morning just before 9am I was waiting for a bus to Morpeth with my 'card' in hand and when the bus pulled up I got on and duly placed my card on the appropriate place. At which point the driver looked up and said, 'You're too early, mate, you can't use the card before 9 o'clock!' Looking at my watch it was at this point around 8.53am. A little naively perhaps, I looked at the guy and said, 'So *what do I do?'* He replied, *'Well, you either pay the fare or you wait for the next one'* (an hour later). Thinking very quickly (for me at least) I said, *'Tell you what, I'll leg it up to the next stop and meet you there!'* Thinking that by the time I'd get to the next stop it would be 9 o'clock. Anyhow, without further ado, I quickly exited the bus and in my best brogues (I have a passion for quality brogues) I sprinted the 300 yards or so, up over the train crossing and on up the incline arriving at the stop at the same time as the bus. I waited in the small queue, got on the bus and once again placed the card on the appropriate spot. *'Sorry, mate, it's only 8.58 and I can't wait!'* said the driver. No time to debate the issue I once again 'fled' from the bus like it was on fire and sprinted up the footpath for another 200yds or so looking over my shoulder once or twice as I tried to out sprint the tired old bus and the bemused driver. Once again I just made the stop as the bus pulled up. I climbed up the steps to be met by the driver shaking his disbelieving head and repeated my now well-rehearsed procedure placing my 'old person's' bus pass onto the machine! Yip, this time it was precisely 9 o'clock and it was all above board. As I turned to find my well-earned 'old person's' seat I was met by several smiling (or smirking) faces, and the driver was heard to mumble, *'pensioner, my arse'* or words to that effect! Good job it was 9 o'clock though – the next stop was over a mile away at Ulgham and three quarters of a mile into this next potential sprint there is a fairly steep hill!!!

Strange how things sometimes go full circle so to speak. If you've read the early parts of this you may recall that as a six year old, 58 years ago, I used to race yet another bus up a one mile incline after Sunday School at Widdrington Village, to save my bus fare. As the saying goes, a leopard doesn't change its spots, although it may well get a wee bit slower!!!

Return to triathlon (at 62) and park runs!

Triathlon is still in my blood – for me it is an event that is the optimum of physical fitness, and with the latter view, the sport appeals to me more than any other. The nature of the event dictates this view. I also believe earnestly that there are no losers in triathlon – to complete an event is commendable and worthy of a place on any amateur's sporting CV. Also despite some people's views, it is not just for the super fit (depending on how you categorise the term 'super fit'), there are few stipulations except that clearly you've got to be physically fit, have some mettle in your psyche, own a bike and you must be able to swim!

Whilst racing on the bike over the preceding 12 years or so, from the age of 50, I think it fair to say I became known locally as a fairly 'classy' cyclist; I had won loads of bike races and in all sorts of conditions. My successes in triathlon (which were far greater than any of those on the bike), it seemed, were long forgotten, in all the circles I moved in, my triathlon years were never mentioned, my running days even less so. Queuing to pay for my entry fee into the Wednesday night Barnesbury '10's, I would occasionally be privy to the conversations of cyclists and triathletes standing around me, talking about how their triathlon training was going, all apparently unaware that the old fella standing next to them had been the best triathlete in the country at some point, with a multitude of wins and at the top of the tree for an extended period of time. I would finish well in front of the triathletes in these bike races even though I was giving them 30 or 40 years. It all got me wondering about the sport again. I would occasionally buy a triathlon magazine when out and about and browse through the colourful pages. Triathlon had always been a colourful sport, but now there was so much eye catching gloss, with cover to cover adverts tempting us all with miraculous equipment that was sure to make the difference and transport you into another realm. Then there was the 'oh so' repetitive headlines regarding *'how to shave minutes off your time'!* And it seemed such a lot of that promise revolved around sleek, top of the range equipment, as opposed to increased physical workload.

In 2013, 30 years after the first National Championships, there had been an article in 220 triathlon magazine designed I think to celebrate the 30 year anniversary of the 1983 event. I'd placed 2nd in that event and my views along with one or two others were sought in relation to that day's competition. It was probably the article that got me thinking about the sport again some 20 years since 'retiring' from it. I knew that I was still very fit, always have been, but began to wonder about how I would figure in today's triathlon competitions.

Where exactly it came from I really don't know, except that at some point fairly early in 2014 whilst rapidly approaching 63 years of age, for no other reason other than to see how the sport may have changed, and how an 'old has been' would fair, I went for a swim. I never mentioned it to anyone, just dug out my swimming trunks and went to Amble baths. Amazed that after such a lengthy lay off, I was immediately swimming for 45 minutes front crawl, barely out of breath and certainly void of any upper body fatigue. Furthermore, my cycling was excellent and especially if I wanted to call myself a triathlete again. I pondered whether to enter an event; there were several locally to choose from. With nothing to lose, I decided to go for it. Logically the nearest event seemed the ideal choice; as such I decided to enter the Northumberland Triathlon on 8th June, the superb venue being only four miles from home.

On the 6th January 2014 I bought a pair of running shoes from Start Fitness in Newcastle and on the 8th I went down to the beach at Druridge Bay and whilst I could no doubt have ran non-stop for a while, I purposefully interspersed the running with fast walking for 39 minutes. On the 11th I did another 32minute jog, tentatively, and on the 13th I was up to 45 minutes but 'slowly'. **At the end of this first week's triathlon training, I have recorded: 2x swims, 5 x cycle and**

3 x jogs plus 3 x weight training sessions and several lengthy walks with my son's dog, Misty! All pretty encouraging really following a 20 year absence.

On the 22nd January I was brought back down to earth, as during a 20 minute jog on the beach I somehow, despite running very slowly, damaged my left calf and was forced to limp back to my car. Despite the calf pain while jogging and even walking at this point it appears looking at my diary that cycling was fine and clearly there was no interference with the swimming I was doing.

Little did I know that for the next 18 months I would encounter running related injuries almost every week! Both calves, left Achilles, left shin, right foot, both groins, glutes, lower back, even occasional knee twinges; the extent of these injuries was unbelievable, and oh so frustrating primarily because my cardio was clearly superb. The beauty of triathlon training is that you are seldom laid up totally, and regardless of the running problems, I continued to cycle daily and swim regularly without ill effects, except that my lower back would give me reminders now and again that all was not well in that area. I got totally fed up with the continuous repetitive remarks from local people especially first thing in the morning as I walked the dog. **'By whatever you've got, it looks sore!'** As I limped along while trying my utmost to appear as casual as possible while grimacing (off camera so to speak) like I was being kicked in the knackers every five metres!

It's been strange in my life really, whenever I've had something that troubled me, something else would come along to either give hope or even rectify the problem. My mother used to say quite regularly 'something will turn up, son'! And 'what will be, will be'! And so once again a chance and fortuitous meeting with a guy would bring relief and optimism.

Two of my best mates in terms of triathlon went back 25 or so years; I had occasionally trained with and even travelled with two local athletes called John Willis and Alan Davison. I loved their company and I found their presence particularly at 'big' events somehow comforting. The Geordie banter used to help me relax, especially when away from home and surrounded by hundreds of competitors from all over the UK. Anyhow after years apart when our paths had seldom crossed, we met again at a time trial event. The two of them were also dabbling in triathlon; as such we decided to swim together in a local lake. On one of these occasions I was fortuitously introduced to another triathlete called Gary Hall. I say fortuitously because Gary was a chiropractor and had his own business! Oh what joy, Gary is a super guy, honest and genuine. As you can imagine with the niceties over, our conversation quickly turned to injuries and how I was struggling so badly. Gary immediately said, *'Come and see me, Mike, I'll put you right!'* The certainty regarding the 'I'll put you right' statement that came with the invite was comforting to say the least. Gary's almost throw away comment could be referred to as a *'self-fulfilling prophecy'* which I would use and advocate as a 'tactic' when conducting Conflict Management training. The very strong theory is that, if you tell someone something often enough, and with a degree of enthusiasm and certainty, you can begin to instil that belief within them. In other words if you want to get on well with someone, tell them what they want to hear, but make sure the accompanying non-verbal body language that accompanies the statement is congruent, on the basis that the visual side of communication is often much more honest than the spoken word! An *honest held belief* is crucial in relation to the successful outcome of a situation. **As an athlete, you've got to believe in your capabilities as self-doubt is a formidable foe!**

I hastily arranged a meeting with Gary, we talked, he diagnosed, he advised, he gave treatment and we have become lifelong friends. I'd like to think that if nothing else I am especially honest. As you will recall from a previous chapter my honesty in the past has caused me problems. Gary made sound improvements especially in relation to my lower back problem, but I still struggle with other sports related injuries. I am beginning to accept, as hard as it is, that despite my abnormal level of physical fitness, I am aging, and with age come limitations. For two years now, ever since I started running again, I have carried a multitude of running related injuries. Not at all surprising if you consider the premise of this book is based on '60

years an athlete'! And the 60 years is up. My body has served me amazingly well, it's inconceivable the amount of physical work I've done, it is simply staggering and I am beginning to realise that there has to be a pay-back! My pay-back has just about arrived in terms of a worn out body; I hastily add the worn out body phrase is from the 'athletic' or 'athlete' perspective. Ordinarily, if this makes sense, I am still 'very' capable of most things physical.

Regarding Gary, what I find so uncomfortable is the fact that in his generosity he will not accept a fee. Once again I would remind anyone who has cared to read any of this – I have never ever received anything for nothing; all my life I've paid my way. With Gary his continuous invitations to *'get in touch as soon as you encounter a problem'* and his total reluctance to be paid (in his words, he would find it offensive) have created a dilemma for me, and I don't really know how to handle it. None of this of course is in any way derogatory in relation to Gary, I just feel like I am arriving for lunch and expecting someone else to pay for it, regardless of having an invite of course. I haven't explained the latter at all well, all I mean is I don't want to be seen as taking a loan of Gary's hospitality!

Back to training preparation for the 8th June; once again the examples below are taken at random:

February reads: 11 swim sessions (45mins/1hr each), 20 cycle sessions, run NIL! Injured!

March reads: swim 12 sessions, 22 cycle sessions, 'jog' 13 sessions (longest 30mins)

April reads: 15 swim sessions, 26 cycle sessions, 'jog' 4 sessions (still struggling with injuries)

May reads: 18 swim sessions, 26 cycle sessions, 'jog' 1 session (on 26th May)

A day's training on June 1st swim 50mins, cycle 2hrs, jog 22mins 'easy'

WEEK COMMENCING THE 2ND JUNE, I HAVE DECIDED WITH MY RUNNING BEING THE BEST PART OF NON-EXISTENT, TO GO TO THE TRIATHLON (as I've paid a £50 entry fee) WITH THE INTENTION OF DOING THE SWIM AND BIKE LEGS ONLY.

The content of a good proportion of my training particularly on the bike was quality intervals; I'd also had a couple of top 3 placings in time trials, but my running was very disappointing and as good as non-existent due to injuries.

8th June 2014 and my first triathlon for 20 years

As I was leaving the house Jennifer called after me, '*Are you taking these shoes?*' Purposefully I'd left them in the sitting room (with no intention of doing the run), but instinctively I grabbed them and flung them onto the back seat of the car. When I got to the park, I went through a routine that I last did when I was 43, the only difference now was that I was 63! I racked my 753 ancient steel bike, I laid out my 23 year old wetsuit (mercifully just about fitting into it) and at the last minute I decided to put out my running shoes thinking that I could at least 'start' the run, it being two laps, and I could quietly drop out after the first lap if I was in pain. At least I'd get two split times which would be interesting if nothing else.

The swim went ok (physically easy), the bike went well (I had the 3rd fastest bike split) and I even completed the run (whilst feeling slightly embarrassed about my pedestrian pace), like running on glass waiting to be cut. From 250 competitors I finished 20th. My transition times were laughable, totally amateur, couldn't get my wetsuit off, couldn't even get my helmet clipped on, 'why didn't my shoes fit?' leaving the transition area hoping no one knew who I was, while being convinced that when I returned there'd be masses around my transition zone **ready to have a good laugh 'at the old guy' who couldn't dress himself properly!**

The day was wonderful, the weather was perfect, the athletes were as warm as I remembered them to be years ago, my family turned up with my two year old grandson, Dan, and we both got our photos taken on the rostrum as I collected the old guy's trophy.

Reflecting on the event over the next 24 hours or so, I began to wonder how I would fare if I got my act together in transitions and more importantly if I could somehow combat my running related injuries. Nothing but optimism, yes I intended to stay with it awhile and see what materialised.

I had entered the Bamburgh Triathlon a few weeks earlier. But two weeks after the Northumberland triathlon, I rang the organisers to cancel my entry, because once again I had major running related problems. Surprisingly, the organisers knew who I was and kindly accepted my cancellation while expressing regret that I wouldn't make it. Going through my training diary, I find that despite a continuation of running related problems, I once again rang the organisers and after apologising profusely asked if they'd let me back in. They willingly agreed, and on the 26th July I finished the Bamburgh Triathlon in 32nd place from 338 finishers. The event was great once again and well organised but the bike leg, invariably my current strength, on this occasion left me totally frustrated – it was out and back on winding narrow roads, lots of bunching with so many on the road and coming and going in both directions, with little opportunity to make it count!

I also did an event on the 31st of August, the Newbiggin Triathlon and finished 35th from 340 finishers. The bike was three circuits and left me once again frustrated – there were just too many groups cycling for me to make any impression, and at one stage I got stuck behind a double decker bus housing a driver training course. But for the first time my running was becoming 'respectable'! I have written in my diary 'big improvement on previous runs, although as it should do, it hurt'!

Worthy of mention is that on the 20th September as training I did my first Park Run at Druridge Bay, finishing 6th overall in 19m 51s.

My running was at last on the up! I followed up the run with a bike session of 2hrs 10mins.

Finally on the 28th September I did the *Kendal triathlon* finishing 15th from 226 competitors, the most pleasing part being 7th quickest on the run, but I finished with a very sore groin, which was to cause me trouble for the next few weeks!

My first year back in triathlon competition after such a lengthy lay off? Encouraging!

My aim for next year would be to get into the top 10! And why not? In 2015 I'd be 64 and that would be '60 years since my first race'!

2015 and just another year of athleticism!

Having made my mind up to continue with triathlon (at least for a while) my training started all over again as from the 1st January. I trained on the bike in the morning and then got very drunk at the Cricket Club 'and elsewhere'!

What is noticeable looking over this year's diary is that as early as 4th January I was now running for 1hr 20mins although slowly and still running with a sore groin. For the most part I was already training twice a day whilst still taking 'our kid's' dog out for lengthy walks most days. As is usual with sporting injuries, the mornings were always worse, but you get used to them and continue anyhow. On the 24th January I did a 19m 46s park run, a PB, finishing 4th from 110 runners, followed by 2hrs 5mins on the bike. My weight was 10st 4lb and blood pressure 116/75, pulse at 42bpm.

On the 7th February I ran another PB with a 19m 39s, 4th from 126 runners. A week later another PB in 19m 21s. Commenting *'couldn't have tried harder, right calf very sore at the end'!*

What could be better? A proud Grandad, and yet another loft bound trophy

I always know when I'm training hard as at a glance there is just so much writing in the diary, and the first few months of 2015 the diary was congested. In February I was averaging four swim sessions, five cycling sessions, and four runs each week, despite constant discomfort

– mind over matter yet again!

On the 15th March I finished 4th in a Duathlon, just five seconds outside of a top 3 place.

Park runs!

Around about this time I remember nailing my colours to the mast so to speak, and told Gary Hall I was aiming for a sub 19 minute park run, a fairly tall order based on my 19m 30ish runs at this time, and how difficult I was finding these. The Druridge Bay run is in very pleasant surroundings, but it's on a twisty, slightly undulating little course on narrow paths, not really conducive to fast times. So the aim was a big ask for a 64 year old, still plagued by painful running related injuries, and especially with the runs taking place first thing in the morning on bitter cold winter days. The early starts with the often freezing temperatures made these 'workouts' particularly hard work for this aging athlete; in fact for me the pain I encountered in these absolutely flat out efforts was nothing short of excruciating, they hurt like hell from start to finish! I would get up at 6.30am for the 9am start, to give myself time to 'ease' into the day. I was generally the first to arrive at the park, at which point I'd stiffly (and embarrassingly) leave the car before walking for 20 minutes or so, then I'd jog a while, wincing as I went into the cold air, then following a bit of cautious stretching, I'd do some strides, before finally just trying to keep warm till the off. Even at this stage I'd be wondering whether to start, still feeling rough! But start I would (of course) and strangely once I was underway all the skeletal and muscular pain would disappear, only to be replaced by 19 minutes of quite severe oxygen debt, running right on the edge while trying to run as if my life depended on it! Once over the finishing line my breathing would ever so quickly (in a small handful of seconds) return back to normal, but now the pain would switch right back to where it all started at 6.30am, into my joints and my muscles. But I'd had 'my fix', and would return home listening to some loud raucous music, before having a couple of poached eggs and a cup of tea. Then take my bike out and do a couple of hours back out into the wind and cold of the East Northumberland countryside!

At the end of March I had a break in proceedings as we departed for a large family holiday in Tenerife. I swam daily and ran slowly every day, and had a great time in this our first family holiday with my two year old grandson – *little Dan! As I write I can't help but smile, the thought of him running around or watching Peppa Pig is so good. He is an absolute hive of physical activity, a blond haired, beautiful and oh so healthy little Geordie laddie, how we all love him, even when he's a little git! In the evening I sometimes look over at Jennifer and know instinctively she is looking at his photos on her mobile – her smile says it all!*

On the 18th April, I achieved my previously identified aim and dipped under 19 minutes running an 18m 57s park run! I was on my mobile to Gary within minutes, said nothing only wrote '18m 57s'! With this time I headed the 1000 named WAVA league – whatever that means? Perseverance and never say die! It wasn't the time; it was the 'journey' getting there! Running, after such a lengthy lay off was hammering me from all sorts of angles. Although I have numerous faults, I've never been a quitter.

As a precaution all my running has been on grass; however on the 24th April I damaged my right foot running, commenting in the diary 'can't put weight on my right foot'. Little did I know that this injury (just another one) would plague me right through to the QE 11 triathlon on the 18th July and beyond. I've still got remnants of it now on the 9th December although I continue to work out every day.

On the 27th April I swam 150 lengths in the morning, walked the dog for 45 mins and rode a lively three hours on the bike later in the day, then went to see Gary about my foot.

I did the Alnwick triathlon on 14th May finishing a disappointing 19th, but only six minutes behind the winner, clearly there was a lot of us very close together, but pleasingly I had the 7th fastest run on the day. Despite my problems I'd come a long, long way in running terms in a few desperate months. **In the afternoon I went to my allotment**

and put my main crop tetties in – *the family had to be fed, you see!!* Then went out in the evening with my mate Tom Maley to the Sour Grapes to watch a band on.

My main aim for the season, the Northumberland triathlon on 7th June!

Almost a year to the day since my return to triathlon, I returned once again for the Northumberland triathlon. A top 10 place was my aim; I was convinced that I could achieve that. I failed, finishing 15th from an entry of 262 competitors. Last year, after such a lengthy absence, I had been nothing other than an optimistic 'bikie' learning to swim and run again. However, this time a year on, and for the first time in 20 years, I could call myself a 'triathlete' once again. I had been in the top 15 times in all three disciplines, the swim, bike and the run. But once again frustratingly losing much time in the transitions.

On the day, there was a gale force wind which prevailed throughout the event. The wind, which resulted in a choppy and quite rough swim, also posed a lot of difficulties during the bike leg. The bike leg for me was a real disappointment; even at my age and with so much experience I made a real tactical error and decided regardless of the wind to use my disc and a deep section front wheel. As a result I spent the cycling leg fighting to simply stay on the bike; I was all over the place. But there are often 'swings and roundabouts' in triathlon events and on this occasion I went on to take three minutes off my run time of the previous year. A few in front of me were slower in terms of the three individual discipline times, but frustratingly on analysis I lost out once again in transitions. But of course I accept fully that transitions are all part of the race. I have a theory in relation to the transitions – sounds ludicrous but as you age, and of course I was now 64, your flexibility in terms of stooping, bending, twisting, standing up quickly, running quickly from a standing start all diminish. So things like bending over while trying desperately to remove your wetsuit or a simple act such as putting your shoes on is not as fluent as it had been many years ago. Perhaps subconsciously you also restrict yourself, and consequently slow down while performing these manoeuvres in an attempt not to pull a muscle or something similar. I'm probably painting a picture now of a geriatric, and of course I'm not – my performances will dispel that – but there are, for sure, limitations, and maybe as simple as transitions appear there are definitely issues for the older triathlete, which aren't readily apparent.

Anyhow, after a day or two of reflection, I was reasonably content. In hindsight, last year I was a cyclist learning to run and swim again (hence my 3rd fastest bike split); this year I had taken a minute off my swim time in a pretty rough and choppy lake, and three minutes off my run (my diary indicates that I only 'had an 'ok' run, and didn't feel great'), although due to the weather and the severe cross winds, I'd lost three minutes on the bike. Looking back on my cycling training leading up to the 2015 triathlon, my times in both training and competitions were comparable to the previous year, so a poor tactical decision in relation to my choice of equipment on the day had probably cost me dearly! But it has to be said, the latter is just me and there would be many others who had less than perfect races. In reality and in the course of a lifetime of racing, there are very few occasions when you have the perfect build up, training wise, and the perfect race! If you get to the race 'healthy', you must make the most of it!

On the 11th June I entered the QEII Triathlon to be held on the 18th July.

As usual I continued to train every day and at least twice a day. Some examples are outlined below.

On the 13th June, I ran a 19m 06s Park Run finishing 5th from 174 finishers, followed by a 2hrs 45mins 'lively' bike session.

On the 15th June, I took the dog out for an hour, followed by a 3 hour bike session in the morning, and ran for 1hr 5mins later in the day.

*On the 20th June I finished 2nd in the Park Run, **BUT finished with a very sore right foot/ankle**, 'can't put any weight on it'! Yet somehow* *went out on the bike in the afternoon and did 1hr 19ms flat out on tri bars, with the usual press-ups, dips and sit-ups on conclusion. The next day undaunted I did 2hrs 45mins on the bike and swam in the lake for 45mins with Alan and Gary quote 'felt good'! Also 'Foot feels ok whist seated on the bike, but slightly painful when out of the saddle'.*

25th June, Walk with Misty 1hr 15m, Bike 2hrs 25m, pm swim 39mins in QEII Lake.

29th June, slow jog Stobswood field 3miles in 30minutes!! Just pleased to get through it!

3rd July, I raced a 10mile time trial in 22m 24s, the next day I ran for 1hr 6mins averaging only 9m14s miles ('aware of right foot painful throughout') and pm swam in the lake for 45 mins including 10 x 100metre efforts.

6th July, only 12 days from the QEII event, I swam 55 mins in the lake including 10 x 100metre efforts and ran 7.35miles in an hour but with a 2 mile effort not flat out in 14 minutes noted 'right foot sore at the beginning getting better later'.

Crunch day just one week away from the QEII event – ran 45 mins very slowly HAD TO STOP foot and ankle became very sore!

On the 16th July only two days before the event, I went through to the QEII evening swim session to tell Barry Taylor, the organiser of the forthcoming triathlon, that I would have to pull out of his event as my foot was just too sore to contemplate it. Barry somehow persuaded me to just do the swim and bike elements and leave the run out! I'd been in this same predicament before a little over a year ago. I went home after the swim and decided 'well why not, I'd paid for my entry, another hefty £50.00, I might as well get something back for it'.

On the day it was once again windy. I did the swim, but could feel my foot on the run up to the bike transition, did the bike leg, limped into the transition off the bike, *and like the complete dick I am* sometimes, I started the run in quite substantial pain. I could hear Jennifer's voice shouting as she leaned over the barriers – 'I thought you weren't going to do the run'! With every stride and every foot plant it got marginally worse, but with an 'I've *started so I'll finish ludicrous attitude'* I carried on. Somehow I'd finished 19th, even got passed by two guys right on the line in a 'sprint finish'. Once over the line I could barely walk at all; the inclination was to crawl, so painful was my foot.

One clear memory of that 'awkward' day was limping around the lake and hearing my name being called. Looking up there was Jim Alder standing and giving me a shout. Pride hurt, and embarrassed by my running pace, I wanted to shout back at Jim – *'hey, I'm better than this, Jim, honestly, got a foot injury'!*

Once it was all over I went looking for Jim, but he'd disappeared. My intention was to ask him if he would consider presenting the prizes, simply out of respect. I thought I'd ask Barry to ask him, but as mentioned he'd gone. I find it sad really, that with so few genuine sporting icons in the North East, and Jim being one of them, that he would barely be recognised on the day. I wanted to shout to all and sundry, *'Hey, do you know who this guy is?'*

On the way home, and with Jennifer sitting patiently in the car, I called into Jim's house, not to stop, just to shake his hand and say a quick hello, but alas he wasn't home. Kathleen invited me in but I declined and went home in silence. Not a good day for me!

Little did I know it then but my season was over! I could barely walk!

So concerned was I, that I limped embarrassingly to the doctors on the Monday, and asked if I could have my foot/ankle x-rayed, thinking there must be a broken bone or two. The Doc wrote out his slip and away I went to hospital. I sat in the waiting room till a 'lady' came out, shouted my name, and I accompanied her 'very slowly' into the x-ray room. She must have been the most unsympathetic !?#! in the whole hospital. Without any pleasantries whatsoever, not even a hello, she said, *'We get more flaming problems with your type, than with anybody else!'* 'What do you mean *my* type?' I said. *'Damned sporting types,'* she replied, before ordering me to 'climb up there', indicating to the bed with a nod. About to do 'her job', I mentioned that the problem was as much an ankle issue as a foot issue. She responded thus: *'Well I can only x-ray the foot.'* 'Why?' says I, 'the ankle is as bad if not worse and it's only an inch above my foot!' Picking up the slip of paper I had given her, she said – *'look, it says here FOOT! Not ankle, it doesn't mention the ankle'.* Stunned by her inflexibility and atrocious manner I asked, 'So how do I get the ankle x-rayed?' *'Go back to your doctor and ask him for another note.'* 'I live at Widdrington,' says I, and she says, *'Your point is?'*. At that point a guy comes in and says actually you can wait in A and E and see if you can see a doctor, but it might take some time. The only comforting thing from my point of view was that some poor sod would be sitting in a miserable house, with a miserable dog, and a canary frightened to sing (for fear of being hit on the head with a rolling pin), in a miserable street somewhere, waiting for her to come home and no doubt grab the remote for the remainder of the miserable night! I am indeed lucky!

All part of '60 years an athlete', but I wonder if Mo Farah would have received the same frosty reception?

As far as the rest of the year went I have been severely restricted with the foot injury (or ankle, I never did find out), still sore but nowhere near what it was. I've also developed a left Achilles tendon problem, but I'm very healthy otherwise.

Summarising 2015, now pushing 65 years of age, and 60 years after my very first race on that uneven bit of pavement, as a healthy little four year old, I have had a top 15 placing in triathlon from 262, a top 4 place in duathlon, a 2nd place in a Park Run and a couple of top 10 placings in cycling time trials! This follows 60 years of just 'trying' my best!

The finishing line!

Just realised that that's pretty much my story to date and brings me right up to 2016. I did mention this as part of my intro; however, I do have some reservations as to how all this will actually read when, and if, it goes to print, so can I just repeat. In keeping with most things I've done, I've sought no outside help with this, and have self-typed every single word of this book while sitting alone with my thoughts in my house. The literacy errors, of which there are likely to be many, are all mine. Blame my education at Stobswood and Bellingham, although you may recall, I did used to do quite well in early English lessons – especially writing 'stories'! There is no doubt though that I could write more, but just like picking on at the remnants of the long finished Christmas Turkey (it's topical at the time of writing), I've had enough, and it's time to stop!

On a personal basis, as it stands currently, it makes sense to just take each day as it comes in terms of any athletic performances. Maybe sooner rather than later I may have to simply 'exercise' to maintain good health rather than 'train' for competitive sport and repeatedly suffer injuries. But as I write I have a feeling that I'm not quite finished competing just yet, I don't think, and even now I still have a couple of sporting ambitions. I haven't ruled out a top 10 placing in triathlon even at 65 – that is possible I'm sure – and a few faster runs in the Park Run events does also seem very much feasible, if not probable. I'll also continue to race on the bike, but it seems my future sporting successes, or lack of them, will be dictated not by fitness or effort, but rather by the amount of the ever reoccurring injuries I get now, as well as the obvious limitations that aging invariably brings, especially on sporting performances.

A final lament!

My body, I fear, is similar to an old pair of cleaned up trainers. On the outside they look fine and presentable, with lots of wear still to come. However, on closer inspection, the leather is hard and cracked with many lines, they don't bend as easily as they used to – the flexibility has all but gone. The rubber on the sole is eroded and the cushioning has disappeared; additionally the glue that keeps them all together is no longer as strong and fluent as it once was. As hard as it is to accept, after such a lengthy active life the shoes must accept their destiny – and regardless of the loyal service they've given over many years and with no other choice because they are so seriously worn out, the shoes must accept their fate and travel unceremoniously to the nearest refuge tip! Although there is a similarity between the shoes and our bodies, there is indeed also a difference. As humans we have been thrown a lifeline – regardless of the state of the body, we've got a mind-set! It's the mind that keeps us hanging around for yet another day, week, and month and who'd bet against many more years. Although the body is at loggerheads with the mind, the mind always wins and dictates the future. The mantra keeps chiming out 'we aren't done yet'! And of course the body simply responds by doing what it's always done and complies with that special computer that is our brain!

As mentioned previously, I don't like some of the current 'in words' so often used by our sporting stars, such as 'sacrifices' and 'get inspired' and as I write, sport at the upper level is somewhat murky and tainted, rather than pure, honest and above all fair; however, in closing if I may, I would say this in keeping with this sporting autobiography.

As far as I am concerned, I truly don't believe I was born with any real sporting talent, not at all. I may well have, through a lot of trial and error and unending effort, just about made the best use of what I started this life with. I was born very lucky in terms of health – I say lucky because I didn't have to work for my health when I entered this world, it was simply a gift I was given. The human body is a phenomenal, wonderful piece of kit – once again in my mother's words: **'Michael, you were born healthy son'!** And so I was, Mam, **thank you!**

And so there it is, '60 years an athlete', all starting in the autumn of 1955 and finishing in the autumn of 2015!

Northumberland Triathlon 2015 – 15th

Appendix

TRAINING DIARIES!

Although I was an athlete way before 1977, and even have training diaries from as early as 1969 when I was an 18 year old Royal Marine serving in Singapore, it wasn't until 1977 that I began to keep 'detailed' accounts of my training. For the past 40 years, at the end of every day, my training diaries have been opened, carefully logged with new details, and then slammed shut till the following day. It is fair to say that no one has ever read these four decades of training detail, simply because no one has ever asked, and probably because I've never had a coach either there has never been any interest in them, and I understand that. However (and it's a late in the day decision to include this chapter), how can I possibly write a book of this nature, titled as it is '60 years an athlete' without a mention of those 40 detailed books, they tell so much about my life as an amateur working athlete.

In terms of sporting ambition, diaries have two main functions – they take you back to where you were, and they assist you in moving forward to where you want to be. In other words (and I hope this makes sense) it is difficult to go forward in terms of progression, if you don't know where you've been, or indeed where you are currently! As an athlete, you need a defined route in order to arrive at your desired destination and achieve your aims, and diaries help you create the path. When you log detail, you create, to a degree, a potential recipe for success; through continuous reflection and trial and error you find what works best for you. And just as important, what doesn't. Diaries are an integral part of any athlete's tool kit!

So, ever since the 3rd January 1977, I have kept detailed training diaries, and lately I have realised what a monumental, incredibly fortuitous decision that was, if only because I really couldn't have given an accurate account of *'60 years an athlete'* without these books. Whilst I have an excellent memory for other aspects of my earlier life and times, the specific detail recorded in my training diaries covering over 40 years, is way beyond mental storage. I would have to have guessed, and 'guessing' in many respects is fiction, and fiction has little place in an autobiography. I am able to state quite categorically that my diaries are little other than pure and honest simple fact, written as they were when fresh in my mind at the end of every day.

In terms of pride, my diaries far outweigh my results; the diaries are an everyday account of my daily consistent and arduous struggle, all designed to achieve my sporting aims whilst at the same time managing both my occupational and family commitments – remember I was never sick or ever absent from work!

What follows are *'random'* samples of training over the years. Obviously it is not possible to give every day accounts (that would be 14,600 days!); however, for the vast majority of these 40 years I trained every day, often twice or thrice a day and even occasionally more, and all the while working full time.

Training diaries

Running with Morpeth Harriers!

3/1/77 – 35mins slow jog, with a few strides.

13/1/77 - I hour fartlek in 'boots', including hill reps.

6/8/77 – a.m. Time trial Chisholms circuit 28m 2s PB. p.m. run at the beach 1 hour.

27/8/78 – a.m. Run 50 mins slowly in woods. p.m. 50 mins road run.

29/4/79 – 17/6/79 – weekly running mileages – 80, 103, 90, 100, 111, 126, 120, 91.

17/9/80 – 26/10/80 – weekly running mileages 103, 101, 115, 115, 116, 100, 121, 135.

26/10/81 – 27/12/81 – weekly running mileages 100, 112, 119, 100, 125, 120, 50, 108, 110.

16/8/82 – 26/12/82 – weekly running mileages 101, 112,115, 123, 113, 93, 55, 104,115, 116, 116,120, 104, 92, 112, 103, 112, 105, 102.

27/2/83 – a.m. 20 miles with Bob Marshall and Barry Mitchell, p.m. 5 miles steady.

Triathlon years!

17/4/83 – 23/4/83 – Run 91 miles, bike 140 miles, swim 8,000yards.

7/8/83 – 13/8/83 – Run 95 miles, bike 220 miles, swim 8,000yds.

18/5/84 – am Run 2hrs, dinner time swim 90 lengths, pm bike 90mins.

1/6/84 – am Bike 3hrs (good and hard) followed by 4 mile run, pm swim 2,500yds (flat out) pm run 5miles (wet).

20/2/85 – am Sea Coal 'humping' (usual good strength session) am – bike 3hrs (undulating), pm run 1hr 10min.

22/4/85 – bike 53mins to work, swim 1000yds, dinner time run 1hr (including 9x70s and 3x 2min 10s efforts), pm bike 2hrs, pm swim 1000yds.

4/5/86 – am bike 4hrs 30mins with John Willis, pm swim 3,200yrds (intervals) pm run 30mins steady.

NOTE IN DIARY 20/4/86 'MOST NIGHTS NOT SLEEPING WELL, DAVID AWAKE SEVERAL TIMES, ALWAYS ENDS UP IN OUR BED – WONDER WHAT EFFECT THIS HAS ON TRAINING?'

3/4/86 – am swim 5,500yds (220 lengths, always front crawl) pm bike 2hrs 40mins (hard effort especially on hills, felt good and strong) pm run 30 mins (6m 30s pace 'sluggish')

11/3/87 – am bike 3hrs 21mins hilly, pm run 8miles 47m 43s (very good session after this morning's efforts)

29/7/87 – am run 10miles (66mins), pm swim 3,000yds (took James and David), pm bike 2hrs 30mins including Barnesbury 10 mile time trial in 24.00.

AT THE END OF THE ABOVE DAY WHILE CYCLING THE 14 MILE HOME AFTER THE T T, I HAD TO STOP AT 'TAITS' SHOP AT CHOPPINGTON AND 'BEG' (I HAD NO MONEY) FOR TWO MARS BARS TO SEE ME HOME –SHATTERED!!

3/3/88 – am swim 3,500yds (couldn't really be bothered), dinner time run 52mins with Ben (springer) at the beach, pm bike 1hr 45mins steady.

18/3/89 – am swim 1hr, am bike 3hrs (windy) pm run 45mins with Ben – feeling fit and strong!

15/7/90 – am Bike 100 mile Time Trial, 2ⁿᵈ, pm run 1hr at the beach – 'no bother at all'!

And so the triathlon training goes on for the next four years up to and including 1994 when, having finished 8ᵗʰ (at 43) in my last National Championship at Guernsey, I decided to retire from triathlon competition – but not other sports. Over the following years I continued to train/exercise daily until ...

2001 aged 50 and Ultra Fit competition!

From 11/3/2001 to the 20/5/2001 I trained for 'Ultra fit' competitions, which were gymnasium based. Exercises incorporated running, rowing, stepping, rope climbing, assorted weight lifting elements, additionally with press-ups, sit-ups, shuttle runs. My diaries during this spell are congested with every day 'specific' training details, with up to 2hour, mainly gymnasium based sessions.

15 years of BIKE RACING from **20/6/2001 up to today 17/2/2016** with a few **Triathlons** thrown in for good measure!

During this period I have ridden my bikes almost every day and raced whenever possible – I was 50 years old when I got back on my bike again and in the next 10 years or so I would win 75 open races and still be there or thereabouts when I was 60. In addition to my wins I'd have 'numerous' other top 3 placings. Recording precise detail will take forever, and in the process will bore both you and I rigid, so what follows is a very brief resume of my continued sporting efforts as I briefly flip through all the intense detail.

23/3/03 – 29/3/03 - 22 'plus' hours training in the week.

Up to the **14ᵗʰ April 2004** I had 178 consecutive days on my bikes – simply training and racing in all weathers, that's consistency!

9/4/05 – am 4hrs in stiff wind, pm 45mins intervals on turbo.

1/4/06 – 9/9/06 aged 55 I raced 28 times and had 20 top 5 placings with 16 top 3 placings and several wins.

2007 - I raced 30 times. I had 27 top 5 placings, 21 top 3 placings and 13 wins.

2008 - I raced 20 times with 13 places in the top 3, all others were in the top 5 except for a 6th, a 7th and a DNF due to being blown off the bike twice!

2009 - 13 races, 11 inside top 3

2010 – Strange but I didn't race in official competitions? But trained just about every day on the bike. England got hammered in the World Cup on 27th June – 4 bloody 1 off Germany!!

2011 – 2012 - Although my diaries are congested with little vacant space, there is little of interest racing wise.

2013 - Once again shows some good performances especially as I am now 62, 2 x 10mile T.T. in 20m 25s, 20m 45s, and 2 x 25mile T.T. both identical in 54m 35s although on different courses.

2014 -2015 I am now a **TRIATHLETE** again. As such, training twice or thrice a day again, e.g. 1/5/14 a.m. swim 120 lengths, dinner time bike 2 hrs, p.m. run 30 mins! I have 3 top 15 places from fields of 250 plus competitors.

2016 – 18/2/16 and whilst rapidly approaching 65 years of age, today I walked the dog for 1hr 20 mins this morning, then ran 6 miles, took the dog out again later for 45 mins and did an hour on the bike!! Just another day in another athletic year!

Are you really sure you still want me as your coach, Ryan! Really?

AGE! (a state of body, or a state of mind? – something to think about, perhaps?)

'A happy family' with Dan, Michael, me, Jennifer, Julie, Sarah and my Dad

Acceptance is a negative word, it's an admission or recognition that signifies finalisation and finalisation is discontinuation, the final article, the end! In any context that's a bit daunting.

Age, or the process of aging (and it's something we've all got in common) need not be negative nor need it be accompanied by pessimism. In today's society we see both men and women in their sixties and beyond running marathons, but we also see kids in their teens incapable of shuffling a quarter of the distance.

Youth and age are merely words; it's the interpretation which is the issue. I believe both maturity and youth are a state of mind. We are what we think we are, old or young you determine your state; certainly I know young people who by action and thought are old, and old people who likewise are youthful, despite their years.

A good positive philosophy is to state with a degree of sincerity and a genuine amount of commitment "next year I am going to be healthier and fitter than this year, that's for sure, and the year after I'll be even better"! Is that possible? Of course it is, why not? Can I gain from that? Of course! Is it possible to get fitter and healthier as you get older? **Absolutely!!**

Acceptance, regarding health is static, it creates apathy, and apathy leads nowhere except perhaps to boredom, and boredom befriends no one.

Acceptance is for the dead, those in graveyards. Us living people, well, we can choose. The choice? We can physically deteriorate, we can remain the same (temporarily), or we can progress and improve – no contest.

I suppose I will be classed in some people's minds as pretty much an old fashioned 'has been' due to my seniority and some of my views; regardless, I can say with some certainty that **'everything starts and finishes with health'.** The fitter and healthier you are, the greater the possibilities and potential, and the fewer the limitations; age need not play a major or significant role.

So be careful with tongue in cheek banter such as "I'm too old for all this", because if you say it often enough, sooner rather than later, you might just begin to believe it! And where does that leave you? I'll tell you where! **BLOODY WELL OLD!!** That's where.

Age isn't a disease, nor should it be feared, but to court it invites limitations, and limited beliefs create limited people, and limited people may ultimately be found wanting when opportunities beckon and choice becomes a necessity rather than a preference.

Winston Churchill once said *'growing old is not for cowards'*. **How apt!**

If you've taken time to read any of this I am truly chuffed, thank you.